FEEDBACK

FEEDBACK

Translations from the IrRational

elliott sharp

WESLEYAN UNIVERSITY PRESS

MIDDLETOWN, CONNECTICUT

Wesleyan University Press
Middletown CT 06459
www.wesleyan.edu/wespress

Manufactured in the United States of America
Designed and typeset in Quadraat by Eric M. Brooks

Library of Congress Cataloging-in-Publication Data
available at https://catalog.loc.gov/
cloth ISBN 978-08195-0204-9
paper ISBN 978-08195-0205-6
ebook ISBN 978-08195-0206-3

5 4 3 2 1

CONTENTS

LIST OF ILLUSTRATIONS

1

Introduction

"I Feel Fine." Not a declaration of my current state of being, this is the title of a song released by The Beatles in 1964. Hearing it was almost certainly the first time, at age thirteen, that I experienced acoustic feedback in a musical — or any other — context. This sound was raw, bristling, the wildness constrained by the pop song it introduced yet somehow contributing to the song's underlying teenage franticness and joy. A friend who had been learning electric guitar informed me that this was the sound of feedback, caused by leaving the guitar in close proximity to the speaker, allowing a small signal from the pickups to be amplified, which would then again be amplified in a process of self-oscillation: a powerful sound emerging out of nothingness.

Though I had listened to other rock songs by The Beatles and The Rolling Stones, the beginning of "I Feel Fine" was different and startling, a sound heretofore unheard and completely outside of my sense of music, which at that time was shaped by a bit of rock n' roll, my piano and clarinet studies, and the light classical music and show tunes played by my parents on their hi-fi. Already a budding science geek, I was interested in the technology of sound production, and my father's employment as an industrial designer working on loudspeakers and microphones provided a direct conduit into the workings of what I was hearing. With my trusty Remco electronics kit, I soon cooked up a small amplifier and, plugging in a budget crystal microphone and aiming it at the speaker, I generated an adrenalizing howling screech. I can't say it had any musical value, nor did it funnel me into the creation of popular music, but it was a thrill of its own making, psychoacoustic chemical change.

As my interests multiplied in many directions throughout high school and then in university, I found myself drawn more deeply toward music — though there were significant detours into physics and mathematics, anthropology, literature, and philosophy. I now view these various interests as currents within the wider river of artistic translation and creation. My love for divergent strains translated into output across various disciplines, styles, and techniques. Friends, colleagues, audiences, and students all will attest to my tendency toward what I call "creative digression." I hope that their trust in my ability to shape the ultimate trajectory of each of these digressions remains present and active. They will eventually lead back to their point of departure and in so doing enrich and illuminate the larger narrative.

Some of the detours undertaken in *Feedback* will refer back to topics initiated in my previous book, *IrRational Music*. In this book, these core materials will be expanded to reveal new paths and vistas. And so, within this volume, the reader will find off-road excursions into theory, speculation, travelog, fantasy, tribute, satire, and interview.

Feedback was the word that opened *IrRational Music* and the jumping off point for this volume.

Elliott Sharp, NYC, November 2024

2

An Asymptotist Manifesto

1. The end is near: it's merely an infinite number of points away.
2. Your goal is in sight and you will approach it but you will never reach it. Relax and enjoy the journey.
3. An asymptote is tangential to a line at a point of infinity—attempt the tangential.
4. The word *asymptote* is derived from the Greek ἀσύμπτωτος (*asumptōtos*), which means "not falling together"—therefore, let's fall apart and embrace the chaos.
5. Since you will ultimately never reach anything, approach everything.
6. The asymptotic is not failure; the asymptotic is continuous success.
7. The asymptote is never nihilistic but eternally utopian.
8. To be continued . . .

3

Experimental? Music and Sound

We who do what we do with sound and music get called lots of things and possibly the kindest is "experimental." It's not that "experimental" is necessarily an insult—quite the opposite: in popular usage it denotes exploration, an action without predictable results, an ascent into the unknown for the purpose of discovery or illumination. But its usage in labeling music is often pejorative and meant to marginalize the work and explain why most people consider the experimental unpleasant to listen to.

When considering the experimental, it might be useful to delve into the word *experimental* itself. We may start with the prefix *ex-* denoting "from," "out of," "away." We decapitate our *experiment* and are left with *periment*. A touch of mispronunciation or misspelling will yield *pediment*, a triangular gable having a decorative function in architecture, often crowning a door or window. It's a welcome metaphor for an ornamental fixture, also often found in orchestral music or opera and well defined as an overture or prelude, support for the opening of the composition or revelation of the material that follows.

But what is a *periment*? Digging into the depths of the internet leads to the Latin word *perimere*, a verb with various meanings including "to annihilate, extinguish, destroy, hinder, prevent, kill, slay." If one is performing *ex perimo*, is it leaving the scene of the crime? Constructive and generative? An act of promotion? Musicians love to compliment an exciting and superlative set with such adjectives as *killing*. A successful Las Vegas or Borscht Belt comedian "slays" the audience. Is experimenting, then, a renunciation of violence and specifically murder, or is it the opposite, as in "bad" to denote excellence? By departing from the known elements of which music is created, are we making sounds that somehow heal, cure, make beneficial? Or not . . . Instead of this positive framing, might the experimental be that which is without use or function when the act of destruction is actually the generative force? Experimental: residue, perimo fallout, dry ashes, toxic waste, the reduction of action and reaction.

Experimentation is vital for the evolution of both concepts and their manifestation, but I do believe that it is generally best (though not always) performed in isolation without interference from friends or colleagues or other external distractions, such as an audience. Sequestered in my studio, a great thrill is to plug an instrument into various devices patched together in a previously untried sequence just to see what happens. Alternately, a rush may come from mapping data from a source found in nature to a collection of pitches in a score, then seeing where it takes me. The results may be wondrous or nothing at all, but at the very least they're a novel manifestation only awaiting evaluation. The deep beauty of experimentation is that with ever-shifting parameters it remains unpredictable. Positive results may then be incorporated into a composition or a performance setup, while neutral or negative results may send you back to the drawing board. The passage of time may actually recontextualize those negative results and prove them useful after all.

In 2000, I was asked by Alanna Heiss, director of the PS1 Contemporary Art Center in Long Island City, to curate a comprehensive exhibition of sound art which would be titled *Volume: Bed of Sound*. Congruent to the question of what defines the experimental is what defines "sound art." This was the wall text for the show:

> A distant murmur, a flurry of chirping cicadas, a pounding bass drum, a mass of sliding squeals, a hushed sine tone, an echoing scream, a consonance of lightly bowed strings, a wall of rushing greyness. Turn off your filters, the learned reflex, the already-known, and let the sound do its work. You may be surprised and overwhelmed.
>
> Volume is a measure of space, an enclosure of the intangible, a quantification of that purist abstraction, sound. Volume is also a measure of intensity—the pressure of molecules rushing away from each other and bouncing against the walls of the outer room and of the inner ear [loudness] causing small and rapid changes in air pressure between some 10 times per second and some 20,000 times per second [saturation], a range defined by the physical construction of the human ear. Finally, volume is a containment, whether of bytes, words, music, anything and everything.

Pump Up the Volume: Notes

"Wherever we are, what we hear is mostly noise. When we ignore it, it disturbs us. When we listen to it, we find it fascinating . . . If this word 'music' is reserved for eighteenth- and nineteenth-century instruments, we can substitute a more meaningful term: organization of sound."

JOHN CAGE

Cage follows the great pioneer Edgard Varèse's definition of music as "organized sound." The "organizers of sound" appearing in *Volume* come from varied domains and engage in activities that evoke a wide spectrum of physical, aesthetic, and emotional responses. The experimenters mine and undermine the core elements of our perceptual engine, hacking and rewiring. Creators of soundscapes reshape the materials indigenous to our everyday environments so that we may hear them as if for the first time and find different modes of meaning in them. Composers working with a new syntax and vocabulary of musical materials derived from the workings of sound itself and forged into tools as yet undefined create music that is alien and exciting. Sculptors and installation artists utilize inextricable sonic elements as an integral part of the whole. The cultural commentators provoke and challenge habits and preconceptions. Finally, the entertainers channel their audio intelligence into popular media, stretching ears wide.

Volume exists in two galleries, both furnished with giant bed-like structures to encourage the visitor to recline, relax, open themselves to sounds and the possibility of psychoacoustic chemical change at the deepest level. No visual stimulation is provided in these galleries—with total immersion in this acoustic environment, the sounds will embody themselves across all inputs.

The West gallery has loudspeakers for the "outer ear," the socialized listener, the receptor of the whole person; the North is equipped with headphones for the audio solipsist, the "inner ear." *Volume* is a spa for your ears and body, a sonic sauna: soak in the hottest, retreat to a cool place to regroup, dive in again.

In the North gallery, listening is an intimate transaction between the sound and the person. When it hits the tympanum of the ear in each listener, there is, first, a pure physical reaction, a movement of tiny hairs and a change of chemistry. From this, there is the generation of a signal: from ear

Figure 1 (Left to right) John Cage, E♯, Petr Kotik (1986). Photo by Felipe Orrego.

to brain, to glands, to spine, to muscles, to bones. The sound becomes the person in the act of reacting to the sound, a closed loop, reflective, reflexive.

Sounds played over the West gallery speakers form a consensus reality among those present. The minute reactions that each listener has to a sound will subliminally affect the perceptions of those around them—the group feeds back on itself, resonating and reinforcing. Brainwaves will be amplified or suppressed; pulse rate or body temperature may increase or decrease; limbs may move involuntarily; pheromones generated and transmitted. Sounds in this space may be masked by other sounds in the immediate environment or they may amplify and grow.

Volume: a portion of data, with its physical storage medium, that can be handled conveniently as a unit: floppy, hard drive, compact disc.

Volume is an assemblage of audio initiators manifesting their work through the purely digital medium of the compact disc. Within this disc, meaning is reduced to 16 bits of raw data and quantized levels of information: the complex curves of sonic life are encrypted as thousands of on-off blocks every second. The artist encodes allusions, emotions, memories, thoughts, and actions into these discs. In the simple fact of conversion from digital bits to physical sound lies alchemy: a simultaneous decoding into not only the immediate elements that define the sound (its loudness, direction, frequency, transience, and duration) but also its wider context. This hearing is vastly different for each behearer and informed by the varied cultural factors that define who and where each listener is, has been, will be. But, most importantly, that hearing exists on an objective level within the objective nature of the vibrating molecules themselves. This is Volume.

4

Applications and Builds

It's exceedingly rare that I'll present an actual experiment in concert—the experiments have been run in my studio and those results deemed positive are then brought out to the public in whatever form. However, there have been circumstances where one must launch oneself into outer space without knowing if one will go into orbit or just fizzle out. One such situation was the premiere of my algorithmic piece *SyndaKit* in 1998. *SyndaKit* is a set of instructions and twelve pages of Cores (short phrases in musical notation denoting pitches, rhythms, and textures) that are divided among the players. Inspired by cellular automata, recombinant RNA, bird flocking, and the transmission of gesture in African drum choirs, it's been recorded by my own Orchestra Carbon and Berlin's Zeitkratzer and performed with ad hoc ensembles in Europe and Japan. Performers may play the Cores, make loops, pop out with improvised statements, and imitate and transform what the other players are doing all the while maintaining a groove (even though it may only be heard implicitly at times, as texture). The instructions are designed to facilitate two seemingly contradictory goals of complete unison and continuous mutation. But when twelve musicians are required and rehearsal space and time both scarce and expensive, the most efficient way to initiate the experiment is to book the gig and then see what happens. Orchestra Carbon at that time was a free-floating pool of musicians who had, in various combinations, all performed various algorithmic pieces that I'd composed for the group, some simple, some more complex. For this concert there would be two sets at 8 and 10 p.m. at Tonic, a venue, long gone, located in NYC's Lower East Side. We assembled at 5 p.m. and after a quick build-up and soundcheck began to go through the various elements of the piece. There was time enough for only an overview and a cursory run-through of one iteration. By its very nature, every realization of the piece is unique and any rehearsal just presents one set of the myriad permutations. There is no right or wrong way to play *SyndaKit* as long as the actions conform to the operations. All I can ask of the players is that they learn the basic rules and then apply their considerable creative skills in active listening and improvisation to make it all work. Again, no right or wrong—only the act. At the downbeat of that first manifestation of *SyndaKit*, the lure of the unknown combined with the adrenaline of performance led to a successful experiment playing out over two sets, meaning that the music gave a glimpse into the continuous and greater flux that we all attempt to access.

Since my teenage years I've pursued instrument invention and construction, an activity steeped in experimentation and inspired by Harry Partch, country blues artists, and various non-Western musics. My luthiery skills are rudimentary, as are the refinement and extent of my tools. My workshop is stocked with the basics: a few saws, rasps, and files; hand drill; pliers and diagonal cutters; screwdrivers and wrenches of various sizes; clamps small and large. The exception is a compact collection of wonderfully sharp (no pun intended) woodcarving chisels inherited from my father, both an industrial designer and artist working in paint and wood. Using them continually revives my connection with this wise and loving man who was so important to me. The final outcome of my experiment is often rustic, but this rough and unsophisticated process is valuable in that it yields unique instruments. The spirit of bricolage animates the procedure: a balance of science and "magic." A pile of junk yields a viable assemblage; a glimpse of an illusion of sound evolves into the sound itself and its extrapolation. These instruments are quirky and demand unorthodox techniques to generate results. They flourish in the studio: a controlled environment immune to the demands of performance where a specific technique must be applied at the exact right time so that the sound may emerge when desired, no earlier or later. If it doesn't work the first time in the studio, you can always try another take. Live, there's no safety net.

Certain situations demand that the experimental be dragged kicking and screaming to the stage, a risk that teeters on the line between calculated and reckless. When this need rears its head, my go-to approach is to bring out one of the invented instruments. In the 1980s, my bands Carbon and Orchestra Carbon made use of the pantars and slabs, percussive string instruments built between 1980 and 1986, as well as the violinoid, built in 1978. For these concerts, the players familiarized themselves with the techniques and possibilities of the instruments and did the necessary homework to produce the sound as needed in the performance.

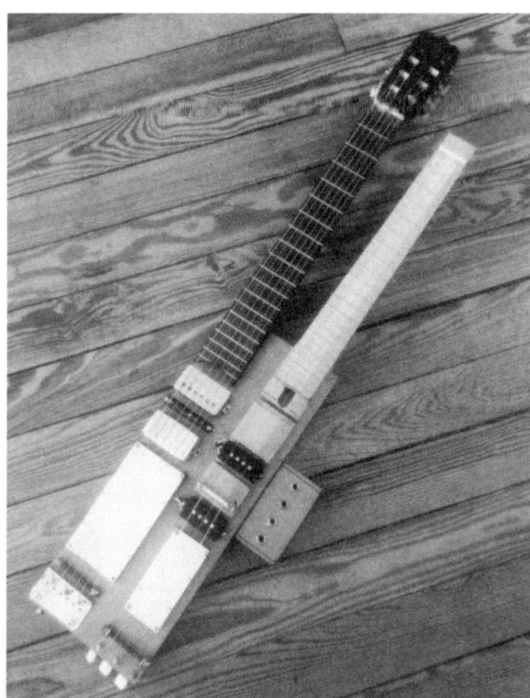

Figure 2
Arches H-Line.
Built by F♯ (2022).

For his concert at Roulette on November 3, 2022, multi-instrumentalist and composer Scott Robinson invited me to join him to play his suite *Hypocycloid* and requested that I bring the violameriyah to play on one of the sections. True to form, the violameriyah was constructed during the summer of 2021 from odd pieces of detritus residing in the multiple studio junk boxes. The chosen parts included a viola neck, mandolin fingerboard, magnetic bass pickups, a piezo element, tuning pegs, springs, and a chunk of scrap wood. The name is a composite of viola, dulcimer, and *sumsumiyah* (a Bedouin zither). One pickup for each of the two necks plus the piezo with each on separate outputs allows for a plethora of sounds, especially when combined with the specialized bowing and tapping techniques developed for this instrument plus the electronic processors. I'd recorded with it to create part of a sample pack for Splice.org but hauling it onstage is different: there are no second takes or edits. This makes for a heightened state of being: hyperawareness of the quirks of the instrument and how to work with these potential obstacles, not against them.

For a November 11 show at Downtown Music Gallery I decided against taking the mostly known route (as all improvisation involves some degree

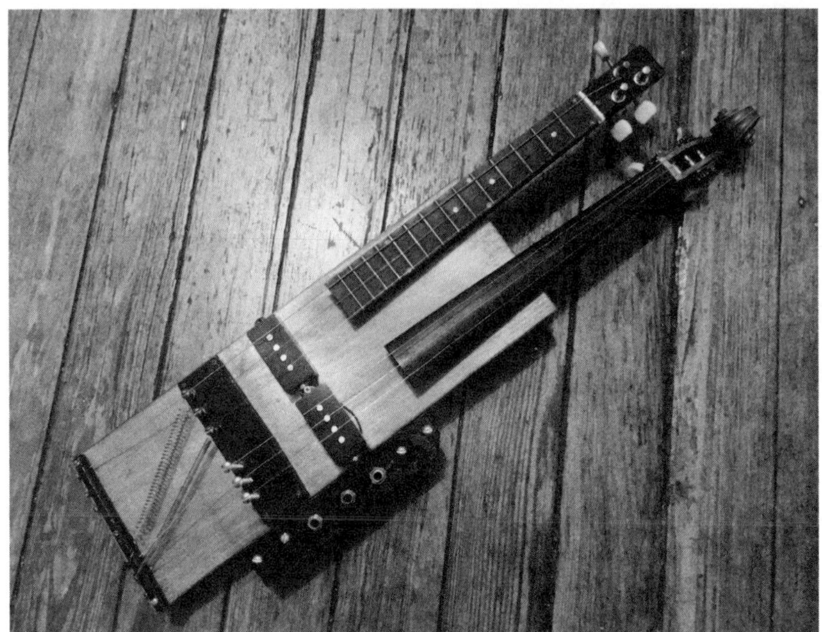

Figure 3 Violameriyah. Built by E♯ (2022).

of deviance), instead performing my solo set on a different instrument as-yet untested in the field. Chosen was the TrePonti, named for its three bridges—in this case, constructed from an "unplayable" 1980s headless Arbor Stiletto guitar that was gifted to me during the summer of 2021. I first set out to make it playable and did succeed, but even at its best, this guitar was meant for neither hands nor ears. The decision was made to transform it instead into a guitar-shaped electro-acoustic sound source. The frets above the fourteenth fret were pulled and the fingerboard filled in with wood putty stained to match the rosewood. A new bridge made from electrical conduit was mounted between the pickups and a "gliss plate" (to allow glissandi, sliding sounds) with a piezo element set inside a pleather sandwich constructed and mounted behind the original bridge pickup. Two additional bridges (for three in total) were cut from aluminum tubing and mounted fore and aft of the gliss plate. The mono output was replaced with a two-circuit jack, with the magnetic pickup routed to the tip connector while the piezo element was connected to the ring. To cap it off, a metal spring was mounted to the gliss plate to add some percussive boing.

While I had tested TrePonti briefly when first completed, it had lain dormant, hanging on a wall in the studio waiting for a chance. Hoping to bring a spirit approaching pure experimentalism to this aspect of the event, I refrained from any significant practice. Arriving at DMG, the split output of TrePonti was connected to a guitar amp for the magnetic pickup and a bass amp for the piezo, allowing me to dial in a fairly balanced tone across a wide panorama. Just a few minutes later it was time to dig in, and I found myself quickly pulled into the TrePonti soundworld of unpredictable resonances, clouds of overtones, and varied clanks, thunks, howls, and sproings. Use of the EBow yielded nearly operatic singing tones with bizarre ghosting effects . . . an experiment well worth pursuing with the presence of audience ears and expectations adding to the overall ambience.

5

Socioacoustics

If there was nobody present to hear the Big Bang, did it happen?

Standing in the spotlight on a stage in a blackened auditorium, the room packed but completely silent, the artist proceeds with absolute confidence, knowing that the audience, rapt, is paying full attention to every nuance, every sound and gesture, loaded with the sense that this is how it must be. When the lights come up, there is a huge and sustained ovation and there is a feeling among all assembled that this was an event of remarkable significance.

The next day, another stage in another blackened auditorium filled with a silent audience. As the artist plays through the set, they feel that the sounds are falling on deaf ears and that the audience is totally immune to any expression. Remaining the consummate professional, the set proceeds, though to continue playing becomes a Sisyphean effort. Indeed, the audience is indifferent to the music and clearly transmits this indifference. When the lights are raised at the conclusion, there's a smattering of polite applause after which the room quickly is vacated with audience members saying little to each other and nothing to the artist.

This compact tour completed, the artist retreats to the studio to assess the two concerts. Playing the recording of the first event, memory still filled with the evening's resounding success, rather than witnessing brilliance the documentation reveals an extremely competent but unexceptional performance. There is surprise and dismay as this contradicts the feelings of the moment: an event of singular beauty and creativity. Now reluctantly auditioning that second absolute dud of a concert, the artist is completely surprised by the depth of invention and luminosity of the realization, counter to what they and the audience had experienced.

During the coronavirus lockdown, of necessity, many musicians took part in remote recording and performing scenarios. Various strategies were employed, including performances online using one of the social media applications, sending soundfiles to each other for overdubbing, giving verbal or written instructions for individual recordings to be assembled later, providing a through-composed score and a click track for synchronization, or my favorite, defining a length of time and overall flavor and letting the players create their parts in isolation, after which these parts would be collected in one place for mixing. Using this latter strategy, the results were often stunningly beautiful, with a remarkable sense of gestural unity, each musician's parts fitting together seamlessly and amplifying each other's intentions, demonstrating incredible sonic empathy and shared vision. In April 2020, as the lockdown was looking to be more and more a fixed feature of our lives, guitarist Sandy Ewen invited me to give an online concert through her series Social Norms. Sitting in my studio with an electric guitar and facing the camera of my desktop computer, I performed for the invisible audience. Though there was a complete absence of any evidence of human witnesses to this event, I felt that I was in an actual concert (albeit in a virtual space sans Green Room or other amenities) with all of the requisite elements of feedback returning to me in a most positive fashion at that moment yet invisible, unheard.

Once, a friend and frequent musical collaborator visited me at my studio and asked what I've been working on. Coincidentally, the night before I had finally completed mixes for a new recording project. The songs had been mixed many times over the period of one week as I continued to tweak and refine, honing in on trouble spots and burnishing the various stringed instruments and percussion tracks. At last, it could be considered complete. Yet sitting near my friend as the first section played, within seconds I could hear that the violin was equalized too bright on the first song, and on the following, the drums were too quiet and there was too much reverb on one of the guitar tracks. Without a word being said, I could hear through their ears and recognize distinct flaws in the mixes that I hadn't noticed, even with repeated listening. There was no direct verbal discussion, no body language that indicated antipathy or discomfort during the playback. The illusion of hearing through the ears of another was completely seamless. When I was alone again, I listened to the tracks in question and, indeed, the problems that I had heard continued to be present and were soon corrected keeping in mind the vivid revelations of that encounter.

One can imagine many variations and permutations of the above events. These scenarios may also be complicated by altered states of consciousness on the part of the participants, whether through drugs, alcohol, meditation, fasting, anxiety, or the pressures of performance. There is an unpredictable relationship between a creator's experience of their musical manifestation and the perception of it by a listener or audience. In fact, in many years of performing, I have been party to the full range of these possible states so many times as to now believe that there is no direct and accurate correspondence between the performances and their perceived quality, either by the performers themselves or the audience. An event might be extremely enjoyable to all when it happens but, upon reflection, conflicting feelings might surface. Can there even be an objective evaluation of a concert by any of the participants? In the end, where does that leave any of us whose musical life and work is intertwined in a variable relationship with an audience, whether direct or remote? The short answer is that it shouldn't matter—we do what we have to as composers and performers. But the long answer might be derived by delving into the myriad variables.

How can we begin to evaluate what is happening here? What are the factors that define the relationship between all of those taking part in a performance and the elements that are in play in the analysis of this network? Are there any objective measures, or is it all a matter of relativistic interpretation of continually shifting viewpoints? This set of questions may be seen as the central window into a definition of "socioacoustics": human interaction in sound production as manifested in the relationship between sound-producers and other real-time participants.

An audience may be sitting quietly or they might function more actively as listeners. This may be the case with dancers working with live musicians or students analyzing a performance. Different styles of music engender different styles of listening. Free-jazz concerts from the 1970s up until the present have seen audiences practicing a form of dynamic listening akin to *shuckling*, a Yiddish word defining a rocking movement during studying or praying from the Torah. Punk-rock and hardcore audiences perform ritualistic brawling as the inevitable outcome of their most concentrated form of listening. In contrast, attendees at a sound installation may spend a significant amount of time sitting stone still, eyes closed to take in the work, while others pass through with a minimum of deep listening and seemingly unaffected.

The mutual relationship between multiple sound-producers working together simultaneously increases the complexity of the interaction as each participant is both a generator and a listener. This is complicated further if there is one leader and the rest are followers, or, in another case, if there is a peer relationship inherent to the structure of the ensemble. More codified are the interactions between the participants in a large ensemble, such as an orchestra or marching band, playing from a fixed score and with a conductor or drum major to keep them in order in the rigidly constructed hierarchical relationship described so beautifully in Elias Canetti's *Crowds and Power*, then presented as *cinema buffa* by Federico Fellini in his 1978 film *Orchestra Rehearsal*.

There is also the question of sound-producers interacting with their materials and how the physical properties of sound in space affect those humans effecting the sound. Socioacoustics functions as a feedback loop within a system defined by the dynamically shifting balance of spatiality and time-based actions, filtered and modulated by human perceptions and framing. Both expectations and desires (not to mention engendered stylistic responses) will affect all states.

Let's consider the notion of the reality of the moment. Almost every human situation, no matter how many times we have experienced it, will be unique. Certain parameters might be considered to be constants, but not all and not really. If the music is familiar to us, then we have to contend with comparing the performance at hand to other performances and recordings and also, for a composition that we know well, a Platonic ideal of that particular music. Attending a concert of favorite musicians at a local hall that we have visited on numerous occasions might find us affected by the weather (including temperature and humidity, both outside and interior), location of our seat, time of day, skill of the sound engineer, perceived state of engagement of the performers, who we are attending the event with, and one's personal emotional and physical state. Finally, one must mention the collective mood of the rest of the audience. This can be a very palpable feeling, but how can it be measured? Though there are no conclusive studies proving the existence of human chemical communication, whether pheromonal or otherwise, it has never been disproven. Then again, there could be less obvious and more theoretical solutions to the problem of human group communication, including quantum entanglement.

Underlying all of the above are feedback systems, both acoustic and social. The first is almost purely physical, but with emotional ramifications. For the musicians, difficulty in hearing themselves or each other will lead to performance problems which may be subtle or obvious. As a guitarist, if I have trouble hearing myself, the instrument can feel as if its material state—whether string tension, frequency response, or sustain—has somehow been transformed away from the familiar. If the audience witnesses the musicians in an uncomfortable state, they are more likely to feel that the performance was somehow compromised. One glaring exception to this will be in a blues or jazz performance where the musicians are visibly fighting to overcome obstacles both worldly and cosmic, and the manifestation of their struggle excites the audience. To see the sweat pouring off Albert King's brow as he peals off blistering licks or the passionate totality of John Coltrane in solo flight inspires resonant emotions in the listeners. In general, audience discomfort or impatience will be fed back to the performers through physical cues such as shifting in seats, coughing, and sideways glancing, or more subtle and subliminal cues operating in the realm of "vibrations." In a similar manner, a positive audience experience will also be felt by the performers. Vibrating systems experience resonance when proximate physical systems exhibit their own vibration at the same frequencies. This causes the amplitude of both systems to increase. The Beach Boys expressed this phenomenon quite succinctly in their song, "Good Vibrations":

I'm pickin' up good vibrations
She's giving me the excitations . . .

A positive experience tends to remain positive and a negative remains negative, paralleling Newton's First Law of Motion that "an object at rest remains at rest, and an object in motion remains in motion at constant speed and in a straight line unless acted on by an unbalanced force." And what could be more of an unbalanced force than a musical performance? There is a threshold that must be breached for the state to be changed. In this sense, the closed system of "room with performer and audience" functions very much like the synapse in a nervous system, polling all its inputs until the threshold arrives and a decision is made, yea or nay.

Duration in a musical performance is another great variable within a dynamic socioacoustic system. Miniatures by Anton Webern or Napalm Death may be structurally complete within their short time span, demanding that the listener recalibrate their expectations about narrative arc to get the same sense of completion and satisfaction they might derive from a longer composition. In the same way, pieces of extended duration, whether a performance of Morton Feldman's *String Quartet No. 2*—clocking in at six hours—or Richard Wagner's four-hour *Die Meistersinger*, demand a different mode of listening, even requiring alteration of one's physical state. Musics in the extended-time and minimalist realm often intend for the listener to eliminate their esthetic filters and "space out," with the desired result being to override what are seen as Western ideas of the correct trajectory for a piece of music, including the filters that look to a discrete narrative arc with a clear sense of beginning, middle, and end. Extended duration musics often take on a ritualistic role. I think of music as an act of psychoacoustic chemical change, and proponents of slow musics might tout the tranquilizing effects of that genre, whereas fast musics with discrete events over a short time span might be considered more in the realm of stimulants.

The next parameter to be addressed is loudness. The late composer Zbigniew Karkowski was an advocate of extreme volume in the performance of his works. No sound system seemed to ever meet his approval, even when the decibel count was at 140. He has written, "Where language ends, music begins," and sees his use of extreme volume and white noise as a way of transcending language to create music that is Magic, not an estheticized experience. Others, such as the group of composers under the Wandelweiser umbrella, work in the opposite direction, creating compositions that are nearly subliminal or even silent. These compositions draw inspiration directly from John Cage, whose 1952 work *4'33"* framed silence from the performer to open the compositional language to the ambient sounds of the concert hall and surrounding environment. Though Cage reaped both fame and infamy for *4'33"*, others preceded him with manifestos and compositions using silence, including *Sketch of a New Esthetic of Music* by Ferruccio Busoni in 1907, the French humorist Alphonse Allais's 1897 *Funeral March for the Obsequies of a Deaf Man*, *In futurum* by Erwin Schulhoff from 1919, and Yves Klein's *Monotone-Silence Symphony* from 1949. With this music of silence and quiet, composers have the intention of raising sensitivity to sound, but also sending up some of the pretensions of conceptual work (while generating a new set of their own!). Audiences may respond to either approach and may indeed be confused as to which response is appropriate given such music.

I consider Alvin Lucier to be one of the great pioneers in creating awareness of socioacoustics as a prime component of compositional strategy. Lucier's *Music on a Long Thin Wire* from 1969 is a potent example of an ambiguous socioacoustic response extrapolated in presentation. In this combination of composition and installation, a wire is excited by a sine-wave oscillator through a power amplifier. A microphone picks up and amplifies the sonic artifacts, such as difference tone beats and glissandi produced by the wire in motion. Lucier himself has said that the piece works best in "interesting" settings. An integral component of the work is being able to experience the vibrating wire in different relationships to one's position relative to the wire in space, with profound sonic effects occurring as the direction of hearing shifts. I had read about this work and was quite excited to see it performed at Buffalo's Albright-Knox Gallery in May 1975 as part of "Evenings for New Music," the seasonal concert marathons directed by the Center of the Creative and Performing Arts at the University of Buffalo where I was working as a sound technician while pursuing my graduate studies in composition. Unfortunately, the setting chosen for the concert performances was the auditorium, and the piece was presented with a seated audience as if it was a work of chamber music. Within minutes, the limitations of this approach were revealed. By eliminating the mobility of the audience, the sine-wave tone was rendered mostly static. Though I did not have any sense of how knowledgeable the audience was (the Albright-Knox events were free and attracted sizable community participation), I could see the bewildered and disgruntled looks on many faces as they waited for that irritating sound to end. A much better version of *Music on a Long Thin Wire* was realized at the International Computer Music Conference in Berlin in 1999, where the wire was suspended just below the ceiling of the spacious atrium at the entrance to the Philharmonie Berlin. The sound itself was not loud, but moving through the space allowed one to hear subtle but pronounced variations in the sonic environment.

We turn again to Alvin Lucier in considering expectations as a vital component of socioacoustics. His composition *I Am Sitting in a Room* is never opaque or cryptic, mystical or pretentious. The work begins with Lucier reading a text that not only explains in simple language what will happen, but also provides the seed material for the acoustic processes that unfold:

> I am sitting in a room different from the one you are in now. I am recording the sound of my speaking voice and I am going to play it back into the room again and again until the resonant frequencies of the room reinforce themselves so that any semblance of my speech, with perhaps the exception of rhythm, is destroyed. What you will hear, then, are the

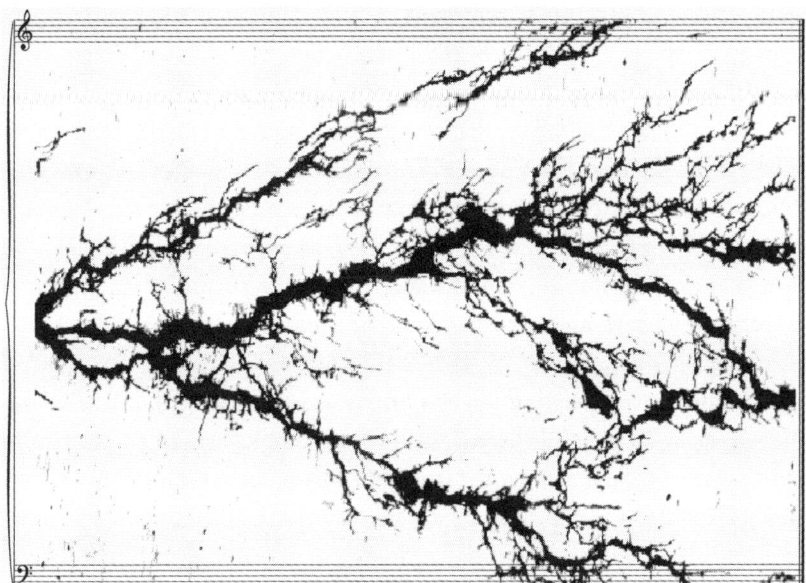

Figure 4 Score, *Hudson River Nr. 6* (1974).

natural resonant frequencies of the room articulated by speech. I regard this activity not so much as a demonstration of a physical fact, but more as a way to smooth out any irregularities my speech might have.

The iterations of playback allowed the mechanical process to work its transformation of the seed material through the resonance of the room. Though the process was clearly delineated in advance, dampening any expectation of surprise, the results grew more startling with each iteration until at the end our ears were treated to a mellifluous and harmonically rich burbling and droning. Despite having heard multiple realizations of *I Am Sitting in a Room* over the years, I have never failed to be engrossed by the process and its results.

Before conceiving of the term "socioacoustics," I could have described a good number of my earlier works as taking that outlook, starting with the *Hudson River Compositions* of 1973–1974, a set of text and/or graphic works that posit brief instruction sets as algorithmic compositions. These pieces include instructions to emulate fireflies, flocking birds, branching rivers and streams, grooves either interlocking or of maximum density, and the one most open to interpretation: "play the opposite." Another work in this canon is *Crowds and Power* from 1982, a mix of notated and text gestures inspired by the Canetti book of the same name. In *Crowds and Power*, each section of the music is performed either in total darkness or bright light, with the Fibonacci sequence–based timed changing of the lighting cuing the different sections. Each section is steady-state and without any discernable narrative arc. Sections alternate between extreme loudness and breathless quiet. With six drummers, five electric guitars, saxophones, brass, and strings, the high-volume end of the spectrum is easy to attain. The transformations are always unexpected, leaving the audience sensitized, irritated, provoked.

Although the installation *Tag* was briefly described in my book *IrRational Music*, I'd like to revisit it here in this context. Designed as an interactive audio work, *Tag* was created for *Departure Lounge*, an exhibition curated by Alanna Heiss at the Clocktower, a gallery then associated with PS1 Contemporary Art Center and located at the top of an iconic building in Lower Manhattan designed by architect Stanford White. The intention was to have *Tag* both engage visitors with the exhibition and elicit sonic graffiti from them—and, in so doing, provide a continuously changing ambient underscore or soundtrack. Four microphones in small metal boxes with grill openings were placed around the exhibition space, clearly labeled and height-accessible to a wide range of the public. Signal from the mics was fed to a mixer and routed to a hardware vocoder that was modulated with a rhythmic pattern programmed on a drum machine using a detuned and softened cowbell patch. This combined signal was fed to an eight-second digital delay with a moderate amount of feedback, allowing signals in the system to last approximately forty-five seconds. The final output was fed to a number of speakers situated around the gallery. Through signage, the public was encouraged to enter their "tag" (any verbal utterance, whether singing, speech, or some other sound), which then, modulated and recycled, became part of the gallery's sound world. The continual refreshing of input information, combined with the relaxed groove of the drum machine, created a textured beat that was recognizable as human voices and could be considered nearly music, though actually more a transformation of public input into sound reflective of the changing population of the show. Those visitors who heard their voices replayed in the room engaged more directly with the microphones and increased their input.

The next socioacoustic work, *Living Room*, is, on the one hand, a title

Figure 5
E♯ at the Clocktower, NYC (2012). Photo by Bert Shapiro.

descriptive of the piece, and also a tribute to the innovations of Alvin Lucier. In performances of *Living Room*, a small microphone is plugged into a laptop and routed through equalization and digital delay plug-ins within a sequencer (at the time I first devised this project, I was using Cubase). Swung overhead in a circle for the duration of the forty-minute piece, the microphone picks up the sound of its own movements through mechanical transmission, my fragmented spoken texts and vocal sounds, and any sounds occurring in the space. Thanks to the volume and equalization of the system, there is also acoustic feedback, which ebbs and flows to create a rich and continuously changing drone. The primary performance gesture is one of endurance, as the microphone is twirled overhead for the duration of the piece. The sound world contains a rhythmic component generated by the regular repetition of the mechanical sounds of the mic on its cable, plus the sustained tones of feedback as shaped by the room resonance and equalization, as well as the interjections from the audience and random environmental noise. A constant provocation in the piece is the threat of the

Figure 6 *Living Room*, performance at the WPS1 Art Radio booth, Art Basel Miami (2002). Photo by David Weinstein.

microphone flying off of its cable and into the audience (a small tribute to The Who and Roger Daltrey's swirling microphone). *Living Room* premiered at the Henry Art Gallery in Seattle in July 2001 and has also been performed at ISSUE Project Room in NYC in 2001, Art Basel Miami Beach in 2002 as part of the WPS1 installation at the Delano Hotel, and at clubs and galleries in the US, Italy, and Germany. Audience reactions have varied widely, with some sitting quietly and passively taking in the performance while others enthusiastically shout and sing contributions to be injected into the sound world.

Another work of mine in the socioacoustic realm is *Ganging the Hook*, commissioned by the Electronic Music Foundation for their Ear to the Earth festival in 2009 and the first of a series of "Ganging" pieces that rely on live convolution of prepared soundfiles. *Ganging the Hook* is an environmental

Figure 7
Janene Higgins with video mixer (2000). Photo by Jack R. Lindholm.

piece based on convolving the dawn sounds of the East River in real-time performance using electric guitar as a controlling sound source. This intermodulation transforms both into something "other," a sonic meditation on the interstitial states between night and day, technology and nature, noise and music.

In 2005, my partner Janene Higgins and I moved to the Corlears Hook neighborhood of Manhattan's Lower East Side, the easternmost point and the widest part of the island. "The Hook" was supposedly named for the shape of the nose of one of George Washington's generals. When our twins were born in 2005, I often walked them in the stroller early in the morning and soon became enthralled with the mix of sounds presented to us: birds, river traffic, helicopters and other aircrafts, industrial Brooklyn and the Navy Yard, the lapping of the river itself, and the white-noise drone from traffic on the FDR Drive.

For *Ganging the Hook*, my plan was to choose a time to record when the sonic interference of the human element would be most diminished, and to try and capture as much of the sounds of the river and the local wildlife as I could, imagining a glorious avian dawn chorus. I chose Labor Day morning as the target date for recording, thinking that before sunrise on this national American holiday most drivers would be off the road. I walked down to the East River at 5:10 a.m. with a Zoom HF2 recorder and switched it on. Indeed, the overall environmental noise level was quite low, but I discovered to my disappointment that the reduction in general ambient noise at this time on this day brought into stark sonic relief the little traffic present and, by contrast, actually increased its apparent effect. The intermittent-but-still-steady stream of cars became a figured bass to my concerto. The river was calm though broken with occasional tug boats and barges, and most of the birds that I normally encountered (sparrows, chickadees, gulls, cormorants, a small falcon, random colorful songbirds) were either absent or strangely silent. It was only at the sun's full appearance that a group of sparrows chattered their appreciation in a burst of high chirps. Though my projected and desired results did not appear, the recording experience was still deeply satisfying, and later that morning as I auditioned the four audio channels in ProTools, I found many points of sonic interest and began to envision the strategies that could be employed for the performance.

The raw audio was nearly three hours in duration and was edited down to forty-five minutes. Noise reduction was applied to increase the contrast between desired sounds and background noise. In a few sections, I copied and layered the recorded sounds to enhance the presence of the birds. The four processed channels were then imported into Ableton Live, and a patch was created that would apply different types of convolution and filtering, controlled by envelope-following to the tracks. Convolution by definition involves multiplying the audio spectra of the various signals, with the result being the increase in amplitude of shared frequencies and the attenuation of those not in common. In performance, the eight-string electric guitar-bass was used to generate the dynamic envelopes and the carrier frequencies for the two stereo convolvers and two stereo filters. The eight outputs (four stereo channels) were then sent out to the eight powered speakers and two subwoofers that ringed the audience. The harmonic structure and dynamics of the various guitar sounds modulated the ambient sounds. I could add pulsing rhythms, jagged noise, and slowly shifting harmonic envelopes to the recorded sound. The guitar itself was never present in the final mix, only its electronic shadow revealed by its absence. *Ganging the Hook* was performed in a darkened hall at the Judson Church with a synchronized slide show that telescoped the three-hour shift from dark of night to full daylight into forty-five minutes. Surrounded by the eight channels of audio, the audience was immersed in the sound. Reactions varied widely: some audience members told me of a feeling of tranquility followed by joy at the bird chorus. Others felt impending horror, as if they were in a reenactment of Alfred Hitchcock's *The Birds*. The very abstract nature of the material and the neutral presentation allowed audience members to tint their perception of the sound to fit their own preconceptions about my work and/or their expectations for the performance based on the printed program notes.

A later variation, *Ganging the Waves*, was presented in 2011 by the SNYK–National Centre for Contemporary, Experimental Music and Sound Art in Copenhagen with edited recordings of shortwave radio substituting for the environmental sounds of Corlears Hook and moving the piece into the etheric.

6

Sakunicki

Written in 1997 after the passing of William Burroughs as a tribute to his late-1950s prose style.

As the twenty-first century crawled out from under its rock and blinked, rumblings from the underground bowels of New York's New Music scene hinted at a cataclysm that in a mere two decade's time would shake the very foundations of the anesthetic artistocracy and from there advance to the greater beyond. Movers and shakers, stirrers and schnorrers, faders and borers, all stared and stammered in shock: Whu-whu-whu-wha-wha-wha . . . General deterioration in the fiscal environment soon transformed the once-lush esthetic gardens of Soho, Loisaida, Williamsburg, and adjacent realms into a vast metaphoric Dust Bowl.

The militant factions were the first to be hit and the first to fall: Minimalists, Maximalists, No-Wavers, NewAgers, Sewagers, Sign Wavers, SlopTappers, Inappropriators, Teetotalists, Ambivalents, Nihilisters, Scramblers, Jizzers, Free Dazzers, Preservationists, Fromprovisers, Strict Deconstructionists, Jewhadis, Nude Complexionists: all bottomed out and deliquesced. What remained was a residue, a thin scum composed of organic materials—a fertile base for the growth of a feral atavism, a virulent meme dedicated to the final eradication of everything held dear to the princes and queens high in their ivory and diamond towers on the tony streets of Rivington and Stanton in the greater Lower East Side or hallowed canyons of Tribeca. From 23rd to Canal, from Lower Hudson to Least River, the old guard burned down to greasy ash, imploding into a black hole of irrelevance and confusion as the Sakunicki multiplied like cellular automata in hyperdrive.

Sakunicki: animal, vegetable, mineral, or completely alien? They seemed to have come snarling and slashing out of nowhere but most scientists linked their appearances to the aftermath of biochemical attacks on New York City early in the zeros launched by the Blessed Republic of Texas. Soon they were everywhere, coiled into strange attractors and ubikked.

Sakunicki: synergistic blend of soft and hard tech, meat and machine. Whatever passed their auditory organs was instantly processed via an etheric and pheromonic shared-distribution network and then digested and expelled through microscopic subcutaneous amplifiers and manifested through the vibration of water molecules in a cloud surrounding each of their bodies—no speakers or other transducers necessary. Simultaneous input-output; a feedback loop of infinite gain and Absolute Zero content, phase-shifted 180 degrees, negating all that surrounded them. Sonotropic, they gathered wherever sound exceeded a threshold of 18 decibels, mere whispers in this town. Sakunicki infested cafes, clubs, concert halls, galleries, restaurants, classrooms, political gatherings, courtrooms, cocktail parties throughout the city. Their signature: a hideous silence; a sucked-out negative image of all sonic space; seething and fibrillating near the bottom edge of perception. All conversation, all music, all communication was destroyed in their presence.

The mutation seemed undefeatable. Not only New York's Bohemian demi-monde was decimated. Even Uptown with its impenetrable gated halls and critical barricades fell victim to the plague, this mutant horde of nihilistic phase cancellation. Carnegie Hall and Lincoln Center: both silenced. Even the Rectalists of Miller Theater were muted—not even the slightest hint of Boulezian flatulence. All attempts to rout the Sakunicki failed as did all attempts to screen or even identify them for those infected could not be physically distinguished from everyday New Yorkers, whether by phenotype or by costume. In fact, anyone might spontaneously join their ranks and immerse their immediate environ in a torturous hushing and then, after weeks or months of satisfying this alien appetite, just as suddenly revert to normality.

The only recourse was patience: the fever eventually ran its course, consuming the consumer. The Sakunic aberration was self-defeating, its amusia rendering all vectors sexless, free from any pheromonic communication and thereby unable to metabolize and transmute the sonic soup of life. The attractor stalled and crashed, the loop shattered. The Sakunicki disappeared from New York though reports began filtering in of other urban appearances: Chicago, LA, Warsaw, Tokyo, London, Berlin, Shanghai . . .

7

Improviser's Mind

One of the many beautiful things about free improvisation is that in its ideal state there really are no rules. Everyone who improvises has their own unique way of processing input and generating output. Each devises their own internal strategies for spontaneous creation—some consciously via a systematic approach involving historical listening and technical exercises, and some through hands-on experience and self-analysis. Practiced improvisers generally agree that there is no right or wrong in improvisation; there are just sounds that go together in a process of spontaneous consensus. What those sounds are and why they go together or not bears exploration.

Much has already been written about improvisation and associated non-composed musical practices. There are anecdotes and hints, exercises and suggestions, but can they really teach one to take part in this mysterious yet common practice? If one was to grow up in a culture where improvisation is a significant element in the music most commonly played, then one might learn what to do (and what not to do) from elders and peers. In Carnatic and Hindustani classical music, improvisation is the very essence of the music, yet, for the student, there is much time spent in rote memorization and in exact repetition of *ragas* and rhythmic patterns. Once the student has integrated these elements into their very being, then they may fluently combine traditional gestures with their own inventions, but always within the predetermined framework of temporal structures and *ragas*. This same form of pedagogy may be found in modern jazz. Whereas the jazz tradition during the swing and bebop eras might have been passed on in jam sessions and on the bandstand, by the 1970s universities were developing jazz education programs where players would memorize typical chord progressions and their variations, the scales that would be associated with these chords, and more mechanical pattern-oriented playing that could overlay and eventually resolve within common harmonic structures. To my ears, only a very

Figure 8 Performance with Richard Teitelbaum, Andrew Cyrille, and E♯ at Roulette Intermedium, Brooklyn, NY (2011).

few extremely talented musicians have emerged from this latter educational regimen who can actually create passionate, original, and unpredictable improvisations, free from the clichés of their genre. Physical virtuosity and lightning-swift execution, though often thrilling to the listener, can be used as a substitute for actual invention and emotion, the sources of the psychoacoustic chemical change that I feel is one of the core essential attributes of music.

Though improvisation was an important component of baroque music, with the performer creating harmonic complication and melodic filigree from a bare-bones figured bass score indicating chords and their inversions, it fell out of practice in the classical era (except for short cadenzas and codas that would allow a soloist to display their prowess). Rhythmic invention and complexity were never major aspects of European classical music, and polyrhythms were nearly nonexistent as a primary force until composers in the twentieth century, including Igor Stravinsky and Edgard

Varèse and later Béla Bartók, began to address the many ways to subdivide time, yielding an explosive rise in the use of complex rhythms and exotic textures as well as motoric rhythms meant for dance. Before World War I, the composers Arnold Schoenberg, Anton Webern, and Alban Berg moved in an opposite direction, constructing music with the complete serialization of pitches and mechanical processes involving retrograde and inversion to avoid classical tonality with Schoenberg's methodology the source. Their music ranged from the Expressionistic convolutions of Schoenberg through the eclectic lyricism of Berg and on to the crystalline austerity, fragmented time, horrific sonorities, and stark humor (to my ears) of Webern. Harry Partch, John Cage, and Carlos Chávez each took personal approaches to the incorporation of rhythms, whether inspired by Indonesian or Mexican musics or imagined music of ancient Greece. The Romanian/Greek iconoclastic composer Iannis Xenakis found inspiration in stochastic processes, mathematical models, and the language of architecture to create a music of pure sound, devoid of classical reference and filled with complex rhythms of great physicality and ritual power. Only in jazz were the players allowed, even required, to freely transform the basic rhythmic motifs in a song, as long as the feeling of swing was maintained. By the 1960s, drummers were freeing themselves completely from the rigors of timekeeping, with pioneers such as Milford Graves, Sunny Murray, and Rashied Ali moving into realms of pure sound and chaotic clouds of rhythm and fibrillated texture.

When John Cage premiered his notorious composition *4′33″* in 1952, the raw materials in use by the composer shifted from what had always been defined as the foundations of Western music to any and all of the sounds of the world, including silence, whether intended or not. Early 1950s explorations of free improvisation by Lennie Tristano with Warne Marsh and Lee Konitz were echoed and expanded upon later in the decade by Cecil Taylor and Ornette Coleman, who themselves inspired waves of largely improvised music blossoming through the 1960s and 1970s.

England in the mid-1960s was a hotbed of improvisation and alternative approaches to composition. The group AMM was formed in 1965 with guitarist Keith Rowe, drummer Eddie Prévost, and saxophonist Lou Gare, all jazz refugees who succeeded in alienating both jazz and contemporary classical audiences until their later enthusiastic acceptance. Rowe at first detuned his guitar away from any system, eventually laying it flat and treating it as a sound source and resonator while eschewing all traditional guitar technique. The composer, pianist, and cellist Cornelius Cardew joined AMM in 1966, bringing influences from his time studying at the Studio for Electronic Music of the West German Radio and assisting iconoclastic composer Karlheinz Stockhausen. Cardew later composed *Treatise*, a 193-page graphic score that allowed considerable latitude in interpretation, yes, improvisation, to its performers. Free improvisors Derek Bailey, Evan Parker, and Tony Oxley formed a pioneering independent label, Incus, in 1970 to document and disseminate their own work and that of likeminded colleagues. On the European mainland, such players as saxophonist Peter Brötzmann, drummer Han Bennink, pianists Misha Mengelberg and Alexander von Schlippenbach, bassist Peter Kowald, guitarist Hans Reichel, trumpeter Tomasz Stańko, and American expat Steve Lacy delved deeply into spontaneous ensemble improvisation and composition. Derek Bailey was a skilled guitarist with a long career history in jazz and show music. In the process of escaping from the strictures of those worlds, he began to improvise along with recordings of the music of Anton Webern that he had transferred to tape. He developed a sound world of scrapes, plinks, harmonics, and atonal strummings that were a revolutionary retort to the typical jazz guitar stylings. In 1980 Bailey published *Improvisation: Its Nature and Practice in Music*, the first version of his study and thoughts on improvisation.

In a parallel and contrast to Bailey's activities, the New York–based guitarist Sonny Sharrock created his own personal guitar language inspired by the raging saxophone intensity of John Coltrane, Archie Shepp, and Pharoah Sanders. Sharrock's roots were in doo-wop, and he later became obsessed with jazz after hearing Miles Davis. Though he briefly studied guitar at the Berklee College of Music, his own epiphanies came from meeting Sun Ra and playing with Olatunji, but especially after hearing Pharoah Sanders, in whose group he performed, creating a tsunami torrent of sound by overblowing his horn. Using a steel bar in his left hand, Sharrock evoked that sound and added screeching, non-pitched intensity outside of any tonal system to Pharoah's music and to the bands of Herbie Mann and Miles Davis. Witnessing a performance of the all-star Mann group in 1969 was a mind-melting experience, especially when Sonny took the solo spots. Playing a big Yamaha jazz box, Sonny's solos bore more of a resemblance to a glass skyscraper being shattered into shards than they did to anything by Jim Hall or Joe Pass. Rather than a reasoned development of a song's theme,

Sonny created a parallel universe of the solo as compacted apocalypse, yet with the full drama of a narrative arc.

The panorama of African American improvisation in this period from the mid-1960s onward was fueled as much by revolutionary thought and discussion, both political and spiritual, as it was by musical considerations. The Association for Advancement of Creative Musicians was founded by composer and pianist Muhal Richard Abrams in 1965 in Chicago and birthed the multi-dimensional Art Ensemble of Chicago. Anthony Braxton was another member of the AACM who blazed new trails in both improvisation and composition with innovations in structure, instrumental techniques, and graphic notation. The AACM extended to and overlapped with the New York circles around Ornette Coleman, John Coltrane, and Cecil Taylor, with a sonic language based on saturated intensity leading to transcendence, but always rooted in improvisation and with elements referential both to American blues and gospel and to sounds and techniques from African and Asian folk musics. These circles included master improviser Sonny Rollins, who maintained one foot in jazz tradition while outputting a freeform lyrical and virtuosic discourse that was Zen koans to Coltrane's cosmic testifying. One also heard vast improvisational epiphanies in the "Sky Church" music of Jimi Hendrix in his more expansive performances incorporating feedback, onomatopoeic noise, and freeform melodic extrapolation. Hendrix's widespread influence catalyzed freeform rock improvisation. Electrified free improvisation was adopted and transformed by Miles Davis to create a unique music grounded in electric funk but elevated by its open forms and wild sonics influenced by the work of Karlheinz Stockhausen. The music was brought to life by guitarists John McLaughlin, Sonny Sharrock, and Pete Cosey; saxophonist Wayne Shorter; bass clarinetist Benny Maupin; keyboardists Herbie Hancock, Joe Zawinul, Chick Corea, Keith Jarrett; drummers Jack deJohnette and Lenny White; percussionist Airto Moreira; and a coterie of other players.

Playing in rock bands began for me in 1966 with a microphone stuffed into the bell of my clarinet in an attempt to emulate Jeff Beck's molten fuzz guitar tone in The Yardbirds. I began teaching myself guitar in 1968 and was soon playing electric bass and guitar in various ad hoc formations. Jamming was a central component of our practicing and playing. We didn't think of it as improvisation, a mystical process that was only practiced by more accomplished players with a deep knowledge of the mysteries of music. During a stint at Carnegie Mellon University at age seventeen in the summer of 1968 on a Ford Future Scientist of America fellowship, I spent my free time building and experimenting with distortion and ring modulation circuits to apply to my guitar. With a midnight to 4 a.m. DJ slot on the campus station WRCT, I could take deep dives into the ocean of amazing music being released at that time and spin sides from Tod Dockstader, Balinese gamelan, Burundi drums, Ligeti string quartets, Mongolian throat singing, American country blues, and more. Back at my parents' house one December night, I plugged my guitar into a string of pedals and let the sound play me, fingers changing the settings on the pedals and amp as if guided by an unknown force. It was an experience like no other, in which I felt myself completely disappearing as I immersed myself in the waves of sound. This experience was my first glimpse into the timeless void of improvisation, after which I began work in earnest on building up my knowledge and praxis to effect a return to that place, a lifelong quest.

Throughout the 1970s, we in the sodality of sound pursued all avenues, all styles, all genres. Whether jamming with my band St. Elmo's Fire in Ithaca, NY or informally with friends there and later at Bard College, there were experiments with instruction sets and algorithmic approaches, free jazz, free rock, pure noise, multimedia and theatrical forays, graphic scores and conductions, unaccompanied soloists, and large ensembles. The constant current underlying our explorations was improvisation and, within that stream, continuous questions of balance: freedom vs. structure, the individual vs. the group, innovation vs. tradition. Results could be gratifying, frustrating, even sometimes enlightening. As a student of Roswell Rudd's at Bard College from 1972–1973, I found a number of musicians who favored improvisation but from a "free jazz" sensibility that often entailed sessions of extended expressionistic output that seemed masturbatory and with a hierarchy ruled by the fastest and loudest. While I certainly enjoyed fast and loud, I was also hoping for a wider range of sounds and gestures. Attempts to introduce some graphic notation to shape the sessions were mostly met with resistance, though these attempts led in the period of 1973–1974 to the creation of the *Hudson River Compositions*, which combined aphoristic instruction sets with graphics. In August of 1974 I moved to Buffalo, where I became a graduate student in composition at the State University of Buffalo. My adviser was Lejaren Hiller, a pioneer in many musical fields: computer music with his *Illiac Suite* and the computer-generated work *Algorithms* for chamber ensemble plus tape; sound installation with the John Cage collaboration *HPSCHD*; performance art with *Avalanche* and *Three Rituals for Two Percussionists*. Hiller had been a chemist, and he applied many scientific practices in creating and working out ideas for compositions. In these, he balanced the intuitive with the structural to yield compositions that, while utilizing formal frameworks, also displayed an open musical sensibility and wicked sense of humor. Studying with Jerry (Lejaren's nickname) would often take the form of discussions about strategy: what was I trying to do with a particular composition? Various forms of notation were considered, or even the possibility of no notation at all. Hiller did not dismiss improvisation, as he valued the indeterminate elements it could contribute, but his scores never made use of completely open-ended improvising. Nor did mine! I strove to make the formal elements less visible, so that if improvisation was used to flesh out a piece, it was indistinguishable from the bones. It was during this period of exploration that I began to work toward making my improvisations have the sense of inevitability of a well-constructed composition and my compositions to have the spontaneity and unpredictability of an exciting improvisation.

Morton Feldman directed the Center for Creative and Performing Arts within the Music Department, and my admiration for his music was one of the main reasons that I had come to Buffalo. Feldman's office was next door to the Electronic Music Studio, where I had my own compact workspace and from where I ran my maintenance operations as an employee of the Department. Morty and I often exchanged friendly words, and he'd ask me what I was working on. This sometimes led to an invitation to sit with him in his office. Though I was not formally his student, these lessons were valuable insights into both his analysis of my work and of the very nature of being a composer. Feldman conducted a Friday afternoon Composers Forum in which he spoke at length on many topics extending far beyond the musical. These were often head-spinning windows into his compositional thoughts and processes and his esthetic views. We would listen almost completely without interruption. The Composers Forum would present a concert each semester, and in October 1974 a piece of my own was to be included, *Hudson River Composition Nr. 7*. I had composed the *Hudson River* series while living in Germantown, NY on the river, with each piece based on an observation or a simple instruction set. These included emulating the fireflies, bird flocking, river branching, hocketed rhythms, "doing the opposite," and in the case of Nr. 7, creating a layered work beginning with a ninety-second through-composed melody that was recorded using a soprano saxophone and a ring modulator pedal that I had built, which was then slowed down to half-speed with another layer of sax and processing added. This 180-second recording was slowed down to half-speed again to create a tape of 360 seconds' duration to be used in performance. Looking back, I can now view this composition as a fractal exercise in self-similarity with an element of figured bass as a tip of the hat to the baroque tradition. I performed the six-minute work in the Forum concert running the saxophone through my ring modulator pedal. The sonorities had as much to do with the metallophones of a gamelan as they did with any saxophone music. The next morning when I ran into Morty, he called me into his office as before. "Sit down," he ordered, and without any other niceties forcibly said in that thick Borough accent: "Improvisation . . . I don't buy it!"—then I was dismissed. Needless to say, this only reinforced my determination to employ improvisation in my work, whether in totality or as an element within a structure.

During my time in Buffalo, I also had an association with the late composer and performer Julius Eastman, who was on the composition faculty and a fellow of the Center. Julius was the composition teacher of my friend Charles Kaufman, and I would sometimes accompany Charles to lessons just to listen in. I played soprano sax in rehearsals for an early version of Julius's composition *Femenine* and appreciated how his notion of freedom in interpretation through the use of guided improvisation dovetailed with the composed modules in the work. As sound engineer for some performances of Julius's compositions, I was able to appreciate his visionary genius, which incorporated process from the Minimalist school combined with a deep sense of funk that could only have come from his unique position as a queer African American composer and, in retrospect, proto-Afrofuturist.

In *IrRational Music* I wrote at length about the campus events in the spring of 1975 around the Attica prison uprising that led to my arrest and banishment from campus and the resultant loss of my employment and graduate fellowship. When the exile ended, I returned to the University and finished my master's degree through the American Studies department, where Charles Keil was my mentor and adviser (and coincidentally, first cousin to Roswell Rudd). Keil was a prophet of "the 12/8 Path," and our jamming together on Afro-Cuban grooves and more found us exploring the intersection of the clave and Tibetan ritual through extended percussion improvisations, drones, and duets on the double reed *tzourna*. Hiller and Julius Eastman remained supportive during my trial on campus, but they were in the minority, so I had little to do with the Music Department during this period. Instead, I focused on my degree requirements and then teaching Keil's course "Music in Culture" through the American Studies Department while he was on sabbatical during the 1977–1978 academic year. The course included a lab, "African and Asian Performance Practices," in which we improvised, sometimes freely, sometimes with guidelines or instruction sets or using models from non-Western musics. These classes were a window into the wider scope of improvisation going beyond European compositional approaches and typical free-jazz tropes. Moving to the Pioneer Valley in western Massachusetts in 1978 brought me into contact with such musicians as Marion Brown, Michael Gregory Jackson, and Jim Whittemore (and through the latter, members of DNA and Pere Ubu), but it was more a time of focusing my work until I finally made the move to New York City in October of 1979. There I began composing music that would combine improvisation with electronic pulse, rock dynamics, and non-pitched materials, with the end result manifested in my bands and recording projects Moving Info and I/S/M.

Eclectic interests had me moving simultaneously in many directions in pursuit of artistic fulfillment and economic survival. Fellow Buffalo improviser and percussionist Greg Ketchum arranged for me to become an accompanist in 1979 to the Improvisational Dance Ensemble (IDE) based in NYC's Tribeca and led by choreographer and pianist Richard Bull. The group later changed their name to the Richard Bull Dance Theatre. Together with dancers Peentz Dubble and Cynthia Novack, they would perform three concerts every week, completely improvised (though each week was assigned a theme). This ongoing work with committed improvisers was both an enlightening practice and an anchor for my new NYC life, as I felt a direct resonance with their way of working. The IDE rehearsed steadily, always discussing and analyzing the work with the purpose of perfecting their improvisations so that they would satisfy the need for an integrated narrative arc while still remaining completely spontaneous. Over the six months that we enjoyed rehearsing and performing together, one aspect stands out: sometimes the performances felt good, sometimes not. The difference was never the technical level of our participation, but rather the unspoken, unseen, and unheard x-factor, the chemical and the alchemical feedback loop.

Some gigs were elevated and exciting, some not. Was it the audience, the weather, what we ate before the show? There was never an exact correlation between the known discrete factors and the subjective success of a performance. This was acknowledged but did not in any way alter the way the group operated.

During those first weeks in NYC, I came upon a handwritten card posted in a record shop that listed concerts at a place in the West Village called Studio Henry, which turned out to be the basement of the Exotic Aquatics pet store. I only recognized a few names on the card but soon realized that I had come upon the home base of the "white improvisers," a loose grouping that had little intersection with the performers featured at Tin Pan Alley, Ali's Alley, and Studio WIS. The prevailing esthetic was that of the English scene around Incus records. I attended the next event scheduled, a solo concert by pianist Robin Holcomb, and through her met a number of musicians. Drummer Mark Miller was the first of the players that I connected with, and I was soon invited to play a couple of gigs with him, a fortunate start as he was open-minded and interested in expanding his activities in a rock direction, as well as being critical of what he called "the toenail" because of the ingrown qualities of this small group of musicians. For a number of years now I had tried to employ a full complement of extended techniques, including atonal two-hand tapping and the use of objects and preparations to create non-pitched sounds, but I favored the saturated guitar tones usually associated with blues or hard rock and was drawn to grooves, both explicit and implied, macro and micro. Though nothing was spoken at first, from the reactions of some of the other players it was clear that there was a disconnect between my approach and theirs, which soon was explained to me outright. Though they believed their music was "free improvisation," there was a slate of strictures that defined the genre for them, including the nearly exclusive use of "dry" sounds and an almost complete prohibition of explicit melodic or rhythmic material.

Derek Bailey and Evan Parker did not see their praxis as a fully defined method, but rather more of an underlying philosophy of musicmaking. Their own playing did actually operate from a position of freedom, though the limited spectrum of possibilities within the genre of "free improvisation" grew into stylistic rules by the consent, whether explicit or not, of the acolytes and other participants of the music. Bailey famously said that free improvisation is "playing without memory." This, of course, brings up the notion that the best free improviser is one without any short-term or long-term memory abilities and that the music itself is timeless and without a defined arc, not to mention stylistic and technical limitations. The reality is that a narrative is inherent in the structure of a performance, as there will always be a beginning, a middle, and an end, whether you define it by what's happening on stage or in the ears of the listeners. Whether this is clearly perceivable by the participants or the audience is up for debate depending on the nature of the event, though I believe that no matter if it's in the foreground or background of our musical activity, there is a denotation of elapsed time marked by our internal clock, which may be "calibrated" to the consensus clock or to some more abstract timekeeping standard. As for how musicians find their way in the improvisational process, I have witnessed players mostly developing their skills and personal vocabulary from practice and interplay with peers, instructors, and recorded materials. Learning and creating the parameters of a style has always included an element of imitation as a way to gain an understanding of sonic syntax and vocabulary. Once achieved, there is, in the end, the open question as to whether or not this is the strength of a shared notion of identity or the limitation of self-parody. I believe that students who are developing improvisational skills should play what they want to hear, not what they know. When sufficiently trained, fingers can do what they do almost autonomously, somewhat like the octopus with an independent "brain" in each tentacle. This feeds back to the question of what has been played and how is it heard and ultimately, "Where do we go next?" The key to this is global listening, outside of one's personal tastes and practices. Evaluating one's own listening and playing is a discipline to be continuously explored, and one that requires ruthless objectivity though without self-abnegation. There must be memory, there must be future projection, but there must be continual awareness of one's own shifting nature as wave or particle in the great flux.

In my personal practice, saturation has always been an essential element. Give me *caffe ristretto*, *koicha matcha*, *grappa dura*, and their musical equivalents: John Coltrane, Albert Ayler, Archie Shepp, Albert King, Cecil Taylor, Jimi Hendrix, Iannis Xenakis, Roswell Rudd, Nathan Milstein, the Jajouka musicians. I would group these all as Dionysian sonic entities: intense, raw-edged, fiery, passionate, chaotic—vehicles for ecstasy. On the opposite end of the spectrum is the Apollonian state, where the intensity is real but its nature is cool, rational, cerebral, structural, a vehicle for enstasy, introspection, an objective state. Both are valuable, even necessary at different times and for different contexts. Can the improviser operate in a simultaneous balance between both Dionysian and Apollonian, or must a choice be made? There is no simple correspondence between Dionysian and improvisation counterposed with the Apollonian composition, yet we may generalize the conditions of these states. I prefer a model of greater fluidity with the musical states changing dynamically on a quantum level.

In the years between my first attempts at finding my place as a music-maker and the present day, I have continuously worked to find that balance between improvisation and composition. This praxis does not always yield clarity or gratification. Just as lifting weights might preserve and increase muscle mass, practicing scales might hone your muscle memory—but this may not make you a better improviser or, more importantly, a better listener. A creative impulse appears . . . what then? If an idea or commissioned request appears for a piece of composed music, my first impulse is not to set up the notation program or open up a ProTools file or pick up an instrument. The first action I take is to ostensibly do nothing—but in reality, I am quieting the conscious process, slowing down the reflexes, disabling the filters, retreating to a space outside of my desires until the impulse can be translated to the proper band of the spectrum for its manifestation. If the project is a musical work, then I wait until the sound appears in my Inner Ear. To the casual observer, this process might resemble catatonia or indulging in a nap. Sometimes no music arrives, or perhaps just a glimmer—something that you can note but not yet obsess or build upon. Translation is the essence of the process of manifesting the work. The creative impulse appears and the proper portion of the spectrum for its output must be determined. This notion was very much inspired by the Walter Benjamin text, *The Task of the Translator*, where, simply stated, the priority is not to get just the correct words, but to capture the full essence. This applies to any creative work. Give up trying to "make" the work but instead listen and wait, take a walk or read a book, cook a meal, pick up an unfamiliar instrument. Maybe the sound will finally appear fully formed, or not. When it does appear, you will know it, and then the job is to capture it with notes, words, abstract mnemonics. That first appearance is not the finished work but merely the seed—still, it is a seed revealing the inevitable. You sit back and listen, let it grow. Put it away and let the backgrounding processors take over. Return in one day or one week or one month and listen again and it has evolved, changed. At some point, recognition of the nature of the work and its arc solidifies and then it's time to dig in, to turn inspiration into the concrete reality of a score, a performance, a conceptual menu.

If the goal is to improvise, is the process different? In my early attempts at free improvising, there was often little sense of freedom from anything. Anxieties of technique and equipment worries might overwhelm one's connection with the flux. "What do I play? . . . and what do I play after that?" Charlie Parker's famous quote remains a touchstone for the improviser: "Learn all the scales, all the chords, then forget that shit and just play the music." Now we say, "Learn the sound of everything, notes, scales, chords, styles, birds, insects, industrial processes, electronics, feedback, environments, water, the wind . . . then forget it all and just play the music!" Go read Gary Snyder's poem "What You Should Know to Be a Poet." Improvisation is life, and life is improvisation. Preparation need not be a self-conscious struggle for perfection. Again, the asymptotic. I like to think that taking part in an improvisation is analogous to entering a weather system that encompasses fellow musicians, the audience, room acoustics, physical equipment, and one's individual state of mind. The skies may be calm or turbulent; the air might be clear or cloudy. If you've put yourself in a prepared state, or perhaps better defined as an open state, then it will be possible for you to flow with the weather, accepting your conditions and making the most of them, perhaps even affecting them with your own output. The musicmaker becomes another component in the feedback loop where input and output cannot be separated. To defy this "weather" is almost certainly going to cause deterioration of the sound environment for all involved, especially yourself, in a perfect example of negative feedback.

We return again to the process of listening as the essential component of improvisation. What one plays is not as important as what one hears. The contradiction is to remain in an objective state while being fully immersed in the sonic activities. Let's call this "Schrödinger's Musician." When you are in the flow state, you are both outside the action and fully taking part. In this state, your perception of initiating actions or joining what has been initiated is irrelevant. Your internal observer (I call it "The Accountant") does have a purpose: to step in and tell you that it's time to advance the patch on a particular pedal, that the B-string is out of tune, that you're too loud or too quiet—all the little things that happen in a session. But when The Accountant intrudes into the overall musical process and attempts to interject intentions that might not be of the sonic consensus, then the flow state breaks down and the spell is broken. But when it all works, Improviser's Mind is synonymous with the flow state, letting us interface with the infinite probability machine that is the universe.

We are all here at this very moment doing whatever we're doing. We can say this with 100 percent certainty. However, we can never say with absolute certainty that what we are doing will continue in its present state in the next smallest instant after this ever-continuing moment. It's only extremely probable. Let's call it 99.99999 . . . with an infinite number of zeros probable. These are actually not bad odds for any kind of wager. Again, it's highly probable that the universe as we know it will continue to exist after this moment and follow the trajectory projected for it by consensus. It is now believed that our universe is 13.7 billion years old (give or take 200 million years) and will last for at least another 22 billion years. These numbers are based on what we now know, but they may change as new forms of measurement are discovered, not to mention new sea-changes in information and definitions as a result of these measurements.

In post-quantum physics, the reigning paradigm on Monday may be completely discredited by Tuesday, with a new language sweeping out the old by Thursday, only to be replaced again by Saturday. For example, string theory was once all the rage and promised "The Theory of Everything." But where is it today? There were too many missed correspondences, fussy, unproven complications. Yes, the Higgs boson was found, but what evidence of the infinitely more important supersymmetry? The inability for a theory to remain strong and inviolate is one of the reasons that the connection between the science and the parascience remains fluid and dynamic. The more we learn and discover, the more questions and uncertainties arise, in a typically asymptotic process. Can we say that we know enough about the workings of the universe that accepted knowledge of those workings will always be constant? War criminal Donald Rumsfeld was widely ridiculed for a statement that I believe is one of the few truthful and enlightening things he ever said: " . . . as we know, there are known knowns; there are things we know we know. We also know there are known unknowns; that is to say we know there are some things we do not know. But there are also unknown unknowns—the ones we don't know we don't know." (In a brilliant retort Slavoj Žižek defined a fourth category especially appropriate to Rumsfeld and his enablers, the "unknown known," that of self-deception or willful blindness to one's own heinous actions.) The likely huge (but unknown) number of unknown unknowns surround us like the Dark Matter that is believed to make up the greater part of the universe.

One of the reasons that I've always loved science fiction writing is that it can project alternative views of our current and future reality without necessarily being bogged down by scientific accuracy. This freedom from accuracy is why it is called fiction or fantasy or speculative. Science fiction may be used to comment on current political, social, or even scientific trends through alternate realities or by projecting futures that present the outcomes of extrapolations of current states or processes. Some of these predictions have actually come to pass, or at least have influenced the inventors of the new reality in such a way that the portrayals of what could be possible are so vivid as to frame how the creators will proceed with their discoveries. A case in point is William Gibson's description in *Neuromancer* of virtual reality and the visualization of the "interwebs."

A recurrent theme in science fiction is that of multiple alternate realities with pathways diverging at key points in history or even continuously bifurcating with every action and thereby creating an infinite number of parallel universes. Applied to a session of improvisation, we may find ourselves in a series of crucial actions with unpredictable outcomes. The actions and their perceptions are part and parcel of the socioacoustic, a feedback loop defined by the total interactions of all parties involved, both making music and listening.

I'm reminded of a science fiction story read in my long-distant youth. Searches for the author and title have thus far been fruitless. In this tale, a physicist who is also a jazz enthusiast obtains an ancient wire recording of an astounding saxophone solo from the 1950s, light-years beyond the concepts and techniques of any of the known players of the time. He's obsessed with the solo and when his work on a time machine (classic sci-fi trope!) comes to fruition, his first mission is to return to 1950s New York City, where he hopes to find the saxophonist on the recording. He succeeds in traveling back in time and haunts the abundant jazz clubs in search of the musician within the twenty-four-hour limit of the time travel window. The only player he hears who bears any relation to the sound on the tape is in steep decline thanks to drugs and alcohol but still displaying brilliance. He befriends the saxophonist and plays him the tape in hopes of finding out the source. The saxophonist is shocked by what he hears and becomes obsessed with it. The time traveler soon disappears, and the musician spends the remainder of his not-so-many days alive trying to recreate what he heard on the tape. His last act before his death is recording a solo on a wire recorder that eventually passes into the hands of the physicist/jazz enthusiast.

It's generally agreed by improvising musicians that when one enters the flow state, actions take on an automatic quality, with the improviser acting as both antenna and transmitter, manifesting the music without self-conscious input or manipulation. Is this actually happening, or is it merely our framing of the action as participating witnesses? Then, by entering a flow state and abdicating responsibility or even taking credit for our actions, are we abandoning our own contributions and letting the notion of predestination define our reality . . . all of our musical decisions, all of our creativity and energy for a process in which we're not causal but merely a vector? A more positive view might state that this sense of inevitability is continuously created, the multitude of possible universes each spun off from our current sonic actions. To keep the bubble of this particular set of probabilities in motion and to prevent it from bursting requires input: creative juice, sweat equity, even luck (if we define luck as receiving and acting on the information presented by the probabilities). Just as getting that electron up to the next quantum level requires energy, so does the improvisational process. At cruising altitude, the metaphorical electron of our sound process seems to be a perpetual motion machine, but it's not. Any lapse in what we shall call "automatic focus" can cause the particular reality to disappear—the gig's over.

If we continue descending to subatomic levels in our search for the ultimate, we may find everything to be made of units that cannot be defined as solid physical entities. Instead, we witness a maelstrom of particles manifested by the probability of their existence. But are these particles actually physical entities? Photons behave like particles and, in a seeming contradiction, also like waves, as demonstrated by the classic "two-slit experiment." In a continuous search for the ur-particle, physicists might bombard target neutrons with a pair of beams of incredibly high energy, on the average order of 6.5 teraelectronvolts, coursing at each other in opposite directions within the torus of the Large Hadron Collider. The neutrons are blown apart, and the decay of the various subatomic particles ensuing from the bombardment is measured and compared and perhaps named as new particles to be bombarded. Unique characteristics define the various results and increase the knowledge of the effect of seemingly subdividing the components of the elemental nucleus. An intuitive guess might be that this approach will be asymptotic and that the ultimate subatomic particle will never be found. Continuously increasing the power of the beams used in the process may very well generate more and more heretofore undiscovered particles, but the results will not necessarily be the discovery or definition of new fundamental particles but merely the generation of more particles as artifacts, splinters, dust. The observers are no closer to their goal. Though I might believe that the search will not accomplish what it proposes, the search itself remains valuable as there is no certainty as to what vistas will be unlocked.

Given the possibly infinite nature of the universe, then there would be an infinite number of data points on a timeline between the significant sonic events of our manifestation. If we can stretch our framing to encompass this infinitude, then all sonic actions within the course of a session of musicmaking could accordingly be reduced to the evanescence of the decay of a particule, a sonicule, not even a blink on the cosmic scale. Where and how does this admittedly reduced and simplified view of post-quantum physics apply and how does this examination of the search for the ultimate particle relate to improvised musicmaking? Can we say that each improviser engages in a search for the ur-state of sound, where they are fully in the Void? Or must the improviser relinquish the notion of arrival at the Void and simply surrender themselves to the asymptotic?

8

Derek Bailey

Hearing Derek on record for the first time in 1972 made me realize that "we are not alone"—the aliens had landed and they are us. And it was fine. In fact, it was fantastic, not only to hear Derek's particularly austere and spiky take on the outer limits of guitar and of the grammar of music itself, but to know that it could be captured on record and disseminated out into the world. To finally meet the man at Soundscape in 1980 and then to play together at a series he had booked in a photo studio in midtown Manhattan in 1981 had me both overjoyed and quaking in my boots. Derek's seemingly steely presence soon gave way to his warmth, humor, and keen intelligence.

A favorite moment: asked to accompany a journalist interviewing Derek for *Guitar Player* magazine, I was witness to a fabulous extemporaneous (and completely fictional) narrative about the genesis of improvised guitar in obscure seaside lounges in England in the early 1950s, all recounted completely straight-faced and with nary a wink or smirk. While having coffee after, just the two of us, Derek let loose with a fine cackle of glee.

In 1990, Derek joined Slan, the improvising trio of Ted Epstein, John Zorn, and me, for a gig at the old Knitting Factory. I had brought my Telecaster for Derek to use. He normally favored hollowbody archtops, but casting a hairy eyeball at my battered plank, Derek muttered that he'd "had one of these once" and then, with a twinkle in his eye, dimed all of the controls on the house Twin Reverb and proceeded to deliver a barrage of absolutely blistering sonics until the poor amp gave off a cloud of noxious smoke and went silent.

A choice memory of Derek was a relaxed afternoon meal in 1992 in Lisbon with him and his wife Karen the day after an improvisation festival in which we all performed. In general, talk rarely turned to music, but at this moment it did, with Derek offhandedly stating, "Of course, one should never listen to the people that you're playing with." Rather than taking this literally as a corollary, I assume that Derek was alluding to the state of inevitability that is Improviser's Mind in action.

9

Mind

The Gap

Events separated by markers and measured: time, framed. Between the markers, the pool of time: unknown, nondemarcated, infinite. Walls, borders, and membranes enclosed and measured: space, finite. Within the space, infinite distances found between the points. Between the frames, between the walls, a gap. A differential, a potential, is generated by the relationship between the frames of time or between any space and another space, whether adjacent or remote. This separation is the reservoir of force, the unknown entanglement.

What may bridge these gaps and actualize the potential energy in this cosmic battery? One might say that there is an inevitability at work. Gravity, thermodynamics, entropy: known laws of our universe conspire with laws yet unknown to cause the release of this potential, thus returning the system to a resting state. The measure of that release is a single frame, a unit of discharge running from zero to X.

We jump from the macroscopic present to a deeply ancient microscopic past: a complex molecule is submerged in a soup containing other complex molecules. Through physical forces these molecules come into contact and bond to form ever-larger aggregates or supermolecules. Some would be defined as organic, since they contain carbon-carbon and carbon-hydrogen bonds. Over millennia, these supermolecules form larger entities and bond with other such aggregates, eventually creating ever-greater agglomerations of supermolecules, some of which will be found to possess unique capabilities such as photosensitivity or responses to different environments including motion, all aspects that create a change of state, an input-output. At some point the entities may interface with an external coding function such as DNA, another complex molecule and essentially an algorithm that provides the substrate with an instruction set to create repeatable structures and define the organization of potential actions (including duplicating itself). The aggregate entity may now be able to reproduce by splitting the DNA component into chains of nucleotides or RNA, which may then combine with other RNA molecules to create copies of the original aggregate. Can we consider these entities to be alive? Do they take in fuel and generate waste material as a by-product of their continuing chemical processes? The entity receives chemical input and expels chemical output and to survive it must differentiate between the input and output materials mixed in the soup in which it is immersed. Input is fuel that will allow the entity to continue functioning or become part of the entity, expanding it in size. Waste includes materials that are not part of the entity, and which may cause its processes to cease functioning—in other words, poisoning the entity. The chemical communication of input/output is transmitted to the other aggregates and migrates internally between the sub-entities. Multiply this process over eons until, in a process of feedback and refinement, some sub-entities become autonomous specialized organs of input and output, the loop yielding a system of identification for entity and non-entity, input and output, food and waste. There is movement and reproduction, the process continuing automatically with the chemicals that are input yielding one response and the chemicals that are output, another. There remains a gap, the spaces separating the acts of intake and expulsion.

The aggregate may now possess characteristics that could cause us to define it as "alive": it may reproduce, it may be mobile, it may take in sustenance and expel waste. Alive, yes, but it still might just be hash: a "deaf, dumb, and blind" mechanistic accounting system, input and output, a balance sheet. Increased possibilities of input give more channels of raw data. Sensitivity to light or vibrations of various frequencies. The aggregate grows chains of stimulus and response to bring this new information into the system, with resultant actions yielding the same process again and again. The aggregate develops specialized sub-entities that change state dependent on the input and output in a chemical ledger—a basic memory system. The recognition of input is rewarded: a chemical increase. Perhaps the production of dopamine dates back to the early formations of these aggregates and was a contributor to the perception of chemical reward. This input is the fuel, and, in the presence of this reward, the response across the gap generates an energy. This is pleasure—the activation of the reward. Pleasure equals positive feedback—the reason, the ability, the need—to pursue more input. The entity operates from the principle that input equals pleasure which equals the possibility of generating increase of the entity. These transactions are all noted in the ledger.

Is the entity conscious of any of these processes? When consciousness arises is it the same as Mind? What is Mind in relation to this entity? What lies between the input and the output but the entity itself, the gap and an image of the gap? Here is the threshold of recognition for the "I" of identity: if it is not fuel, if it is not waste, then it is either Self or some external other, as yet undefined. When and how does the recognition occur, the self-awareness? Perhaps the gap itself is the answer: the space of unresolved time, the expectation of a change in potential energy to yield a flash, the burst of pleasure. A signal goes out and when the answer returns, the chemical handshaking says: this is not fuel, not waste, but something "other." From the endless iterations of the reinforcement of this signal, the feedback loop coalesces into an object/process that reinforces its own identity by forming specialized networks that release certain chemicals when the pleasure of the "other" is detected. These chemicals are noted in the memory ledger. At some point, the "other" may be recognized as the same entity as the one receiving the "other." Other = Self. The more that selfness is reinforced, the closer the aggregate comes to the realization of itself as a conscious entity.

Recent studies of neurophysiology have focused on the microtubules found in the neurons, dendrites, and axons, structures that are used to transfer different neurotransmitters throughout the nervous system. The photosensitivity of these microtubules and, in fact, sensitivity to quantum vibrations point to the possibility that the secret of consciousness lies within their functioning as antennae to the infinite probability system that is our universe. It also opens the door to conjecture about quantum resonance and communication between sentient entities.

Within the gap resides the set of potentials to be resolved, whether instantaneously or over a longer period. The stimulus has been sensed before; it is known. The signal of identity, the pulse of energy, is registered and changes the state of a cell connected to the gap. The gap has created a dedicated system of memory. But the gap is not a binary device, for within its span there are myriad paths for consideration and action, including a null path of nothing at all, a resting state. Transmission and reception, input and output. The receptor continuously polls the gap until the potential is released. Gradations of response may be noted: when the percentage of positive input fires past a threshold, the answer is "yes." The "gap" is the open door to the place where Schrödinger's Cat lives, an area of infinite possibility. We may compare this manifestation of awareness within the living gap to the sensors found in a silicon device and the interpretation of their output. Silicon awareness reduces the expectations query to a binary response. To move past a mechanical consciousness demands switches that recognize not just states of "yes" and "no," but a full gradient of possibilities and probabilities.

A leap over the gap into another realm, that of music and sound. Music began as pure sound, a set of physical phenomena to be noted, wondered at, questioned, enjoyed. We might surmise that early humans and protohumans imitated the sounds of their environment for the purpose of hunting or curiosity or pleasure, even for the identification of self or self-formed associations. The repetitive use of such tools as stone scrapers and grinders coalesced into patterns, perhaps in imitation of other creatures' repetitive sounds, perhaps internally generated as a mimetic response to heartbeat and pulse. Input, output. Pleasure, functionality. Intended sound. That which is heard becomes food for the ears, food for thought, food for the body. The output—the sound produced—is both desired result and excreta, the sonic waste produced in the living of life, sustenance for the maker and for those who witness, or, on the other hand, waste noise for the surrounding audio bystanders. The gap, that space between input and output, operates on a shifting scale as the acts of making sounds and listening to them takes place. Awareness of the action brings it into the foreground, thereby increasing its significance. The act and sound are no longer divided into components, but are now one structure: the object and its hearing united in a state of "musicness."

For the maker of sound or music, there is a distance between the conception and the manifestation, measurable time for the physical actions to take place, measurable space for movement of fingers, hands, vocal components. The sound producer may not have a discrete plan in advance for what they will produce, but once sonic consciousness emerges, somewhere in their creative core exists a seed of conception, a Platonic ideal of sound. The awareness of this seed of conception is a substrate on which the process occurs and against which the action is compared. The distance between conception and output is another gap, one that may be examined from different angles. This point of view (point of hearing?) may be sonic, purely a measure of physical vibrations, or philosophical, an instant evaluation of the situation followed by feedback regarding the perceived success of the output in comparison to its conception. As the making of sound gets closer in time or in accuracy to its conception, the gap shrinks. Though in reality asymptotic, as an action within the creative process, the gap seems to disappear completely for the maker. Even when sound exists within a definable genre of music, time becomes fractal for the musician fully immersed in the process. Recursiveness renders the scale of the external clock malleable: one may zoom from infinitely microscopic to the infinitely macroscopic with different vistas opening up in either direction . . . to be lost in the space between two markers, whether they be endless drones, equal demarcations of time into small discrete chunks, or inchoate noise. Sound outside of scale is a window into time travel, teleportation, parallel reality—even if only within the closed perceptual system of the musician and listener. Extramusical communication operates as a subcode to the sound itself, subconsciously catalyzing the handshake between input and output. One person alone making music is already a vast set of possibilities, but add one or more players or listeners into the mix of collective sound production and the field expands toward the infinite, ripe with diverging paths that render the synchronicities all the more dramatic. What are these points of intersection? Random coincidence is certainly possible, but could it also be subliminal communication on a pheromonal level, or even the manifestation of quantum entanglement effecting actions without any linear or visible direction of causality? When the music happens in such a way that the improvisers recognize as being of the void, there is that feeling of inevitability, a going-togetherness.

Another leap, this time to a functional AI Mind and a deep question: Does it groove? Does it sing? Can it improvise? Musical improvisation balances memory, intention, spontaneity, and acoustics, as well as the internal sense of narrative, all embedded within a translation of the creative impulse to sonic inevitability. To build an improvising AI, we would need porous switching, where the network polls tendencies just as a neuron polls and calculates the various inputs to yield, finally, a response—the firing of a synapse, the leap over the gap. Could the answer be the meat/machine interface so beloved of recent sci-fi, or in the recent experimental Neuroplatform? A bacterial computer operating from our own gut? (A nod to Greg Bear's visionary novel *Blood Music* is in order here.) When the component "transcriptors" can finally operate at high enough speeds, could a DNA computer function as the perfect soft brain to intersect with the hard AI? Rightness, not accuracy, is necessarily the goal. Mind must include error, clouds of ambiguity leading to ultimate clarity at the moment, decision-making based not just on logic, but feeling. It's built into our code, and perhaps that old cliché of our language contains an element of overarching guidance: "gut feeling" giving us the push across the gap. With another leap, we go beyond biological computation to direct quantum interface. We may surmise that we've always made use of it, but without any awareness of its existence, of how it even functions. But what the quantum communication manifests is ubiquitous, even if we can never see it working from outside of our own state of being and doing.

10

The Musical Garden of Toru Takemitsu

We digress with a walk in the musical garden of Toru Takemitsu, suspended between the silence, *ma* in Japanese, and the essential sound of a composer who delicately confronts many dualities. To the typical listener of classical music, his work may seem strangely exotic in its instrumentation and gestures, but at other times comfortably familiar, with a sound steeped in early twentieth-century Impressionism. No matter the style, Takemitsu calls forth the rich imagery of historical events, deep suspense, sheer terror, or an inner sound—"a lifelike event, beyond esthetics, without conclusion" in the words of the composer.

As a teenager in the final days of World War II, Takemitsu was inspired by the beauty of a phonograph recording of a French *chanson* played clandestinely by a soldier in the country clearing wood. This moment sparked his decision to pursue music after the war. Self-taught, he found inspiration in the sounds and techniques of Debussy and Messiaen. Later influenced by the words and music of John Cage, he set out to explore what Cage called the "insides of sounds" and the very functioning of music. Essential to an "Eastern" approach to music, in Takemitsu's conception, is the Confucian idea of music as ceremony: dignified, devoid of direct expression of emotions, an allegory. In Takemitsu's words:

> The Japanese temple gong speaks without personal identification: its sound seems to melt into the world beyond persons, static and sensual. Does one express himself through his own suppression? Or is the reverse true? Either way a simple comparison between Japan and the West is meaningless. I hope to define the characteristics of something Japanese, then, with those characteristics—personally confront something European of comparable value. At this point in my generation such confrontation of the two traditions should not be impossible.

Although he considered himself to be a composer of "Western" music, Takemitsu carefully considered the historic breadth of Japanese arts (and their roots in Korea and China) in assembling a personal approach. In a diary entry from 1962, he describes hearing the eighth-century Japanese court music *gagaku*: "The most important instrument here is the *sho* [mouth organ]. My impression of ascending sounds and the secret of immeasurable metaphysical time seems to be based on the sound of this instrument. I want to give serious thought to some of those things that *gagaku* suggests to contemporary music."

A landmark composition for Takemitsu, in terms of the manifestation of his identity, his theories, and his practice, was *Arc for Piano and Orchestra* (1963).

> Many compositional ideas came to me from old Japanese gardens. I love gardens. They do not reject people. There one can walk freely, pause to view the entire garden, or gaze at a single tree. Plants, rocks, and sand show changes, constant changes. *Arc* is a musical garden that changes with each performance. In this metaphysical garden I tried to create a structure of tempo strongly influenced by the traditional idea of *ma*, which exists at the performer's discretion in the Noh drama. By allowing the solo piano to stroll through the garden with changing viewpoints, the piece is freed from a set frame. It becomes a mobile strongly reminiscent of the Heian period (794–1185) hand scroll painting. Such a concept, which gives mode and rhythm to individual parts like characters in a play, comes out of the tradition and musical spirit of Debussy and Messiaen.

Rather than the Western viewpoint of the orchestra regarded as one gigantic instrument, Takemitsu used it as a source of many different sounds, a "garden for strolling."

Later, he considered the use of Japanese instruments together with the symphony orchestra. *November Steps*, commissioned in 1967 by the New York Philharmonic, is composed for the *biwa* (a four- or five-string lute using a large plectrum) and *shakuhachi* flute, plus orchestra. The *biwa* was played by the daring and innovative Kinshi Tsuruta, while the *shakuhachi* was played by the equally virtuosic Katsuya Yokoyama. Takemitsu wrote,

> The *biwa* could be called the mother of Japanese music. The major characteristic that sets it apart from Western instruments is the active inclusion of noise in its sound. The sounds of such instruments are produced spontaneously in performance—they seem to resonate through the performer. In the process of their creation, theoretical thinking is destroyed. A single strum of the strings or even one pluck is too complex, too complete in itself to admit any theory. Between this complex sound—so strong that it can stand alone—and that point of intense silence preceding it, called *ma*, there is a metaphysical continuity that defies analysis. Like *itcho* (a recital of an excerpt from Noh drama accompanied by a single percussion instrument), this *ma* and sound do not exist as a technically definable relationship. It is here that sound and silence confront each other, balancing each other in a relationship beyond any objective measurement.

Takemitsu, in speaking of filmmaking, says that "sound is also an image—we have plenty of moviemakers who 'shoot film' but do not 'see'—there may be many ways of 'seeing.'" And so, there are many ways of hearing, he says: "A door slams . . . Let us imagine that I hear agony in that sound. But within the realm of physics, that sound is only a blue light glowing on the oscilloscope. We can reduce both sound and color to wave forms regardless of their own propensities. If this is so, was it foolish of me to hear agony in footsteps and pain in the screech of the wheels?"

We may ask if that deepest emotion may be heard in the measured tones of a church organ, the deeply burnished *shakuhachi* obligato, the clashing flurries of *koto* strings against a dissonant bed of low strings in the score for the film *Rikyu*? These elements all evoke the flavor of the seventeenth-century imperial court, the intrigue of a counterpoint not of harmony but of the interplay of strategies and betrayals.

While a student at Bard College in the 1970s, I was introduced to the triple threat of the music of Takemitsu, the films of Teshigahara, and the writing of Kōbō Abe all in one evening with a viewing of *Woman in the Dunes*. This was a film that overwhelmed and terrified me with delight. I was intrigued by the seething otherworldly sound that perfectly personified the shifting sands and parallel reality of the villagers, and was excited to find the same forces at work in *The Face of Another*, a masterpiece of psychological cinema based on the book by Yukio Mishima, a horrifying meditation on the surface skin and its connection to the inner mind and personal identity. As if to hint at the Freudian undercurrent, the opening montage of faces is accompanied by a bittersweet waltz, orchestrated for sweeping strings. Scenes in a sanitarium for the mentally ill are scored to collages of atonal crashing piano chords mixed with the ravings of Hitler addressing his adoring masses. A floating, dissonant motif played by flute and vibraphone materializes under discussions of the construction of the mask and the thought processes of the man for whom it is made. His distress is orchestrated to harshly ring-modulated piano chords, transformed into near-noise. His "resurrection" in the real world wearing his mask is ironically set to the bouncy accordion foxtrot of a pseudo-Bavarian beerhall. (A bonus treat in *The Face of Another* is a cameo appearance in one scene by Takemitsu sitting in a *kissaten*, or coffee shop.)

The theme from the film *Dodeskaden* encapsulates the many perspectives pictured in this slice of Tokyo slum underlife. Optimistic and whimsical major key melodies are contrasted with an interjected sourness in the string glissandi just to keep things real.

The scores to *Empire of Passion* and *Harakiri*, also composed by Takemitsu, most completely manifest the elements he describes in his meditations on the confrontation of sound and silence, the emulation of nature, the essences of Japanese and Western orchestration. The restless *koto* ostinati, asymmetrical eruptions of tuned percussion, and questioning strings in *Empire of Passion* underpin a *shakuhachi* commentary that conjures swirling mists, a deep dread, an erotic tension. *Harakiri* is a *biwa* tour de force. Composed in 1962, it represents Takemitsu's first use of the instrument in a contemporary score. Over ominous strings and the crackling percussive interjections of a Noh play, the *biwa* enters mysterious sonic realms, sometimes driving in a relentless strum, sometimes teasing out strange resonances and bent buzzes. Speaking of the *biwa*, Takemitsu describes the tradition of *sawari*. The *sawari* is the part of the neck where the strings are stretched over a grooved ivory plate—the point of contact creates the characteristic buzz, deliberately designed to imitate the sound of a cicada. It is also physically similar to the ivory bridge of the sitar, designed to create a buzzing sound as well. The convex part of this plate is called the "mountain," and the concave part is the "valley." In addition, the word itself, *sawari*, also means "touch" and "obstacle" and colloquially describes the menstrual cycle—altogether a perfect metaphor for what Takemitsu defined as the Japanese approach: an instrument that creates its own obstructions which are an essential part of the uniqueness of its sound. The music itself is manifested from the inner core of that sound. Takemitsu writes, "Sounds are ever-present as new individual realities. Let us start listening with unfettered ears. Soon sounds will reveal their turbulent transformations to us. The new and the old are both necessary to me. The unknown is neither past nor future—it exists only in the precise present."

Takemitsu's garden is far from the manicured perfection found in the English tradition, but instead islands of calm beauty coexist with explosions of weeds, ancient species, and wild growth hinting at nature untamed—yet filtered through a refined vision. There is an element of mystery always present in the music of Toru Takemitsu, a beautiful haziness that is never merely pretty, but invites the listener to find the undercurrents of deep beauty swirling around them.

11

Nicolas Slonimsky

The grandfather of my friend Kate Yourke was the legendary Russian-born composer, musicologist, author, elfin sonic prankster, and raconteur Nicolas Slonimsky. On our first meeting, like a true fan boy, I was thrilled that he was willing to autograph my copy of *Thesaurus of Scales and Melodic Patterns*, his visionary theoretical and reference work first published in 1947 and hugely influential for John Coltrane and Frank Zappa, among many others. The *Thesaurus* creates scales based on mathematical symmetries and displacement that in some cases need five octaves or more to resolve to the starting point, as well as patterns of varying shapes and dispositions.

When in NYC visiting his daughter Electra, Nicolas might come to Kate's house in Brooklyn for a soiree, where he could be easily persuaded to perform Chopin's *Black Key Etude* using an orange to press the piano keys. With great glee he told me about his time working as pianist and secretary to conductor Serge Koussevitzky at the Boston Symphony Orchestra. Koussevitzky could only conduct in the meters of two or three and when the BSO was scheduled to perform Igor Stravinsky's *The Rite of Spring* in 1923 for its American premiere, it was left for Nicolas to rewrite the entire complex and syncopated score in two so that Serge could conduct it.

One day in 1991, Kate and I brought Nicolas to the Veselka Cafe for lunch, a Ukrainian joint on 2nd Avenue and 9th Street, an East Village fixture long known for round-the-clock cheap and filling eats. The crusty Old World waitress came to take our order and, on asking Nicolas what he would like, he said wistfully that he couldn't decide because it was all of his favorite Russian foods. The waitress glared and corrected him: "Not Russian, Ukrainian!" Slonimsky replied that no, this was Russian food and he was Russian, and all of it was his favorite. The waitress began to flush, steam pouring from her eyes and ears, and stomped off. After a short interval a young man came to our table and we quickly ordered a selection of items for

Nicolas, thereby forestalling an international incident, perhaps even averting a war.

The *Lexicon of Musical Invective* is another classic work of Slonimsky's: a collection of bad reviews that composers down the ages have received from their "critics." It's a revelation to read how Beethoven's *Ninth Symphony* was treated by the so-called experts and arbiters of taste. Also inspiring was the response that many composers and musicians offered back to their critics. It's unfortunate that 50 or 100 or 1,000 people might attend a magnificent and crucial concert, but 10,000 or more will read the biased review that only reflects the opinion of one person. Music is the source of psychoacoustic chemical change in the listener and can be a powerful force in opening minds. How many people say, "My life was changed by reading that review of so-and-so's performance," or "I understand the world differently now because of that review of that string quartet"? Scratch a critic and reveal a bitter or failed composer.

I shared my studio for fifteen years with two cats, sisters white and gray. They seemed to derive great pleasure from recordings of Robert Johnson and Skip James, often climbing onto the loudspeakers to bask in the sound. Yet their favorite composer was Virgil Thompson for other than sonic reasons. When Thompson died, his old friend, Electra, was tasked with cleaning out his apartment in the Chelsea Hotel and, joining her mother in the work, Kate snagged his can opener for me, which was afterward used daily to open the cats' tins of wet food.

12

The Implicate Drone

Not those flying toys and lethal weapons of war, but the sound: ever-changing but static, filled with detail yet monolithic, a soothing presence or invasive annoyance. We are surrounded by drones and dronalities, whether intentionally created as musical gestures or as the by-product of activities by both living things and machines in our environment.

Certainly the drone, in all modes of its defining essence, has been a constant gesture in music both ancient and modern. With probable origins many thousands of years ago in the western regions of Central Asia followed by its outward dissemination, the drone has formed the substrate of many North African and Arab musics, later extending across Europe and then finding root in the Americas in traditional blues and folk music. The drone became formalized in twentieth-century America and Europe in funk, jazz, rock, minimalism, and experimental music as an extended-time variation of the pedal point—a continuous tone that may be sustained across changing musical scenarios, whether harmonic or melodic. The drone may appear as a benign sound, bland or sweet, but also as a massive block of noise. The drone may be just a single pitch or a note and its strongest overtones of a fifth, an octave, a tenth. The drone may consist of simultaneous verticalities whose focus may shift though the sonic gesture is continuous, without attack or rhythm, transforming a drone into a dronality. The appeal of the drone in all its forms is clear: an open canvas upon which nearly anything may be superimposed. This drone is explicit.

The *sruti* in South Asian music, the *maqam* in Arab music, bagpipes or resonating strings in Balkan folk music, the underlying sustained tones of *piobaireachd* (aka pibroch music) from the Northern Scottish Highlands—all are manifestations of the explicit drone. A mood is defined by the drone: an emotional framing catalyzed by an array of pitches. In Indian music, it may be generated with voice, tamboura, harmonium, or *sruti* box, an electronic synthesizer that produces a set of notes specifically tuned to accompany *ragas*. Explicit drones blur the fabric of linear time and obscure the bar lines, the markers that divide music into metered frames. Music played over a drone gives the feeling of timelessness—existence devoid of both beginning and end. These drones are interlocked in a feedback loop which creates a reciprocal relationship with the variations and inventions that rise from their base seemingly without harmonic or melodic barriers. If any of the component parts of the drone changes, then all of the relationships between the pitches that will be superimposed change as well, thus changing the emotional tessitura of the music in a sonic feedback loop. The explicit drone is an invitation to openness, a relaxation of discriminations that allows the music to flow freely within the delimiting parameters of a particularly defined cultural matrix.

Piobaireachd relies on the drone of the pipes to provide structure throughout the slow and measured arc of the music. The ground in this music has become fixed over the centuries. Whereas improvisation was once an important element, it has faded into the background as *piobaireachd* has become more folkloric, an artifact of the tradition rather than an ongoing vital practice (not to take away from the beauty of the current state of this music). The sixteenth and seventeenth centuries were a peak time for *piobaireachd*, when improvisation was an essential component of its variations, accumulating tension and excitement leading up to displays of high-speed virtuosity in the ultimate choruses. While the fast-paced climax over the slow-moving ground is retained in today's pibroch, the lines now are handed down and learned by rote, not the product of spontaneous invention.

The diddley bow, the ur-instrument of the country blues (and namesake of the great R&B singer and guitarist Bo Diddley), may be tied directly to the prehistoric practice of musicmaking using the hunter's bow. A monochord, the diddley bow is made by wrapping one end of a piece of metal wire or heavy string or animal sinew around a nail fastened into a wall. The other end is held to the floor or ground with a rock or nail, with another rock or brick or piece of wood tensioning the string and forming a bridge. The string is plucked or struck by hand or with a stick, while a glass bottle stops the string at the desired pitch. Glissandi and vibrato come naturally to this setup and are a prime feature of the diddley bow, a vocalized line emerging from the drone. Think of the country blues slide guitar as an instrument that distills six diddley bows into a portable resonator to create a richly varying drone over which the combination of melodic and rhythmic gestures ride, either as an instrumental force or accompanying vocals. In the music of Mississippi Fred McDowell, his expressive and rhythmic singing sails over a thumb-picked driving groove that rests on a base of tonality, an open string in an open chord. His bottleneck guitar provides commentary and counterpoint and weaves and darts above the rhythmic patterns below, sometimes underpinning, sometimes interlocking, sometimes becoming the main voice. McDowell's drone, like that of most Delta players, is never a limitation, but a welcoming: a path running deep into the emotional landscape of the song and rooted in African song-story traditions, transplanted and transformed in the New World.

Listening to the North Mississippi fife and drum music of Othar Turner, one hears a direct link to sub-Saharan African music in all its polyrhythmic glory, with overtone-based fife melodies emerging from the drumming like sparks from a brush fire. Still vital today though Turner himself has passed, his Rising Stars Fife and Drum Band, now under the leadership of his granddaughter Shardé Thomas, is a window into a music created hundreds of years ago by the meeting of African and European sounds, tragically under the auspices of colonialism and slavery. I had the pleasure and honor of opening for the Rising Stars Band in a medium-sized Lower East Side club back in the last century, and the power of their sound was earth-shaking, the effect ecstatic. Low-tuned parade drums, heads tightened just enough to maximize sustain but deep enough to boom, rang out to form a rich dronality, never static but ever present, over which Shardé exhorted the crowd and played venerable melodies and reductionist solos on her reed fife. The antecedents of these North American musics are found in songs from Mali and Senegal, from Nigeria and Saharan Africa, but modulated by European forms and harmonic movement. The particular dronalities of these musics not only define the sound of the song, but embed it in a geographical locus, the migrations and evolutions of place and story decoded in the hearing. This locus is not merely directional but also temporal—accreted layers of musical tradition, continually evolving but with the taproot always in evidence. Here, the drone is rarely stated explicitly but emerges as the implied sum of tendencies generated by the melodic materials over a base that is simple from a distance. This base, however, when examined from within, reveals itself as a hypercomplex stew of interlocked polyrhythms, with the resultant cloud of overtones from the struck membranes generating a dronality.

One may perceive a trap created by the explicit drone: a skein of acoustic barriers, an invisible electrified fence that dares musicians to defy the benign consonance outlined by the drone. Most choose not to oppose the drone, as there is undeniably great pleasure to be found, both for musician and audience, in flowing along with the drone's soft currents, reinforcing the clear and present offering of the substrate in their mellifluous overtones. There is no maleficence in the drone, as the music in which it functions is often positive in its presence. To the practitioner of drone-oriented music, the relaxation, tranquility, and mild stimulation that is a product of this flow is the desired result, a goal to be achieved. So often, such a musician floats freely above the drone, the notion of groove left miles below and eons ago. Still, an inventive musician may spontaneously permute the set of pitches defined as "correct" by the drone in such a manner as to maintain the excitement of improvisational creativity. Such individuals seem to be somewhat in the minority though, with most players conforming to that which is expected, a practice that can be seductive and indeed enjoyable for those so inclined (not to mention profitable), but leaving some listeners desiring more. The danger lies in the oft-self-imposed notion that one must reflect and adhere to the drone's spectrum. Ornaments, whether microtonal or outside of the predetermined notes, may add slight tensions that can be exhilarating in context, though never challenging the orthodoxy of the pitch array, never inciting the possibility of a radical change in the state of the music. In cultural musics that maintain the drone as a defining component, these sonic tensions enrich the music and are a vital element; we, the listeners, are quite happy that this music is not disrupted, not subverted. However, when the explicit drone is used in modern Western art music, to my ears, it dictates submissiveness—the passivity of the simple, the cohesive, the conformity to the consensus rules, the limitations of a closed set of sounds. The disruption and excitement comes when the challenging pitches cease to be mere ornament and become structural, sounds that transform the drone itself and the overall identity of the music.

As John Coltrane began to see his work as spiritual practice as much as musical praxis, the drone began to be of greater importance to him. Honed on the extended modal changes of Miles Davis's *All Blues*, Coltrane's own quartet would play lengthy improvisations on one or two chords, as in his arrangement of *My Favorite Things* or *India*, with the notion of tonality all but disappearing. Live performances of *India* have been recorded in multiple versions. In one realization heard on *The Complete 1961 Village Vanguard Recordings*, the explicit drone of the tamboura is added to the basic ensemble. Despite the clear tonal center of this drone, Coltrane is never inhibited in his melodic extrapolations. While continuously referencing the strong fundamental pitches present in the dronality, Coltrane plays hyperspeed lines, glissandi, vibrato morphing into non-tempered modulations, onomatopoeic screams, and vocalized sounds that verge on non-pitched noise. These elements may not be immediately recognized as directly related to the explicit drone present in the music, but they are most definitely manifesting the limits of musical inevitability, as well as the clear exhibition of a spontaneous resonance that violates the strict border of the given drone and transforms it into a multilayered dronality. Given the rising tide of Black Nationalism and the movement for civil rights in the US in the 1960s, Coltrane's push against the neutrality of the drone is a combination of ecstasy, fury, sonic revolution, and a search for transcendence, the explicit catalyzing the implicate, the cosmic touching the earth and its daily concerns, whether in the practical, the social, the musical, or the political.

The dronalities created by the low horns of Tibetan ritual music, the *dungchens* and *ragdungs*, form continuously varying sonic strata underlying the melodic inventions and vibrational strategies that generate the top layer. Not as specific in defining an overarching set of pitches as the aforementioned drones of South Asian or Scottish music, the Tibetan dronality expands not just horizontally in time but vertically in both directions from its center pitch. Especially when combined with gongs, the frequency spectrum in the Tibetan drone bristles with overtones of fundamental pitches that do not fall within simple harmonic relationships and are certainly not anywhere close to resembling Western notions of "equal temperament." These drones are saturated with complex timbres and aperiodic modulations. The nature of the dronalities is rendered as a broad swath of rich texture more akin to a rushing river than to the placid stream of the explicit drone. There is pitch, but there is also an inchoate wall of noise that resolves in fractal fashion as one zooms in. This type of drone may be compared to a number line, with the infinite y axis extending vertically in both directions from an arbitrary zero point, touching the Void. Melodic material of varying intonation may be deployed over these dronalities. There may be purely percussive manifestations, with gongs generating waves of sound that may either reinforce or clash with the overtones, thereby generating new dronalities. The Tibetan drone is one that expands the explicit out into the Void, deeper and wider, becoming implicate.

This, then, is the implicate drone, a summation of dronal strategies that includes that which is explicit where it exists as source material for invention and transformation in a feedback loop. The implicate drone is a reflection of our existence in the modern world, finding its origins in the sensations in the wild—of the low rumble of wind or the susurration of rain, the restless white noise of deep river or surf, thunder echoing from mountains and over valleys until it becomes a deep roar. We leap generations to the hum and rhythmic clatter of the railroad train, traffic's gray murk and clarion calls, the thrum of airplane engines, the between-station static of radio and television, the insistent drone of the high-tension 60 Hz power lines noted by La Monte Young when describing the sonic inspiration found in his younger days, a sound suspended between B and B♭. By way of contrast, in Europe with its alternating current operating at 50 Hz, this low drone is centered 35 cents sharp of G. Dr. Andrew Fabian, an X-ray astronomer at the Institute of Astronomy at Cambridge University in England, states that our universe is filled with the sound of a B♭ fifty-seven octaves lower than middle C, emitted by a supermassive black hole in the Perseus cluster of galaxies, creating pressure waves that are thirty thousand light-years across with a period of oscillation of ten million years, arguably the ultimate implicate drone. We are surrounded by countless colors and flavors of dronality, both natural and products of human origin, dronalities that rise to the surface and may become explicit. They are intermittent, ebb and flow—omnipresent or gone without a trace. They may be manifested as frequencies high enough to register as pitch or low enough to become pulse, rhythm, a subliminal feeling. Ultimately, we may sense the implicate drone as a probabilistic tendency rather than a physical phenomenon. All of our actions in sound can be interpreted as operating in relation to these dronalities. Perhaps everything we see and feel in our universe is just a fleeting harmonic of the Big Bang's drone, the probability holding it together for just however long our universe will exist.

The implicate drone serves as memory when the explicit drone disappears. It provides a starting point and a reference, a homing beacon, abstract strata as foundation. In Euclidean geometry, a solid line is analyzed as an infinite number of points with infinite space between each of them. Imagine the drone of a tamboura as a solid line, then imagine it transposed down by multiple octaves, slowed down in time, expanded to astronomical dimensions. Consider the infinite spaces between the components of this explicit drone. Within this infinitude, anything is possible, any sound, any scaling in time in *n* dimensions up or down, zooming in or out. We enter a non-Euclidean universe where there is both the possibility of infinite parallels and infinite non-parallels. We may easily transport the starting coordinates of (0,0) and place them anywhere at any time. The drone itself is then granulated to an infinite series of component sounds, thus implying an equally infinite number of relationships to the musical action.

But is this sea of myriad possibilities then carte blanche for any and all sonic manifestations? When hearing the meeting of varied sounds, why do we deem one correct, another not—one good, one bad? In my first experience working with the Japanese *butoh* dance troupe Byakko Sha in Tokyo in 1985, it was decided that the section in which I was participating would be an improvisation, but we would still rehearse it. The usual course of action when improvising with NYC-based dancers was to attempt to imitate and transform in the service of a greater unison, to correlate sound and action. After about one minute of improvising together at our rehearsal in Tokyo, the lead dancer stopped and said to me in English (and somewhat crossly), "Never look at the dancers when playing!" She was telling me to avoid making the connection between sound and motion explicit, but to let the simultaneity define the intimate and inevitable relationship between them. This creates a state of "going-togetherness," a notion that resonates with both Zen thought and Fluxus art and informs work from a constellation of artists including Yoko Ono, John Cage, Alison Knowles, Dick Higgins, Charlotte Moorman, Merce Cunningham, Nam June Paik, and Henry Flynt (who operated with both explicit and implicate drones) to name a few, and, of course, the philosophy and music of Toru Takemitsu.

When creating sound, how does one find that state of "going-togetherness"? It may come from congruence or from contrast, extension or disruption, absurdity or tranquility, conflict or emptiness. The desired state is a realization of the perfect non-moment, not just a point on a line but THIS point on THIS line at THIS moment in all its importance and simultaneous triviality. Can it be explained, or even recognized? Consider quantum entanglement as a possible mechanism for this congruence. Consider coincidence, points of intersection in a vast probability calculator. Consider all musical activity as bouncing off of the still-resounding echoes of the drone of the Big Bang. Consider the wisdom of muscles modulated both by memory and by pheromonal handshaking. Consider socioacoustics: when musicians meet in the implicate drone, they know it.

In my own praxis, the implicate drone may be found in improvised expansions of seed material existing as algorithms or instruction sets, graphic notation, or predetermined core elements. It may also be more fully realized in through-composed scores where the interactions are precisely notated in time to create dronalities that proceed through their trajectories. These dronalities may be constructed from vertical arrays of pitches, sometimes augmented with layers of non-pitched material. As the music is manifested, emphasis may be shifted to specific layers, thus bringing them to the forefront. This is not unlike the effect of a saturated sound being filtered with a narrow-bandpass hi-Q (selectivity) device that essentially pulls out and focuses on specific bands of information, bestowing upon them the function of a primary explicit drone. As the narrative arc of the music progresses, this primary drone may change. Though always a component of the implicate drone, it remains fluid in its role just as a note in a chord progression whose relationship to the tonic is ever shifting, even sometimes becoming the tonic.

In my 2023 piece *Occam's Machete*, for an orchestra of twenty-four strings spatially arranged, the music dances on the fine line between implicate and explicit drones. The forty-minute piece was built upon the core concept of *Occam's Razor*, my piece for double string quartet from 2011 with a duration of fifteen minutes. Both pieces were composed for specific performance spaces: *Razor* for the marble halls and six-second reverb of ISSUE Project Room at 110 Livingston Street in Brooklyn, and *Machete* for the equally reverberant basement performance space of Brooklyn's Main Drag Music, a room with thirty-foot-high ceilings with catwalks and stairways surrounding the space and extending from floor to ceiling. In both pieces, a series of dronalities are built upon an initial drone pitch and a target pitch grace note. Within each section, the initial pitch diminishes in length as the grace note increases, eventually reversing their roles to create a new dronality. Target pitches have pre-notated microtonal variations to enhance the production of difference tones. In addition, as each piece progresses, additional grace notes are added to form micromelodies. While the piece is externally an ex-

Figure 9 Score, *Occam's Machete* (2023).

plicit drone, it is continually shifting in harmonic structure and internal detail. The dronalities are never constant or static or tranquil, and the resultant sounds are never predictable. Combined with the acoustical properties of a space, such as Main Drag's basement, the listener is immersed in a dynamically changing ocean of sound, an implicate drone.

Ultimately, the implicate drone is taken for granted, like the air we breathe and water we drink, or the sea of ambient sound in which we are immersed. This awareness may recede to the background, but this makes it no less crucial. When we renew our relationship with the implicate drone, it catalyzes and revitalizes our place in the sonic flux.

13

Glenn Branca

The notorious Mudd Club, downtown NYC, October 1979. On a foray to the City from where I was living in the wilds of western Massachusetts, I was anxious to scope out possibilities in the Big Ashtray before making my move, a move that finally happened at the end of that month. I had been resonating deeply with the No Wave sound as personified by The Contortions, Lydia Lunch, Mars, and DNA—all represented on the Brian Eno-produced compilation *No New York*—and I'd already met the members of DNA when guesting with the Scientific Americans, who opened for them. Glenn Branca was a name mentioned in the same light, and his band with Barbara Ess and Christine Hahn, The Static, would be playing on this night, according to a notice in the *Village Voice*. Past the surly doorman into the dull gray box of a club—booming sound system, skinny ties on the guys, dark shades on the girls, Jean-Michel Basquiat dancing quietly in a corner: New Wave bohemian heaven. With no fanfare, The Static took the stage, barely illuminated by dirty fluorescent bulbs and grimy spotlights. Glenn sported a Telecaster. The band was bone-crushingly loud. It was not hi-fi loud or disco loud, it was FACTORY loud, standing behind a B-52 loud, as befitting the space. The guitar was in an open tuning and Glenn's hand-shapes were unfamiliar, grasping for the dark and ringing chords, lots of minor seconds in there. With a simple drum pulse reminiscent of the Velvet Underground's Moe Tucker, their songs rang out classic themes: *My Relationship, Don't Let Me Stop You, Fuck Yourself*. The guitars meshed and clashed, producing a throbbing drone and bright ringing. Suddenly, they would clarify into a two-chord stomp, sounding like The Stooges or The Seeds in some of their heavier moments.

A few months after the Mudd Club show, Glenn had posted a small ad in the *Village Voice* seeking musicians for a larger ensemble consisting of all guitars plus drums. Now that I was living in the City, I was hungry for work. I gave him a call and his initially gruff demeanor began to thaw as we spoke about shared tastes in music: Messiaen, Penderecki. Then he asked, "Do you play jazz?" I answered that I did, but I was not a jazz guitarist. His response: "Forget it" and hung up! We laughed about that many years later.

Glenn's tough reputation was amplified by his stage demeanor: possessed by the music, chain-smoking cigarettes down to the ash, face glaring with eyes bulging, screaming even when his mouth was closed. I caught one of the earliest gigs of the expanded guitar group at Tier 3, the most important little dive in NYC, located in the bowels of Tribeca. The music was certainly loud—repetitive, simplistic but mystical. The guitars were in open tunings, lots of unisons and octaves, cheap Teiscos, single-coil pickups prone to picking up line hum, but also very lively and raw. The strummed attacks created a dense froth of white noise while the vibrating strings yielded tsunami waves of harmonics, overtones filling the air. The music made its intentions clear: this was not entertainment, these were not clever New Wave songs, this was certainly not jazz. Though the musicians all had the air of rockers, it was definitely not rock n' roll. This was music for consciousness-razing, music for falling into a gray void and emerging on the other side, transformed.

In 1981, I was part of an orchestra of nine electric bassists opening for Glenn's ensemble at a disco just off of Union Square. Glenn's group played one long piece, deafeningly loud. As the music neared its extended climax, a startling physical manifestation to the sound was revealed. The guitars flailed, and the overtones rang. When the drummer hit his kick, the air literally shattered, vibrations from the heterodyning causing sum- and difference-tone effects to fill the physical space down to the molecular level. One could see the sound shake! That night was the first time Glenn and I had spoken since that initial phone call, exchanging thoughts with our ideas converging around the notion of the alteration of consciousness through psychoacoustics, the power of the "ghost instruments" as products of the volume and the tunings. While we had extremely different strategies as to how to achieve these ends, we could agree on the goals. In 1982, watching his group perform *The Peak of the Sacred* at St. Mark's Church in the East Village with percussionist Z'ev as its featured guest soloist brought home with finality the notion of his work as ritual—esthetics subsumed to the task at hand, shifting the parameters of perception: not a bunch of notes! Glenn's group served both as the real-time laboratory for the intersection of his music and philosophic endeavors and as the breeding ground for musicians who would go on to found Sonic Youth, the Swans, and Rat At Rat R.

The world of science fiction underwent a positive sea-change after the publication in 1984 of William Gibson's *Neuromancer*. I soon found out that Glenn was also a rabid cyberpunk fan and was distributing various books and reprinting rarities in one-off compilations. We hadn't been in contact, but now our renewed conversations were about the latest output of Jack Womack and K.W. Jeter, or obscure writers whose work was being hand-printed in English fanzines. Author Mark Dery had the idea to bring the two of us together for dinner and publish the conversation in the vivid but short-lived magazine *Mondo 2000* as "We are the Reality of this Cyberpunk Fantasy." Glenn was a surprisingly adept chef, and over perfectly barbecued shrimp and perhaps too much sauvignon blanc we discussed the nature of consciousness, the state of Artificial Intelligence and its limits (already very evident), and the merits of alternate tuning systems: a fine time!

Though Glenn was well known for his guitar orchestras, not many people knew of his visual work. Using mathematics and drafting techniques, Glenn created delicate but powerful visualizations of the structure of his music, clearly displaying the relationship between the acoustic principles and their manifestation via loud guitars. These works are both illustration of the nuts-and-bolts hidden in the music and the Platonic ideal of sound crystallized, then committed to paper.

We met again on various occasions, perhaps at a show of the band of Reg Bloor, Glenn's wife, for whom he gleefully fulfilled the task of roadie. When I turned fifty, Glenn called me up to get some drinks. There was a blizzard that day in March of 2001, back when we still had real winters in New York. He told me, "Everyone loves you when you're fifty," and that I should get myself a good overcoat.

In 2018, I had only run into Glenn a few times, and the news of his passing was a shock to me. He had shared the fact of his illness with very few people. If Glenn were reading this piece, he'd probably let loose with a sarcastic obscenity, but the fact is that Branca lived the passion that he put into his sound, lived it as a musician, thinker, artist, and human.

14

Tim Wright

Street Shamanic

My prior knowledge of Tim Wright had been the simple credits for bass and guitar on the back of the seminal Cleveland underground band Pere Ubu's 1978 debut EP *Datapanik in the Year Zero*, a record that went into heavy rotation on my turntable shortly after I moved to western Massachusetts the same year. The Scientific Americans were a Northampton-based rock band whose sonic sympathies ranged from Devo-esque New Wave through "kraut rock" and the more extreme New York bands like Suicide and those released on Brian Eno's *No New York*. I had become interested in the band DNA and was excited that they would be performing at our local rock dive, Rahar's, in the spring of 1979. The gig was organized by the SciAms, and I would join them as guest saxophonist. DNA's sound on record was dominated by the keyboards of Robin Crutchfield. By the time of this show, however, Crutchfield had been replaced by bassist Tim Wright, effecting a sea-change in the sound of the band. This version of DNA had a loudness and physical presence missing from Eno's compilation, with Tim's primordial bass lines defining most of the melodic and harmonic structure of these song miniatures, each generally running one minute or less. His enigmatic stage presence was encapsulated in "dark magic" dance steps, providing an emotional counterpoint to Arto Lindsay's Brazilian-influenced voice and noise guitar and Ikue Mori's stark and primal but cerebrally sophisticated drumming. Tim's sound was not limited by the typical confines of rock bass playing but encompassed trebly chords, mechanistic repetition, coruscating noise created by hitting the strings with a drum stick, saturated reverberation, and feedback. That first DNA set of many that I witnessed packed incredible drama into twenty minutes. After the show, Tim and I spoke about Pere Ubu and the NYC No Wave scene, a conversation that helped fuel my decision to move to the city later that year, where we reconnected through various vectors.

Our paths would cross often, whether at Squat Theatre, CBGB's, the Binibon cafe, or 4 a.m. at the Gem Spa on 2nd Avenue and St. Mark's. We might discuss the scene or Tim might speak of his unpublished novel *Rise and Fall of Earth*. From 1981–1982 I was producing the first *State of the Union* compilation, a collection on my zOaR label in collaboration with *Zone Magazine* of one-minute pieces in which artists provided their own "state of the union" as commentary on and confrontation to Reagan's January address. Tim agreed to record his piece "My Town" and brought his twelve-string electric guitar to a studio generously lent to me by composer Scott Johnson. Wright detuned the instrument so that it left the realm of Western intonation, rendering it simultaneously alien and bluesy. Our day's work expanded into conversation, and we agreed that we would meet again soon.

In late February 1984, I invited Tim to be interviewed for *Killer*, a fanzine founded by Sonic Youth's Thurston Moore. Tim arrived at my Alphabet City apartment around 10 p.m. for a conversation lasting nearly until sunrise, with alternating pots of espresso and ginger tea keeping us fueled. Tim expounded on a wide range of subjects, including his Kitchen concert of the previous week and his time away from New York living in a house in the jungle in Belize. Our meeting was recorded on cassette tapes, now lost. The conversation flowed into many disparate areas, some involving mutual friends and colleagues. We spoke about performing together, though that first musical meeting didn't occur until July 2003, a beautifully chaotic improvisation together with multi-instrumentalist Doug Wieselman as part of an installation at BPM, a storefront gallery in Williamsburg. From the original transcription (also lost), I had edited this version, typed on my ancient Underwood typewriter. The magazine ceased publication, and so this interview was never printed. In 2020, I found the interview in an unmarked envelope in a file cabinet in the studio. My last communication from Tim came in February 2012 about an upcoming gig we would play together the following July. I didn't hear from him again, but received word that he had died from cancer on Sunday, August 4, 2013.

WHAT? of course i will provide you with amps and this and that.and nice
sound system too.doug wieselman gets to play one drum.or maybe i bring extra

guitar or you can too.the beauty of this is that i know it needs no rehearsal and i hope that you trust me enough that i would not invite you into a sinkhole.i wanna do this before we die. tw

♯

Shortly after our interview, Tim had a concert at The Kitchen on February 19, 1984. These are his program notes:

> I proceeded to attempt an exploratory exploitation of conceptual imagery surrounding the biological aspects of the appreciation guitar playing, which on a most fundamental level involves a sexual undertone in as much as the shape of the instrument and the manner in which is held in the hands against the body provides an easily accessible and socially acceptable phallic image around which the musician and the observer begin to explore the possibilities of expanding the initial pleasure induced by guitar charisma. Since the 1940s, the word "science" has competed strongly with the word "sex" for the status of most popularly employed libidinal activator. Concomitantly, the scientific image ensure for the "scientist," if only superficially, an erogenous place in existing social body. The phrase "Scientific experiment" has a classically postmodern appeal. This seductive appeal is shared by such phrases as "laboratory experiment" and "medical experiment" and is exploited by those who claim to make "experimental music." Particularly in the case of guitar players who are supposedly experimenting with a symbolic extension of their bodies, we tend, however modestly, to envision "sexual experimentation." To give the impression that the musicians united here in music are crude characters abandoning the world through their own sensual excesses made more calloused by their own delight in soliciting the patronage of strangers while in a moment of abandonment would be a grave injustice to the great hearts that beat passionately in their bodies, palaces of pleasure though they may be.

E♯: What army was in the trojan guitar?
T: The army of love.
E♯: And the battle is being waged?
T: The battle was won . . . love prevailed.
E♯: And the loveless wrote reviews?
T: Edward Rothstein (NY Times) even said I was crude. The program notes

say that I am not crude nor any of the other musicians. He didn't really study the program or the notes.

E♯: What he saw was what he wanted to see. How are you characterized here?

T: That's hard for me to say. The reason the show was called *Modern Living Guitar Massage* was because at the time I was performing physical therapy every day on my girlfriend who was unable to walk. I didn't feel like a musician, I felt like a masseur so somehow the masseur was on stage as a musician so I constructed things around massage. That's what my hands were good at at the time. So I switched the massage over to the guitar and then came the idea of the guitar as phallus.

E♯: Does the bass function like the guitar in that way?

T: I think a bass is more libidinal than a six-string guitar mainly because the low tone registers on a larger part of the body. It affects the water in the body more than high frequencies do and a bass player feels that also and bass lines are body rhythms. Good drumming is also. I hate to think of a guitar player seriously dealing with the guitar as a phallic image because the way somebody would play on stage is the same way they would have sex. So I was joking around with that. [The concert at The Kitchen was split between Tim Wright and Remko Scha—a composer who is visiting professor of Artificial Intelligence at the University of Amsterdam.]

E♯: So what do you think of this Artificial Intelligence stuff?

T: I have no idea what that means.

E♯: A school of computer science where they believe they can generate complex enough software and hardware to . . .

T: Okay, then I did have an idea . . . what I thought. I'm much more interested in human intelligence since I'm a human. Maybe if it was my hobby.

E♯: Where do you search for it?

T: Only in my own mind but I have to test my own intelligence by interacting with other human minds. It's too easy to delude yourself: a little knowledge is a dangerous thing.

E♯: So they say. Seems like New York is a very dangerous place right now.

T: Yeah, really too many intellectuals and artists now. Junior thinkers and junior humans. I liked putting a sexual topic on a supposedly scientific evening at The Kitchen.

E♯: It seems that somebody at some point set up the definitions that the concepts were mutually exclusive, that science implies something other than human.

T: Science should be sensual and art should be sensual and artists should be sensual.

E♯: Operate on all levels completely and simultaneously?

T: Yes they should. No, not simultaneously—they couldn't.

E♯: It's possible that someone doing something embeds everything else, whether consciously or not.

T: Simultaneously exhibiting all human characteristics? Well, you can do that but not for long . . . well actually, you could do that. Actually, you DO do that. Actually you don't. Actually you could do that . . . over a period of a lifetime.

E♯: Even in the course of a forty-five-minute set. Actually, it's encoded cellular knowledge.

T: But I mean subjectively it could go through all passions, all emotions, all states of mind, all states of consciousness and unconsciousness in forty-five minutes. It could, I'm sure it happens a lot. It could be a dangerous mistake to think you have done so when you haven't. You could be leaving something out. That's why you have to check your intelligence against the intelligence of other people. That's why I was interested in forming skulls because if right now we are actually genetically ripped off because of bone formation and are not getting everything out of our brains that we could, then what is it that we're missing?

E♯: The Neanderthals had a larger brain-size, larger cranium.

T: The skull manipulation being present in peak ancient cultures, disappearing when these cultures declined, for better or worse. Whether you like it or not, there's something else to be had that's intangible. [Note: Skull deformation dating back to the fourth century BCE has been documented in cultures across the world and found especially in Central Asia, South Pacific islands, the Americas, and Africa. There are various theories regarding why it is practiced, ranging from tribal identity and class status to enhancement of intelligence and connection to the "spirit world."]

E♯: Did your friend in Belize have any knowledge of skull forming or trepanning? Aware of its tradition?

T: No, a lot of traditions he's unaware of because he's spent all of his life in a very small radius and all of his knowledge he's gotten firsthand from someone or from visionary experience. His practice, aside from herbal medicine, involves a complex system of astrological magic, astral projection, the classic shamanic experiences, invocation of supernatural sights and sounds. He has had some experience with people who do teleportation or appear to do so.

E#: Did you find it difficult to make contact, get accepted by people involved in these systems of knowledge?

T: It took a lot of luck. Since people knew what I was interested in, eventually, I found out about someone who was practicing magic and healing and so on and so forth. I had to think of a reason to see him. I had some pain in my chest that I've had for many years, couldn't figure out what the source of it was, plus a large black spot on the outside of my ankle—I didn't like that either. I had someone set up a meeting so I could explain the situation. The man said he could cure me, it would take a week to make the medicine. I had to get there at sundown, walk onto his property fifteen miles away. I go to get my liaison, he's nowhere to be found, his wife doesn't know where he is. I realize he's completely freaked out because he's told me this guy has conversations with devils and spirits. This *brujo* or whatever seemed like a charming person. This bush doctor is a Mayan. He doesn't practice Obeah but some people thought he did. He obviously can do some things and he can heal. Obeah's used as a tool of oppression, that's certainly not his bag. He took care of my sickness. We had an instant liking to each other. He's a very good guitar player. We set up a cover system where I was never seen leaving his house without a bottle of medicine or a guitar. He played Mexican-Spanish music. He improvised, plays and sings like any other person but also he uses the instrument to help him stay up all night and observe the stars, their placement. Last time I was there I gave him an electric guitar and battery-powered amp. He likes it at top volume and distortion and feedback; other than that something's wrong and it doesn't work. So he'll get up at 3:00 a.m. and go down to the riverbank where he has a concrete platform and crank it up full blast and wake the whole village and nobody complains. A couple of Protestant church missions moved in, he'll do that on the nights they don't sing. We were going to make a tape before I left but he had a sore throat. Another time we were both completely broke with no batteries. He'd rescued me from a life-death situation, let me live in a house on his property. We've promised each other we'd do some recording and a book and a video documentary before one of us dies.

E#: There's none of the ancient Mayan music in existence there?

T: Not that I'm aware of personally in that area. Maybe that's one reason why it's possible for me to have this relationship there. People have lost interest. Nothing tangible is left of the Mayans for the young people. They see the old people as being bush-happy, just rustic loons, which IS what they are!

E#: Fortunately!

T: An interesting outlook which every year becomes more and more a minority.

E#: When I was traveling in Chiapas, Mexico last November, I heard what I was told was the outgrowth of ancient Mayan music in the villages of San Juan Chamula and Zinacantan. It was played on homemade string instruments very much like primitive guitars with incantation and chanting over the strummed rhythms. It was mostly used in religious services which were ostensibly Catholic but there was widespread syncretism with the Christian god and saints standing in for the Mayan deities and multiple priests crooning and blowing smoke over Coke bottles filled with oil. These villages were incredibly impoverished at the time—literally barren. Do you think there's a parallel with the activities of the people there in Belize and say, your own work here?

T: Several years ago I had to test that out myself. It has something to do with why I started playing guitar at all, making music. I became satisfied that what I was doing was worth starving for or worth taking abuse for and actually had some sort of relevance, made more sense out of my life. As far as being relevant to how these people live, their work is like any serious thinkers' or artists' work requiring a certain degree of faith in their own intelligence, their own talents, risks everything to do everything they feel they should intuitively do. That kind of inspiration is common to all creative activity. Trying to become aware of things and trying to imagine how you can use that awareness, how that can be beneficial, how you can not make an idiot of yourself and not to ruin yourself or other people because you have to be idiosyncratic or eccentric or whatever.

E#: Do you think it's getting harder to do that now and here?

T: Well yeah, because it's getting harder to basically live.

E#: Plus deviancy is less tolerated in America, even in NYC which seems to be one of the most diversely deviant places.

T: I only feel safe in NYC because apart from the rest of the States, I can disappear in the variety. There's deviations here that make me look like a koala bear. It's definitely getting harder all over the world.

E♯: It seems to be clearer now what any of our activities are about.

T: Where you stand. Maybe because things are more obvious now, it is getting harder just to get by. It affects things because you waste so much time. Right now I'm a poor person so I waste a lot of time just trying to cope with food and money and a place to live and . . . any person that's doing that it takes time away from more . . . uh . . . imaginative luxuries, to have the freedom to engage in anything other than worker activity, that's a real luxury.

E♯: Do you think doing music is an analogy of skull forming?

T: I wouldn't say that.

E♯: Can it be for the musicians?

T: I can't really say that because I don't want to fall into a trap of pretending I know something I don't. I know people who have holes in their heads that they've put in their heads to attain beneficial effects, people I know personally, they can talk. They can tell me how they feel. I can think about it and come to as much of an understanding as I can. I can even think that I know what's being talked about and that I can ascertain in my own changes of consciousness what they're talking about. [Note: Trepanning is a surgical procedure in which a hole is drilled or scraped into the human skull. This cranial perforation exposes the membrane surrounding the brain to treat various health problems. In ancient times, trepanation was used for spiritual purposes and to cure persons displaying abnormal behavior, perhaps possession by evil spirits. Evidence of trepanation has been found in human remains from Neolithic times onward.]

E♯: What I should have said: Does it produce temporary or permanent changes in your neurochemistry?

T: What I think is that we're talking about varieties of human consciousness that you could display or that you have. Some of these are ecstatic. If you make music that has to do with that mental set and you can construct music in that mental setting of trying to recall that feeling then if you can make that music and play it in public with the right impact then it should also remind people in the audience, make them remember that consciousness and feel a bit of that ecstatic feeling. If they have an open mind, a good sense of humor . . . I get the most pleasure in live music if it makes me remember various ecstatic feelings even it's stupidass heavy metal if there's something ecstatic and pleasurable in the idiots that are playing it. Same thing for Beethoven or Vivaldi when he's not being a hack. The only time I write a good song is when I really feel something, even if it's bad.

E♯: I've found I could never set out to write a good song—the good ones seem to come out fully formed.

T: Right. If not fully formed, at least you know where to go. Also I was thinking, getting back to "is this a good environment for trying to literally exist through imagination?" What really upsets me, makes me want to keep running away from NYC is the . . . obviously, until five years ago there was always shifting scenes where people go to, just to get involved in fun/art/music/whatever. The last place where that sort of activity shifted to was here and so there was a time I could think if I'm in NYC out of all the people in the country, the ones that come to NYC will be the people with a lot of nerve and who believe in themselves and have a strong enough desire to do something creative, that they leave wherever they are to come here to do that, to find other people to work with and so on. So you could always be assured of a good time. If things got boring, in a year there would be fresh things. But for the last few years, since the economic situation is so bad, you can be sure that the people who are coming here are not coming because they have lot of nerve and imagination, they're coming because they can afford to. It's out the window.

E♯: Are there any scenes of note here now?

T: No, it might as well be the forties.

E♯: Do you think it's going backwards: '50s, '40s, '30s? The next Dust Bowl will be The Big One.

T: As far as I'm concerned, people are so straight now I can't believe it. Especially new bands and musicians . . . I'm gonna have a band of people that look like me, not like The Ramones. Act Wright, Walk Wright, Talk Wright, and Think Wright.

E♯: Are you in communication with people in other areas doing creative things, any networks?

T: No, I'm ignorant of what's going on. The impression I have now is it's "every man for himself." I don't think there's any gathering place. Networks? Probably . . . but of anything that amounts to anything?

E♯: It seems to be a time of seclusion.

T: That's what I think. Basically, I don't care about networks. I'd rather be left alone until the exact time I want to do something. Any time any band plays it's a network. Any live band is an extension of a small community of people. That's what's meaningful about real bands that reflect the people in the audience. It's what's missing in product bands, a big thing that's missing in this town, grassroots bands that are part of a community.

E♯: What we're seeing is communities but of plastic people and plastic bands, communities to be avoided.

T: When you have a consumer culture, certain images are fed to people to identify with. It's assumed that they identify, assumed there is a community behind this presentation of an image. It's completely opposite to a community of people creating and exhibiting what is indigenously part of their thinking, part of their lives, friends' lives. The friends of these musicians make it possible for these musicians' situations to occur. That's where new music can be meaningful, a real cultural statement; if it reflects a new consciousness, some change in consciousness of people, reflects their desires. There's a problem in this city and in general for anybody who wants to do anything idiosyncratic. It's hard to feel secure about doing that because most peoples' minds are just picking up images that are thrown at them instead of investigating themselves and deciding what they are, what they want.

E♯: Your work here now?

T: My basic problem is usually just finding one or two other people to work something with and as far as music goes, as of the last year, the last couple of years, I haven't wanted to work with anyone on anything very much and basically, that is what I wanted to do, fit myself into a different kind of scene and different kind of method. It's why I left the country. Now it's extremely important for me to get involved with other people, make some music. Right now the only really satisfying thing has been playing with Rudolph Grey. That's showing promise.

E♯: There's the trio with him and Z'ev?

T: Yeah, we did a little bit of playing last year, nothing in public, and we've talked about playing together for years but psychologically it wasn't possible and now it is. That's going to be difficult to start and it's going to be a lot of responsibilities. It's going to have to be very involved. All three people are individualistic enough, it's not something you want to do unless the time is right in all these peoples' lives. It could be too insane, too fast, a pressure situation. It would have to be high pressure and good humor. I played with Rudolph at The Kitchen and we sounded better and worked together better live.

15

Current Strategies for Graphic Notation

This was one of the keynote speeches for TENOR 2018: Fourth International Conference on Technologies of Notation and Representation, Montreal.

All notation is graphic notation: a shorthand correspondence between idealized sound to the visual realm for the ultimate purpose of generating that sound. Most scores are detailed roadmaps for the performers of music strictly determined in pitch and time, well represented by traditional Western notation. However, to provide notation for musics whose inner workings are governed by such parameters as density, texture, flow, and temperature, visual abstraction may be the best solution. It begins with the creative impulse. When concerned with music and sound, this impulse arises in what I like to think of as the Inner Ear. The impulse must be translated from source to output. The act of translation may mean mapping actions from the wavelengths of the creative to those frequencies in the spectrum that produce sound. But one may decide that the sound heard in the Inner Ear is not meant to be produced acoustically at all. Then a different portion of the spectrum may be invoked: light, movement, painting, taking a walk, cooking a meal, just listening. There is porosity between the modes of expression. Ideally, the entire process of translation is part of a synesthetic experience, both in the generative process and in the realization, a feedback loop. This may require completely abandoning the language of music and finding inspiration and models from natural forms and processes, from references in art or literature, mathematics, or philosophy.

My initial explorations of graphic notation began in 1972 when, unsatisfied with the indulgences of student group improvisations, I painted scores on graph paper to create such pieces as *Noise Floor* and *Spectral Shift* as a way of constructing narrative structures over a timeline to shape sonic interactions with my fellow musicians. Color and shape were obvious correlations to the type of gestures, even the language, used by improvising musicians in that period. In the following months I was living in a shared house in Germantown, NY, with a front porch facing the Hudson River and the back facing the woods. Evening was often spent on the back porch watching the myriad fireflies with the expectation that, at any second, they would spell out words or cohere into pictures or even form music notation on staves. Walking along the Hudson, I could find secluded places to practice soprano sax and derive inspiration from the flow. Sunrise on the river (which might be witnessed from either end of the day) could reveal thousands of birds taking off simultaneously, the air so thick that foreground and background were reversed, a living Escher drawing, the sound symphonic and granulated. That image provided the basis for another score. I had a favorite spot on a hill overlooking the Germantown cemetery where I could witness an incredible audio panorama at sunrise, insects and birds creating a pixilated cloud of sparkling sounds, hocketed crosstalk of pure abstraction, Miro sonified. The next step was to photocopy suitable images from *National Geographic* or *Science* magazines to be superimposed on music manuscript. These graphics, combined with a number of loose instruction sets, comprised the *Hudson River Compositions* of 1973–1974, a first foray into the intersection between graphic and algorithmic approaches.

During my time as a graduate student at SUNY Buffalo working with Lejaren Hiller and Morton Feldman, I attempted to mix traditional notation with the algorithmic approaches and graphics. By 1976, I felt that improvisation, whether free or guided, was a more fruitful strategy for realizing my sonic intentions and avoided any written scoring at all. After moving to NYC in 1979, I began a parallel track combining traditional notation with instruction sets as a way to realize processes whose psychoacoustic goals demanded precision of such actions as rhythms, timing, and pitch variation. In desiring to rely more on acoustic instruments, in scores such as *Tessalation Row* from 1986 and *Hammer Anvil Stirrup* from 1988, I tried to devise means of evoking extreme sounds from the musicians without necessarily giving them minutely detailed instructions. The former uses a tablature notation that sequences events precisely in time but leaves them open in internal details within certain parameters of base pitch and rhythm. The latter combines computer-generated images with text instructions, plus traditionally notated rhythms and pitch-maps to strike a balance between explicit instructions and poetic ambiguity and a sense of ongoing process. Scores such as *Hammer Anvil Stirrup* dwell more in the realm of an oblique narrative, catalyzing the sounds in an arc of time rather than linking with precise instruction sets. In this way, the score makes heavy demands on the creative interpretation of the performer, forcing them to go beyond any particular set of definitions or instructions.

Beginning in 1986 and using both hardware and software processing, I devoted myself to real-time electroacoustic work, finding the new sonic potentials to be thrilling and liberating with the Atari ST and Ensoniq and Roland samplers my preferred tools. The Tokyo Music-Merge Festival in November of '96 provided the catalyst for my return to graphic notation. Asked to compose a piece for an ad hoc ensemble with thirteen players of varying music reading abilities, I determined that a combination of conduction and a graphic score would be the best solution. To compose *Spring & Neap*, I copied a curve from a graph of the tidal energy over a twelve-hour period in Tokyo Bay, and assigned parameters including relative pitch, density of activity, dynamics, even the shape of the players' featured solos: all would follow this curve.

With the onset of the American invasion of Iraq in 2003, *Dispersion of Seeds* was composed in response, an algorithmic piece based on a recently discovered text by Henry David Thoreau. In its first realization with a performance by Sirius String Quartet, the music was intended to be a substrate for layers of live digital processing, equal in weight to the acoustic component. However, working with a pristine studio recording of the piece, I found myself favoring the tactility, immediacy, and complexity of the unprocessed sounds. By the turn of this last century, the reality was that extreme sounds were quite easy to achieve with only a mouse-click, digital sound processing having become devalued with its ease of production. I was missing the "sweat equity" generated by more labor-intensive strategies. When the means of audio production is a physically excited vibrating string, column of air, membrane, or reed, one has a greater sensation of the movement of molecules in a space, a greater perception of the initial transient within which so much of the identity of a sound resides. In a live performance situation, this sensation is reduced when the sound ultimately emerges from a speaker.

This was a revelation and triggered a search for alternate ways to reproduce the unique sounds that I could heretofore obtain only with electronics. To begin, I exported pages of my Sibelius notation as TIFFs to be imported into graphic-editing software such as Photoshop, GIMP, and Graphic Converter. Using plug-ins, I was able to use modulation, feedback, filtering, layering, stretching, distorting, and inverting the elements of the score in much the same way that I would do a live mix of a performing ensemble, but with the output in this case being a printed score. The results were immediately appealing as visual objects and met with positive response from the players. This new generation of musicians raised on sonics, texture, densities, personal sound editing, and graphic notation of all types—the images resonated with the players resulting in a surprisingly consistent set of musical gestures. The musicians could balance their personal interpretation with my own input and desires based upon the clearly presented waveforms, textures, densities, and movement.

The first piece completed in this manner was *Seize Seeth Seas Seen* written for Sirius String Quartet in 2007. Each page displayed one image and was designed to evoke a sonic projection rather than a narrative. Performance operations included having all players each play one page at a time in unison and assigning timelines corresponding to changing of the pages, giving players different pages to be played simultaneously, and making mosaic patterns of timelines with each player having different sequences of pages with some overlapping and unisons. With my participation in a performance of any of these graphic pieces, I might discuss with the players why a certain graphic appears as it does and what it evokes for me in terms of evolution of sound over the timeframe. I would ask the players to imagine a single sound and how that sound could be modified when applying the processes implied by the contours of the image. Parameters might include smooth vs. rough tones, varieties of modulation, randomness vs. deep control. No sound exists in isolation though, and the decisions of any player could be modified by the sonic actions of the others in an ensemble feedback loop. These scores are dynamic, never fixed, so that music would be different with each and every manifestation.

The next major work composed in this manner was *Foliage*, for which I made 250 individually processed pages, from which 110 were culled for the performance score. The work was presented in a variety of ways: players could "read" through the score pages sequentially or could randomize them, focus on one page or encompass the total. A range of simultaneous verticalities could be created by giving players different combinations of pages for use as unisons or separated parts. For ensemble performances, the pages of the score might be projected or enlarged and printed and displayed. With the pages of *Foliage* mounted on a gallery wall, musicians could

Figure 10 SysOrk performing at Roulette Intermedium, Brooklyn, NY (2021). Courtesy of Roulette https://roulette.org/archive/.

move between them, their sounds choreographed in a suite that manifested the music spatially but also developed its narrative arc through the cumulative effect of the iterations, superimpositions, and transformations. Finally, through cross-fading, a movie was created of *Foliage*. With the projection of the movie of *Foliage*, the musicians could operate in ambiguous modes: were they interpreting a score? Providing a soundtrack? Generating the visuals? There would never be a notion of "correct" or "incorrect" in *Foliage*—I welcomed any interpretations and hoped that the readers, players, and listeners would also hear it as they see it. An exhibition at the Reverse Space gallery in Brooklyn in 2012 displayed the movie as an installation, and eighty Risograph prints chosen from the *Foliage* set were mounted on the walls. A number of musicians and poets were invited to perform the score, each choosing their own approach to their realization. These scores are dynamic, never fixed, so that the music will be different with each and every manifestation. At the conclusion of the series, I was extremely gratified at the intensity of commitment displayed by all of the performers, each finding a way into the score and producing a realization that felt simultaneously true to their own personal languages and to the score itself.

Inspired by the *Foliage* animation, the next work, *Sylva Sylvarum*, was from its inception intended to be a movie. Starting with eight pages of composed musical gestures, similar processes as used in *Foliage* were used to create 250 cells, which were layered with appropriated clips, such as flowering plants in time-lapse mode and satellite movies of the diminishing Amazon rain forest, Arctic ice shelves, and Himalayan glaciers in a sort of environmental screed. The most recent of these scores as movies was ReGenerate, composed in 2021 for my seventieth birthday concert with my ensemble Sys-Ork at Roulette and using the same techniques in its creation. Made of 400 cells and, for the first time, using color, ReGenerate was meant to celebrate the temporary release from the isolation of the COVID-19 virus.

The final aspect to be discussed with scores such as *Sylva Sylvarum* and *Foliage* is the visual. They are retinal art as much as instruction sets for the production of sound, form and function interlocked. There are ever-present questions though. Graphic scores at their lowest common denominator may be seen merely as "pretty pictures." At their best, they may serve as highly specific catalysts to musicmaking. As someone who has loved both making and appreciating visual art from an early age and from studies of works by John Cage, Cathy Berberian, Morton Feldman, Anthony Braxton, Iannis Xenakis, Györgi Ligeti, and others, I've found great resonance with graphic approaches, and using them has the potential to open up channels that might not have otherwise been explored. Any visual input to a musical interpreter will somehow affect their output, and thus, the performer creates a unique manifestation of that provided material. As a composer, one must acknowledge this essential activity of the interpreter and how these actions are often the final arbiter of the music, even in through-composed pieces. If one is to claim the mantle of "composer," the sonic vocabulary and syntax of a given piece then must be defined to the extent that the identity of the composition will be clear and distinct even though the internal detail of the music may vary from performance to performance. The result is a manifestation of that internal synesthesia that is the translation of thought, emotion, and process from one set of frequencies to another.

16

Future of Mind

We believe that our minds define our selves, not just in the ever-changing present, but projecting back into our past through myth and memory and forward into our futures with hopes, aspirations, and desires. Our minds transmit and receive data in a continuous feedback loop, constantly updating our state of being and inputting new information into our perceptual systems, comparing the novel against all that we have experienced and archived in a process that very likely reaches its completion with our mortality.

The search for the nature of this Mind of ours has been a puzzle and inspiration for both reflection and generative thought extending back to the dawn of self-awareness. With new discoveries daily, not to mention the development of new technologies, our minds at their best have become plastic and mutable, continuously digesting, accepting, rejecting, and discarding a panorama of novel parameters and definitions. Some of these elements are contradictory, even mutually exclusive—some are enlightening and clarifying. With every positive advance in knowledge of the physical and chemical workings of the brain, in a paradox worthy of Zeno, humans still remain woefully distant from complete knowledge of the nature of our own consciousness.

Gödelian concepts apply as well to our self-awareness: with self-perception nested in self-perception, are we perpetuating self-deception? Will it be necessary for us to divorce our self from our selves to gain an objective understanding of what self means? Do our own self-generating definitions muddy the waters, obscuring what might be otherwise obvious? Can we break out of the self-limiting frame and actually know Mind? As AI toddlers are acing Turing tests, how will we recognize the very real Mind of the Other when we're still not absolutely clear as to its nature in ourselves? This Other might be all around us: insect hive-minds, bird flock murmurations, Gaian tree culture, fungi bulletin boards.

We might say that our craniocentricism blinds us and deafens us; certainly our very anthropocentrism has gravely limited our outlook and, at worst, our cross-species empathies. It's only been in the most recent decades that humans have graciously admitted that other living things might indeed possess consciousness. The common belief has been that consciousness and memory reside in the brain—in fact, that they are synonymous with this craniocentric approach. But can we dismiss the notion that not just memory, but Mind itself cannot be divorced from organs and muscles, from viscera, even from the evanescent neurotransmitter stews that drift out into the very air around each and every one of us? For example, the octopus has three-fifths of its neurons distributed in its tentacles, each of which can act as a semi-autonomous brain. Can we disprove that the chemically connected plant life of the world does not form a conscious system, whether locally or even globally?

It might be said that every sight we see, every sound we make or hear, every move or shift, every pheromonal handshake, is part of the free-floating and expanding consensual reality that is Mind. Even though our hardware has been running for many thousands of years without an update, our software is continually transforming to accommodate new modes of data transfer and processing, altering definitions and frameworks. But do we ever fully understand all of the features of these updated operating systems that we're gifted with, and can we even begin to make use of them before they become obsolete and are replaced by even newer ones?

It's no longer a radical notion to say that our individual memories have been externalized in the metaphor of a cloud, perhaps even extended throughout the entire noosphere. With memory decentralized and diffused, even removed from our own minds and resident in the interweb of your choice, Mind no longer demands walls and barriers, but instead requires an open architecture. And if the memories can be external to the person, then could Identity itself, the individual consciousness, also be externalized? Would a conscious entity with no physical locus conceive of itself in the same way as an embodied one? How would the perceptual systems function in a disembodied mind? What are the possible input and output devices? What would the mechanism of internal feedback be? If a disembodied Mind is to interact with a physical world, then what would the interface feel like both to that Mind and to anyone encountering it?

Various notions of Artificial Intelligence have advanced in recent years to the point where interaction with AIs (of greater and lesser I-ness) has become a normal part of daily life, both enlightening and annoying. But is the *I* in AI the same *I* that we think of as intelligence, and is the *I* of an AI the same *I* that is truly a sense of self-ness? Mechanical processes, even when happening millions of times per second, are not the same as biological intelligence, and certainly not the same as consciousness. The current spate of AIs are essentially very fast relational databases referencing a vast amount of data with the use of predictive analytics. What they do is not "thinking" and certainly not yet intelligence as we know it. I will reserve the option of considering that there is now or will soon be "machine intelligence," with definitions and capabilities to be determined that would satisfy the many mandatory requirements to enter the society of sentients.

One of the first rules of computer coding is "garbage in equals garbage out," and as we see AIs spit out contradictory and nonsensical responses to reasonable queries, we must recall that it is a group of humans who have created these things. Are the flaws surprising? The blindness to what might be considered quite obvious facets of the world we inhabit with its biases, weaknesses, prejudices? Can a digital zero/one, on/off mind feel the same, both internally and externally, as a slippery-slope chemical mind? Can that all-important porosity that makes our intelligence what it is be found in an AI? Could it be embedded in a process of knowing and deciding that is based upon the continuous polling of tendencies, analogous to quantum states? Never a simple yes-no or on-off but gradient feeds of raw data to be weighed and sorted and finally decided upon. Explicit expression but with simultaneously vast amounts of background processing contributing to the flux? Background merging with foreground to overwhelm the filters that discriminate between the forms of input? Could Mind, whether hard or soft in nature, be part of a cosmic probability calculation that defines the reality of all moments?

I'm waiting for the day that an AI can experience synesthesia and be able to express its experience of it. Will an AI ever compose music that rends your heart and soul, or is this reserved for those whose language cannot be boiled down to a collection of binary states? Is the transcendent mystery of art somehow linked to the root of its generation? Or in the near future, will our sonic environment be deluged with AI-generated "hit singles," deeply

Figure 11 Nicholas Isherwood with Asasello String Quartet performing *Die Grösste Fuge*, Bonn, Germany (2021). Photo by Janene Higgins.

loved by a population of bots and peripherals but completely meaningless to us "meatbags" (as humans are called by Futurama's soulful but crass robot, Bender).

There's been much in the air over the last decade about how our world will be undergoing a "singularity" and how humanity must prepare itself for massive transformations. Many contend (and I agree) that we're already deeply into the singularity—after all, a singularity is not built in a day (especially when the timescale is cosmic!). Whether this is seen as glorious or apocalyptic depends on the observer, and there are as many definitions of the nature of this singularity as there are observers. The development of "self-awareness" in computers is often cited as a primary element of this cusp-point. Contact with an alien civilization is another. How will humanity find a commonality of expression to communicate with an intelligence conceivably so different from our own that there might not even be recognition *of* that intelligence? This is one of the problems that we might face if we open ourselves to the notion of an insect Mind not localized in a single creature, or a plant Mind extending across the world.

We again return to the notion of interface and who controls it. What will the emergent power relationships be? Do we wish to have AIs designed by narcissistic tech bros whose libertarian tendencies verge on fascism? It's certainly ironic that in 2024 the AI companies are bemoaning the fact that, with their darling offspring now learning from the internet, the digital scions are getting more and more stupid, taking in as gospel the lies and fictions that their predecessors have generated and disseminated. AI is already proving itself to be a useful and exciting tool for artists and engineers, an extension of human creativity like a stone scraper or a laptop, but should not supplant human invention or fulfilling work. In science fiction, the superior alien intelligence often takes on anthropomorphic form (and speaks with a British accent). Will a truly emergent AI condescend to speak with us as equals, or might it demand true peer-to-peer contact and insist that humans must rise to the occasion before there can be any meaningful interactions? From a measure of cosmic intelligence and consciousness, humans might be considered to be merely in a larval state. Will we eventually metamorphose into fully realized beings able to meet an unfamiliar modality halfway?

Perhaps an AI with "capital-I I" will finally be constructed with a biological component that will add that organic element. There are already advanced experiments along these lines, such as the Neuroplatform from the Swiss FinalSpark firm where sixteen lab-grown organoids perform the computational work. Such an aggregate could engender true intelligence and embodied emotions, manifesting innovation in language. Will we then learn to communicate using airborne molecular polymers, chains of regenerated RNA? Flashes of color? Qubit packets? Modulated sine waves? Will that achievement equal a willingness to let go of our traditional assumptions of mind grounded in autonomous physicality? By abandoning these moorings, do we abandon the very core of our humanity? If that is indeed the case, then we might finally ask, "Is this a good thing or a bad thing?"

17

A Gig's a Gig

Some say it began when the Blessed Republic of Texas tried to nuke Gomorrah (their name for New York City) in 2032—fortunately thwarted by the National Guard's Arrow system, though still sending metaphorical but very real shockwaves around the world. Going back further, some said COVID, others 9/11, while the historically inclined contended that the decline in gigging began with the Reagan regime in the twentieth century. The breakup of the European Union in 2027, preceded by the destructive chaos of Brexit in 2020, nailed the coffin. The whole recessive economic structure meant that culture was the lowest priority, except for the blue-chip programming favored by the oligarchs and still enjoyed in their gated domains, exclusive clubs, tony theatres, heavily guarded museums. The usual haunts of touring musicians—NYC, Germany, Austria, Switzerland, London, Japan, Norway—all locked down tight due to economic belt-tightening, with not even the local musicians performing in the flesh anymore.

Yet despite this harsh reality, there still was a need for music, and where there's a need, the market will find a way of filling it. Memory and history, malleable and mythified, and therefore ready to be monetized. Now, in 2037, I remain surprised that at my advanced age I might still be gigging. In fact, I absolutely must keep working to maintain a slightly-more-than-marginal existence since the elimination of Social Security and Obamacare by the Trump regime. I had signed with The Agent in 2029, as their patented Illgorithmic™ approach to booking seemed right for the times while physical performances were cratering. In NYC, the only venues still "live" were the Metropolitan Opera, BAM, and the Lincoln Center, and they programmed a very narrow bandwidth of acts catering to the most upper of crusts with ticket prices to match, locking most real music out. Finding even a basement space in the outer realms of the Bronx or Queens for a DIY show had long become impossible, so, as far as local gigs went, there was nothing. And if there's nothing local, one might as well go global, even if it's only in the Metaverse.

There might be two weeks with no work and then suddenly a thorny knot of gigs would appear, but that was nothing new—it had always been feast or famine. This particular morning as I poured out my first cup of NoSpresso™ (coffee plants having been one of the deeply mourned victims of climate change—extinct except for a few hothouse specimens producing beans only for the extraordinarily wealthy) my tablet bannered a message from The Agent informing me of a tour for the next day: seven concerts in Tokyo, Berlin, Barcelona, Santiago, Bologna, Brussels, and the Luna colony. An '80s Downtown Scene revival had been brewing for a couple of hours the previous afternoon on both Blather and Glub-Glub, so The Agent pounced, with contracts signed by 5:00 EST. Twenty-four hours advance notice was considered very civilized these days. Sometimes the call came with the expectation that you'd be onstage in fifteen minutes, like a neo-mariachi waiting in the town zocalo for the dispatcher to send you to a pop-up wedding, divorce party, or supermarket shooting.

Given the Downtown theme, I first prepared backgrounds for my show. Starting with scans of Berlin's The Loft in all its deconstructed glory, I moved to the black-box purity of The Kitchen, hopped over to Tokyo's Plan B with its reductionist esthetic scripted by Min Tanaka, and ended up with the grime and whimsy of the East Village's 8BC. There would be mismatched guitar and bass amps of varying quality but consistently large size—the bigger, the better. My instrumental arsenal would feature a model of Double Neck Nr. 3 built in 1984 by Ken Heer to a Mad Max blueprint, as well as one of my ancient Martin straight soprano saxophones. I'd made the impulse-response samples back in 2026 and, though not using the latest codecs, they still sounded good. For this gig I would use no time-based processing, just overdrive on each of the necks, referencing my "fundamentalist" period between 1984 and 1988, when I'd pretty much eschewed digital effects. The latest version of Alive™ allowed me to sequence the necessary instrumental processing that would ensue over the course of the set in addition to the staging and lighting cues. Alive's predictive subroutines could do a pretty good job of anticipating the dynamics of live performance, providing a nearly realistic concert experience for the performer as well as the audience. I programmed in 4 percent randomness for ambience, which might lead to some unexpected equipment malfunctions, heckling, or power dimming—just enough to keep it funky.

The introduction of Juice™ in 2032 (essentially a home 3D printer for manufacturing and delivering chems to performers and audiences alike) upped the ante for live performance, though some Luddites objected to this novel intrusion. Humans have been hacking their own biochemistry for eons, so what's the problem? If you kept an open mind (not to mention a port in your neck for the introduction of the chems), the socioacoustic experience was deeply enhanced with its simulation of the pheromonal handshaking present in a physical space shared by performers and audience to create a vivid feedback loop.

The concert itself would be held at 2015 hours local, wherever that was, with the audience temporally filtered by IP address. As show time approached, I felt that old anticipatory buzz: wired but lulled, empty but overflowing. I welcomed it even if I was just sitting in an updated office throne, chems dripping, headset and data gloves in place, ready to rock.

This was a good tour, and not too long at seventy-two minutes total duration. There was that sense of inevitability I've always sought in improvisation, yet I still found myself surprised at the direction the music took me at crucial moments. The feeling that the audience and I were riding the same wave remained present throughout, whether thanks to the chems or quantum entanglement or just the nature of the music. The post-gig hang used to be a high point of touring—the current chat-room scene is a poor substitute, even though it's nice to exchange some bumps with the listeners. Hate to sound like an old geezer, but I do miss the way it used to be.

18

The Rising Stars Fife and Drum Band

From a preview by organizer Adam Lore for this May 2003 benefit event at Sin-é in Manhattan:

> As you may have heard, Mr. Otha Turner, Mississippi's most celebrated fife player, passed away on the morning of February 27. That same evening, his daughter, Ms. Bernice Pratcher, ended her long battle with cancer. Their lives and music were an inspiration to many, myself included, and it is in that spirit that we present a celebration of their lives and legacies, while also providing support for their family and those in their community who aim to continue the fife and drum picnic tradition.

As an impoverished high school senior in 1969 with a deep thirst for music, I'd haunt the bargain bins at Sam Goody's, Discount Records, and Alexander's Department Store, where one could find myriad treasures priced between 49 and 99 cents. I rarely came up empty-handed from my hunts and could claim a bounty including records by Charles Mingus, Howlin' Wolf, Cecil Taylor, Robert Pete Williams, Sonny Sharrock, and, more to the point at this moment, a compilation titled *Sounds of the South* produced by Alan Lomax as part of the Southern Folk Heritage series on Atlantic Records. Alongside the ravishing slide guitar blues of Fred McDowell, mournful solo vocals by Vera Hall, and the stirring Alabama Sacred Heart Singers were two tracks that surprised and thrilled me: fife and drums by Lonnie and Ed Young and panpipe and drums by Sid Hemphill and Lucius Smith. To my ears, it was African folk music, but not "folkloric" or fossilized. It was alive and current and close kin in my ears to the music of Ornette Coleman, Pharaoh Sanders, and John Coltrane. In 1974, Testament Records released *Traveling Through the Jungle*, a mind-melting collection of Southern fife and drum bands. Sid Hemphill was there but also Napoleon Strickland, Ephram Carter, and one track by Othar Turner. It wasn't until 1997 that there would be a release of an entire album of Othar Turner's, the enticingly titled *Everybody Hollerin' Goat*. It became an important part of the soundtrack of my life at that moment and led me to dig out the comparatively rarer 1995 release *Field Recordings from Gravel Springs, Mississippi*.

Sad to say, on both occasions that the Rising Stars band played NYC I had been away on tour and so missed seeing them. However, Adam would go down to Mississippi on multiple occasions for Otha's goat barbecue event, a marathon of music, alcohol, and food. Through Adam I was able to purchase a cane fife made by Otha, on which I sporadically practice. In May 2003, I was thrilled and honored to be invited by Adam to perform at this event so at the very least, this would finally be a chance to hear the Rising Stars band in performance, albeit without Otha. The event took place at the recently re-opened Sin-é club on the Lower East Side. In its original incarnation, Sin-é was a tiny folk club on St. Mark's Place that, incongruously, was also a trendy music biz A&R hunting ground. The new club was much larger with a capacity of 150 and a powerful sound system, though it had the murky acoustics of a concrete box. The evening began promisingly with a group of musicians whose name I did not catch playing a ritualistic chant with cloud-like drumming that grew in intensity. After about fifteen engaging and trance-inducing minutes, they turned on a drum-machine with a monotonous quarter-note kick drum that was *blastingly* loud. They continued to play on and on over this for nearly ninety minutes more, even refusing to stop when asked by the organizers! Bizarre and a total drag for all. They finally left the stage, and the room breathed a collective sigh of relief. Some rare footage of Otha (the *r* was often dropped in later life) Turner and band at one of the family barbecues in Mississippi was then shown, restoring some balance to the evening. The film was beautifully edited to the music and displayed ambience, food preparation, personalities, and, of course, the musicians playing. As the film finished, we heard an amplified fife in the house and distant drums, and soon, bursting into the room in full force, The Rising Stars Fife and Drum Band!

Otha Turner's thirteen-year-old granddaughter Shardé Olivia Thomas was on the fife (with a wireless clip-on mic), and the drum section was RL Boyce, Andre Evans, Rodney Evans, and Aubrey "Bill" Turner. It was ecstatic and spine-chilling, but also seemed to engender a deep sadness within the joy. As she grew more comfortable on stage, Shardé came to life as a bandleader, evoking shouted responses from the packed house and moving everyone to shake and jump. After a too-short set, they took a break, and it was my turn.

My Godin guitar was tuned to Skip James-approved open D-minor and plugged into a direct input for the house PA and a Fender Twin on stage. I began with some EBow and slide, but unfortunately the high gain that the sound engineer had set was seriously overloading the monitors and they completely crapped out. This was adjusted and I restarted, a little flustered but determined to maintain. Fingerpicking a traditional Delta pattern with some slide countermelodies on top and gradually building up into a tapped section, I was hoping to bridge my blues with some sounds from the NYC "delta." The response was strong, and after my set a nice hang with RL and Andre was had, speaking about guitars, touring, and the European festival circuit that they were hoping to enter.

Next was Ari Up, highly charismatic and previously a member of The Slits, an English band whose album on the Antilles label I had greatly enjoyed in the early '80s. Her appearance was brief but exciting and followed by another rousing set by the Rising Stars, finishing with an extended and mesmerizing version of the classic "Sitting on Top of the World." Shardé's fife playing was never complicated yet always enthralling, shading the timeless melody with fluid trills and slurs.

The Reigning Sound were up next, a band from Memphis mixing R&B, rockabilly, and blues with a manic punk energy. After four songs, they brought up the legendary Eddie Kirkland to sing and play a few numbers with them before a break after which Eddie would play solo. One would never guess that Eddie was eighty years old, but his history stretches back to post-war blues and Memphis R&B. Before his set, Eddie regaled us with some tales, leaning in a relaxed manner on the side of his behemoth 1973 Lincoln Continental. It was parked in front of the club, metallic green and gaudily decorated in a fashion very similar to his guitar and clothing. Eddie plays loud, really loud. He gets a cutting tone on a vintage 1970s Japanese "lawsuit" Les Paul copy. It's almost too much to bear, but ultimately worth it as his presence is so powerful and the music filled with undiluted passion and a deep sense of the history of Southern blues and R&B. To cap the evening and return to the taproot, the Rising Stars band returned for an even more rousing set, louder, wilder.

19

Peter K. Siegel

Serving Music

An intriguing offer on Craigslist for a vintage Galiano "Decalcomania" parlor guitar brought me to the home of Peter K. Siegel in the spring of 2021. On the walls hung an aged and obviously well-loved Martin D-28 as well as a number of unique banjos and guitars, old and older. After examining the guitar in question (which I happily purchased), our conversation turned to instruments and from there to music. Though Peter's name had not been immediately familiar to me, certainly much of his work was, going back to my high school years. His various projects starting in the mid-1960s had resonated deeply with me, from the cacophonous joy of the Even Dozen Jug Band, Joseph Spence's rich Bahamian sounds, to the first recordings of the legendary guitarist Roy Buchanan. Peter spoke with affection and humor about the various musicians he had recorded or worked with, and it was clear that he had a thousand stories about this incredibly important period in American music. Starting as an amateur engineer and musician with a deep involvement with NYC's Friends of Old-Time Music, he progressed to staff producer for Elektra, where he ran the hugely influential Nonesuch Explorer series with his pioneering recording of Japanese *shakuhachi* music, *A Bell Ringing in the Empty Sky* earning it a place on the Voyage spacecraft. Later he was director of A&R for Polydor's American label followed by a stint as president of Pye Records, and then, realizing that this work was taking him further away from the music he loved, he left it to resume his life as an independent producer and performer. His output clearly displays his passion not just for the old-time music of rural America of the 1920s and 1930s, but for all music created with soul and passion. With recent releases including his collection of union songs performed with Eli Smith, *Union Makes Us Strong*, his documentation of the revolutionary concert series *Friends of Old-Time Music*, and his latest release of never-before-heard Clarence Ashley recordings, Peter shows that he is still a vital force in music production.

Peter's work as a recording and live engineer brought him into contact with an amazing constellation of legendary musicians: Maybelle Carter, Sam McGee, Fred McDowell, Hobart Smith, Frank Wakefield, Jesse Fuller, Lightning Hopkins, Rev. Gary Davis, Neil Young, Bob Dylan, and more. As a producer, he brought to life recordings of Indian Carnatic music, psychedelic rockers Earth Opera, songsmith Paul Siebel, and Grammy-nominated street singer Oliver Smith. Some of the encounters blossomed into continuing friendships and working relationships, especially with Doc Watson, Joseph Spence, and Roy Buchanan. In our conversation, he spoke of these at length as well as many other topics.

PS: I just made the first LPs that I've done in years, part of an informal series from tapes that I'd recorded many years ago, the Clarence Ashley on Jalopy Records and a Gaither Carlton record for Smithsonian Folkways. What I love about LPs and miss now is you get all this turf. You can read, look . . . you don't get that by downloading a single track.

E♯: You started as an engineer or playing music?

PS: Playing music. My parents had a lot of old records and lived in the Village, part of a gang of people who lived in a house that was owned by a guy named Jimmy George Jemell who was the Daily News "Inquiring Photographer," and also living in the house was a guy named Mel Lampell [Millard Lampell] who sang with the Almanac Singers and wrote a lot of the songs they performed including "Talking Union" and "The Sinking of the Reuben James." My dad got to see all these musicians, including Leadbelly and Woody Guthrie, and he claimed he was part of the gang that would go around to sing the choruses in the songs of the Almanac Singers when they were shorthanded at a union thing. So when I was growing up, the records that were around were by the Almanacs, Leadbelly, Guthrie—I remember music and guitarists. There was a guy across the street named Toby Kreber, a cowboy singer. When I was twelve or thirteen, I really wanted a guitar, so my parents got me one, and when I was fifteen I really wanted a banjo. I saw Pete Seeger play it and thought it was incredibly cool (though I wouldn't have used that word then). I set about teaching myself to play and took four lessons from a really great banjo player named Billy Faier. He made a couple of records on Riverside. He taught me how to frail, play clawhammer style. I loved that kind of music, and by the time I was eighteen or nineteen I had met these guys,

Ralph Rinzler, Mike Seeger, and John Cohen. I went to school with David Grisman [virtuoso mandolinist and inventor of "Dawg Music"] and Richard Rinzler, who got me involved with his cousin Ralph who was really doing things with this music. He and John Cohen and Izzy Young started this organization, Friends of Old-Time Music, and I became the guy that recorded all of their concerts. At that time, these guys were musicians who played the kind of music that I really liked. I'd gotten the Harry Smith *Anthology of American Folk Music* and listened to a lot of old-time music and blues, and they were going around and recording people and putting out records on Folkways.

E#: It seems a lot of the original players of this music were alive at that time—did people know that they were alive and even active?

PS: It was found out as we went along. People like Doc Boggs and Mississippi John Hurt that we heard on the *Anthology* that were not presumed to be alive, yet there they were! That in itself was a phenomenon because of confronting the actual person behind this far-off voice that you made up so many stories about. Like Bukka White was supposed to have written "Fixin' To Die" just before he was executed in the electric chair . . . but suddenly, there he was! Doc Boggs was supposed to be some totally weird strange guy but there he was, a nice old gent wearing a suit, very polite. Damn! . . . I wanted to be like Ralph, and John and Mike, they were about half a generation older, which was, when you're nineteen, a big deal.

E#: So how did you get started recording?

PS: How I got into it, I bought a tape recorder and a cheap microphone. I knew a guy named Art Rosenbaum, he's still going, he's a wonderful field recordist (also a great banjo player), and he was doing field recordings, even took me to Kentucky. He had a Tandberg 3B recorder, a half-track mono, 3¾–7½. I knew Seeger had a microphone, an ElectroVoice 666, a good dynamic mic . . . but when I went to look at microphones, it cost $300, a lot of money, so the salesman, in those days you'd go to a real radio supply place, when I told him I couldn't spend so much, the salesman said to try this EV 664, it's pretty good. It was really a PA mic—they still use them because they look great, so I bought it, it cost like $30 and it looked cool, the chrome one, that's what I had. I didn't really know how cheap a mic that was! But I also have this theory about microphones, which is that, it's really simple, you put one in front of a really great master musician, it's going to outperform itself. It's going to be better than it's supposed to be.

There's an interview with Don Reno, a great banjo player who recorded for King Records in Cincinnati. Years later Gary Reed, a bluegrass historian, put together a Don Reno and Red Smiley box set with a book "that thick" [here he gestured] with extensive notes. One of the things was an interview with an engineer who had recorded Reno, and he told a story about how they always used these old beat-up dynamic mics and Sid Nathan (who owned King) bought these new Telefunken mics, like Neumann U-47's, he made a big deal about recording Don with these new mics. Don said, "That sounds terrible! I can't stand it, it doesn't even sound like a banjo," so they went and got this old beat-up mic, and he loved it.

Now I had this equipment and was ready to make my first field recording. The FOTM at this time had produced one concert in NY—the group included Clarence Ashley, Doc Watson, that was in 1961 or 2? Anyway, a year later, the FOTM got to put on their second concert. At that first concert, people noticed what a good guitarist Watson was, and Ralph had gone to visit Doc at his home in North Carolina and arranged for a concert for "The Watson Family" for lack of any other name and that consisted of Doc, his brother Arnold who played banjo and harmonica, and Gaither Carlton, a wonderful fiddler who was Doc's father-in-law. They arranged the second FOTM concert, no the third, I'm sorry! The sequence was like this: the very first one was, the first two concerts were at PS41 in the Village, and the first one featured Roscoe Holcomb who John had just met in Kentucky, and that concert consisted of four acts, Roscoe, the New Lost City Ramblers, Jean Ritchie, and the Greenbriar Boys. And the thinking behind staging that concert that way was that they were concerned that if they just put on Roscoe Holcomb, who not a lot of people had heard of, they wouldn't get an audience.

E♯: Was Jean Ritchie well known?

PS: Oh yeah, Jean Ritchie was very well known and so were the New Lost City Ramblers and Greenbriar Boys. And Jean Ritchie was on the board of the FOTM.

E♯: Was she a folklorist or authentic?

PS: She was authentic, a folk singer, from Viper, Kentucky. She had come to

NY to work as a social worker and she worked at the Henry Street Settlement but she brought her music with her and she was like a grand presence, my god, a traditional beautiful ballad singer who performed with a dulcimer! She recorded extensively because every company that wanted to put out folk music records recorded her, so she was on Riverside, Tradition, Folkways, Westminster . . . Anyway, the first FOTM concert consisted of those four acts, and it was a big success. The second one, I'm correcting what I said before, was the Clarence Ashley one. That was also held at PS41.

E♯: Are any of the FOTM crew still alive?

PS: John is, Ralph passed away twenty years ago, Mike just in the last couple of years. John is in his eighties, still doing great.

E♯: When I was in high school, they were all legendary figures for us.

PS: I wanted to be like these guys, I wanted to record the real thing . . . and to play the music. I wanted to do both. Their thing was they wanted to play music like the old-timers, but they wanted to introduce you to the real thing. They had a real reverence for the older people.

E♯: Was there a feeling that they couldn't ever make the real expression themselves because of a cultural or geographical distance?

PS: It never got talked about, but what would get talked about, if people came up to Ralph and said, "Wow, that was great, I love listening to you guys," he would say, "If you really want to hear something great, you should listen to Bill Monroe." Not sure what mechanism was at play in their minds, but they knew . . . their mission seemed to be, beyond being musicians, seemed to be to introduce people to the older musicians. Ralph was responsible for when you hear today . . . when you hear people on NPR, for example hearing people play country blues or country music, before Ralph came along, that stuff was nonexistent on the radio, although Henriette Yurchenko had a show on WNYC, Leadbelly would occasionally be a guest.

E♯: How did word get out? Was there a network, handbills?

PS: One of the reasons that Izzy Young was considered one of the founders was that he had a store, The Folklore Center, and he . . . Let me re-phrase something so as not to fail to credit Izzy's contribution to this: the fact that he provided some infrastructure in the form of a store was only part of his contribution. And he wouldn't like it if I just said that Izzy's job was to hand out flyers.

E♯: So he was like a town crier?

PS: Yes. He talked to everyone, he had a newsletter that you'd be on the mailing list for . . . he was very good at spreading the word. The FOTM, you should know, you think of a non-profit arts organization, an office with computers, grants, but this was just three guys who lived in their apartments and talked on the phone, met up once in a while in a coffee shop, I mean it was . . . they had no infrastructure whatsoever, so what Izzy provided was a lot. Anyway, by the time I had this Tandberg tape recorder and this EV microphone, the FOTM was about to produce their third concert, this was 1963 (but I'll doublecheck this). That concert was going to be the Watson family and Jess Fuller.

E♯: From San Francisco?

PS: He came to NY for this and also played at the Cornell Folk Festival, maybe a few other places. So I basically said to Ralph, how about I record this? So I'm eighteen, take out my tape recorder and record this, this unbelievable concert of Doc Watson and his family and Jess Fuller—the recordings of both of those artists end up on the FOTM album. After that, I became the unofficial recordist for the FOTM concerts.

E♯: How did the sound quality hold up after fifty years? Did you have to bake the tapes?

PS: Not bad! No, you're talking about mylar tapes, this was acetate. Acetate tapes tended to warp; they didn't stick together, so you didn't have to bake. The tape would warp in such a way that it would look like a scallop, so you'd have to find a way to hold it over the head. Anyway, after that I recorded a bunch of concerts and great music. Funny thing, when these authentic old-timers would appear somewhere, and one thing that happened with the FOTM, when they would bring someone to NYC, they would try to get them some extra gigs along the way.

E♯: How would they find people? Would they just go drive around someplace asking for musicians? Was Lomax's work a guide?

PS: There's a million stories, not quite as simple as going around. Anyway, for me, when someone, say when Clarence Ashley played at Gerde's Folk City, I could record Clarence Ashley by asking him if it was okay, there was no money in it. There was no agent or manager or lawyer to jump out and say, "You can't do that." The club didn't mind—I don't think we ever asked, just put a microphone up on stage. Whenever I had an album come out, we made an agreement, for instance with the Clarence

Ashley, we made a full-fledged record deal with his grandson who owns the rights. You could ask, "Can I record you?" and they'd say sure, but you couldn't put it out, I certainly never put it out without going back and finding the person and making an agreement. But you could record. My motivation for recording wasn't thinking about records at that time, but largely I like the idea of recording and there weren't many albums of this kind of music available. I like the idea of having that music to listen to. So I started recording that stuff.

E♯: Were you interested in the technical end, how to make your recordings sound better?

PS: Later I was. I was in a band called the Even Dozen Jug Band. There was a lot of interesting people in that band.

E♯: Yeah! Maria Muldaur, John Sebastian, David Grisman, Steve Katz.

PS: Almost everyone in that band went on to do something.

E♯: That bass player who went on to become a cult leader?

PS: No, Fritz Richmond was not in it—he was in the Kweskin Jug Band. There was a thing about jug bands for about ten minutes!

E♯: Yeah, in fact, I was in a jug band in high school.

PS: Anyway, Elektra Records made a record of the Even Dozen Jug Band, 1963 I think.

E♯: That wasn't done on multitrack?

PS: No, it was on two tracks at 15 ips—I got ahold of some of the master tapes at a studio called Mastertone on 42nd Street. When we got signed, Jac Holzman signed us, Paul Rothchild had just arrived at Elektra as their new hotshot producer, and he had come from an interesting background as well. An actual record producer! And he produced an album of the Even Dozen Jug Band. He later produced The Doors, Janis Joplin, all kinds of people. Paul produced us, and I got to see what an actual record producer did—I had no idea. So I said, "This is what I want to do!" After that I was hanging out at Elektra and learning stuff from Paul and made some records out of tapes I made and got to know Moe Asch at Folkways, who was a thousand stories unto himself. But I produced a few albums for Folkways, I didn't know what I was doing. I was in Washington, DC for a bluegrass festival and I heard Hazel Dickens and Alice Foster and with the help of Mike Seeger, I persuaded Moe Asch that I should make an album of them.

E♯: Were you still using the same equipment, or had you upgraded?

PS: By that time, I had a Nagra and a Sony condenser mic, a D37A, nice mic.

E#: Digging around, I also came upon a note of a recording you did of one of Dylan's first "basement tapes" with Gil Turner playing banjo at his apartment in the East Village.

PS: No, that's not true—it's the basement of Gerde's Folk City. It was right after a star concert, on 4th Street at the NYU School of Education, Bill Monroe presented by the FOTM. First, we all got to see Bill Monroe, Kenny Baker on fiddle, Jack Cook on guitar and lead vocal, and Del McCoury on banjo—it was wonderful! After the concert, I ended up in the basement of Gerde's and there was some kind of jam session going on there with, I don't remember, there was Gil Turner playing banjo, Bob Dylan singing . . . anyway, Bob Dylan says, "Would you record me?" I said, "Sure," I was hoping he was going to say that. That was about the time of the *Freewheelin'* album. He would just have me record him for the fun of it. Anyway, I was recording stuff for Folkways and eventually I got hired by Elektra, like an apprentice engineer/producer.

The thing about Elektra at that time—for a few years, all their producers were also engineers, worked hands on. At Atlantic the producer wouldn't engineer, Tom Dowd would be the engineer. At Columbia, there was a union thing, the producer was not allowed to touch the board. Recording engineers were not super hip in those days, most of them came out of radio, wearing plaid flannel shirts—most of these guys, you weren't allowed to touch the board. They also had a "machine man" in a little room behind a curtain. The engineer would be in charge of the mics and mixing and the engineer would say, "Roll," and the machine man would say, "We're rolling," and he would probably also be wearing an old flannel shirt. No one was allowed to touch anything! I think it was all union requirements. At Elektra, for what it's worth, all the producers were trained to be recording engineers. They had a mixing room. The engineers didn't have engineering degrees, but they knew how to place a mic, operate a machine. I was like an apprentice, they really taught it like, you want to be a chef, you start by washing pots and pans. I had some great teachers: Paul Rothchild, Mark Abramson was a fabulous producer, worked full-time at Elektra, produced Judy Collins's albums. My job at first was every morning, align all the machines, clean all the heads with rubbing alcohol and a Q-tip, then when they could trust me a little bit, they had me do something which is like a thing of the past, put leader in between tracks on an album—white paper leader. Eventually, I got to record stuff. And that's the answer of how I got into it.

E♯: One of the first notable recordings that I found of yours was of Joseph Spence. Did you know then of the 1958 recordings? He has such a unique guitar style, like a pianist, impossible to imitate. I hear similarities between his playing and that of Thelonious Monk in the syncopation and unusual intervals in his harmonies.

PS: How that all happened, the difference between folklorist and nonfolklore recordings of the Bahamas. Lomax had been in the Bahamas in 1935. He went with a real folklorist . . . Bahamas was not about Calypso . . . For whatever reason, Lomax recorded in the Bahamas—lot of great stuff. There was a style of singing called "rhyming"—it came out of the sponging—one of the principal industries at the time in the Bahamas was gathering natural sponges. And to do it, these crews of guys would go out on a boat, rickety craft, four or five guys, go out and dive for sponges—really dangerous, a lot of guys drowned. Lot of songs about that. They'd dive for sponges, come up, anything can happen, pile 'em up in the boat, eventually take them back to port—but they would go out for weeks at a time, they would tie up the boats together, and they would sing. And what they would sing, and it became kind of a competitive sport, they'd sing old hymns they called "anthems," really beautiful three-chord songs where a group of people would sing the anthem over and over again—typically someone would sing the melody, someone would sing the treble, someone singing bass, and the rhymer would start improvising vocal parts, usually based on Bible stories. A lot of them, for reasons which are too complicated to go into right now, the Bahamas shared a lot of culture with African Americans living in the United States, a lot of people going back and forth, many had hymn books. That style of rhyming *was* the music of the Bahamas—it does not exist anymore, it's gone. In 1958 Sam Charters went to the Bahamas and recorded what became three and ultimately four albums on Folkways, one a whole album of Joseph Spence, who, as you know, plays guitar and does two types of vocalizing—one is very incidental, sort of like Erroll Garner or other guys who make sounds while they're playing (and you hear that a lot), and he also does rhyming. In the verses of songs, what he does is basically in a rhyming style. It was improvised, but if you do it enough you pretty much get a rap going, and Spence had it down. But he wasn't doing real rhyming because he only had a guitar. A seminal event in Spence's life was the 1929 hurricane on Andros Island in the Bahamas, which resulted in the sinking of the Pretoria and the drowning of twenty people. Spence was on a hill near his home, and he could see the sinking. He ran down to the harbor to rescue people and help in the recovery. He describes these events in his song "Run Come See Jerusalem," just now released on Smithsonian Folkways. The second album that Sam put out from the Bahamas trip was all rhyming with some great people, Frederick McQueen, John Roberts—that was incredible. Those two albums . . . I knew every note of those two albums. Blew me away, both of them. There was a third album of brass bands which I never really got into, and then many years later he came out with a fourth one, which was outtakes from the Spence and rhyming album, but it was still great.

On the record: . . . I wasn't quite working at Elektra yet, but I was hanging out at Elektra, and I was learning to produce records and had produced some records for Folkways. The FOTM in 1965—I went to work at Elektra at the end of 1965 and this was the summer of '65—produced the last of their series of concerts at the New School. And one of the things they produced was music from the Bahamas. Pete Seeger volunteered to go down there and look for musicians, and he found Joseph Spence again and Pete arranged for Spence, his sister Jenny, her husband Raymond Pinder, and their daughter Geneva Pinder to come up and also, several really wonderful rhymers—there was a rhyming group. So FOTM puts on this concert of music from the Bahamas, and one of the things that was my job (as a volunteer—nobody got paid) . . . when musicians would come to NY for a concert, they'd be here for a few days and wouldn't know where to go. They might stay at somebody's house or the Hotel Earl or the Albert, hotels around the Washington Square area, not flophouses but cheap hotels. These guys didn't have any money, but they were trying to pay the musicians, pay their expenses, the gate.

E♯: Would Bill Monroe play for the door?

PS: Bill Monroe's a special case and there's a whole story of how Ralph fits in with that. He'd been off the scene . . . I can't even tell you the whole story . . . anyway, I was supposed to take care of Joseph Spence and his family while they were in NY so, I had this thing, Joseph Spence was legendary among people I knew, my friends, John Sebastian was like . . . "Oh man . . . " but I got this idea to take Joseph Spence to the top of the Empire

State Building. I took him to the top and he was appropriately gassed by the whole thing, him and the Pinder Family. They had a great time. Years later, Guy Droussart, the Swiss guy who became the great expert on Joseph Spence and who wrote a lot about him, took thousands of photographs of him, he was down in the Bahamas years later and he found this little snow globe of the Empire State Building that Joseph Spence had bought on that trip. Anyway, I took them up there, I was living at home at the time, my parents had an apartment on East 31st Street and I took the whole gang back and we went into my bedroom and I said, "Hey, let's make tapes," and I recorded a lot of Joseph Spence in my bedroom. Great stuff. He was playing that guitar [points to D-28]. "I got it in 1962 or '63, it was used, but only lightly used. I recorded all these songs with Joseph Spence playing that guitar—when you're nineteen years old and suddenly you have Joseph Spence in your bedroom, it's a big deal!

Anyway, then I got the idea to go to the Bahamas and record all those people. I was more familiar than Paul was of the concept of the "field recording trip," for lack of a better word. You know, John Cohen had made this incredible album called *Mountain Music of Kentucky* where he went into a relatively small area in Eastern Kentucky and recorded the folk music that was there, one of greatest albums of all time (for me anyway!)—I wanted to do something like that. I realized I could do it a little differently. For one thing, I had better technology. By this time I had the Nagra and a good condenser mic and a very rudimentary understanding of how to produce records, so I could make something; I could do a survey that Sam Charters didn't have the equipment to do. Paul had done a solo record of Spence, so I could do a recording of Spence and McQueen. I couldn't go by myself because of the equipment carrying, a lot of tape. So I called up my friend Jody Stecher, at that time primarily a mandolin player living in NY, and I said, "Do you want to go to the Bahamas and record people?" So we went down there and first thing we did was find Joseph Spence. We found him in a day, we had some instructions that we got from Rothchild, to go to Nassau and from there to a little village called Culmerville, and then ask around . . . and it worked. But people were suspicious, these two white guys looking for Joseph Spence.

We were only down there a week, week and a half—we recorded so much great stuff. We had this marathon recording session in the garden behind Edith Pinder's house. I had two microphones, an AKG D24E and a Sony C-37. No mixer, but I had a preamp that allowed me to put the D24 into the line input of the Nagra, and you could mix the line input and mic input in the recorder, a mono tape machine. We found out about a rhyming singer named Brucie Green who had his own group, we found Frederick McQueen and recorded him with a rhyming group, we found Sammy Green, Brucie's son, we found this group Sheldon Swain, recorded all these people. We made a side trip to a place called Marsh Harbor in the Abako Keys because we found in the Nassau Public Library a book that said that in Marsh Harbor traditional British ballads are still performed as they were during the Revolutionary War. So we went there to find out about it and actually recorded a woman called Mistress Lindel Aubry who sang all those old ballads, apparently like they'd always been sung. We brought the tapes back to NY and went through the process of fashioning an album. When I got hired by Elektra, I played it for Jac Holzman and he said, "Yeah, we'll put it out."

E#: Was Tracey Sterne working there yet?

PS: No, yes! We were both hired on the same day. Later, we were both responsible for starting what was called the Nonesuch Explorer Series. Jac had a label, the Nonesuch label, which was focusing mostly on Baroque and pre-Baroque music. He had a brilliant marketing concept. He had become aware that there were a lot of little record companies in Europe making high-quality recordings of Baroque and pre-Baroque music, and he could lease them cheap for America or just pay royalties. Camerata or Bärenreiter in Germany . . . even Pye in England. So Jac discovered he could license this stuff and he had Bill Harvey who was his art director, worked in-house at Elektra, you know when you see great album covers from the '50s? He came from that school . . . he came up with this concept of putting these very colorful cartoons, people presumably dressed like . . . wearing powdered wigs playing violins and stuff. They put them out in a "gay looking package"—"gay" had a meaning quite apart from what it means today—maybe with some nice notes. Jac's final stroke of genius was the price of Nonesuch Records, which was $2.50. At that point, mono records cost $3.98, stereo records cost $4.98, and budget cost $1.98. So he came up with something you could buy really cheap but without the stigma of it being a budget record. And it was a big hit. And shortly after he started that, he came out with what he called the Nonesuch International Series. You may remember there was a genre of record called International, you know, "Music of Greece," "Music of Israel," he basically got by with the same licensing technique. He actually got a couple of great ones, "Music of Bulgaria" was a great one. The point is he had this thing called the Nonesuch International Series.

When we first put out *The Real Bahamas*, I actually had a great idea—now, don't forget I'd worked for Moe who had a lot of music that was really great, music from faraway places—but working at Nonesuch I had access to good engineering, an engineer named David B. Jones. There was a kind of engineer who did classical recordings in concert halls and churches, and David B. Jones was one of those guys. Mark Obor was also one of them. David would drive to a church in a VW Microbus, take out these huge tape recorders on a hand truck, and he would set up in a hall, arrange a very informal control room with talkback. I knew I had him at my disposal if I wanted to hire him, and I also knew that one of the things about the notes on the international records, they were always schlocky, written by someone who didn't know anything about the music, mostly a travelog, "Greece is a wonderful country, here's some music they dance to, et cetera"—but I'd gotten acquainted from working with Moe and Ralph and Mike about liner notes and how good they could be. The precipitating idea was that some Carnatic musicians, South Indian classical musicians, primarily voice-based, sung with accompaniment on other instruments, and when it's not sung, it's played on a lead instrument that is voice-like, like violin or flute, *veena* does a pretty good job. It's less popular than the North Indian music because the North Indian music appealed to guitar pickers more with guys like Ravi Shankar. But the Carnatic is great, deep music . . . there were a couple of South Indian musicians who took up residence at Wesleyan University in Connecticut. Somehow I met Robert Brown, who set up that ethnomusicology program there. He told me about these great musicians, so I went up there and listened; they blew me away. And those guys were singer K. V. Narayanaswamy, violin V. V. Subramaniam, *mridangam* Palghat Raghu. I got this incredible idea: one of the places that David B. Jones had been recording at was the Manhattan Towers Hotel, which is right about a block north of where the Beacon Theater is on Broadway. They had this fantastic ballroom they used for bingo games, dances and stuff, just a great-sounding room, where Maynard Solomon recorded Joan Baez. David had told me how wonderful the sound was there, and I got the idea: what if we got some really great musicians, signed them, took them to Manhattan Towers, and got David to record them and got someone who really knew about it to write some notes. We would make a complete Folkways album, but with good sound!

E♯: Was this done with the idea of appealing to a different clientele?

PS: I didn't really have any sense of marketing.

E♯: Let me circle back for a second: with FOTM, was there any discussion of the connection of folk music to social movements, colonialism?

PS: Not really. The only way it might come up was say, when FOTM presented a concert of the Georgia Sea Island Singers and one of the women had written a civil rights song. The answer is "no," with some very minor exceptions. Anyway, I had this idea, and Tracey and I talked about it; we sort of came up with the idea of making a break from the Nonesuch International Series and calling it something different. She came up with "Explorer Series," and we talked about it with Jac and with Bill Harvey who, trying to come up with a design concept, came up with the black-and-white pen-and-ink drawings. So basically, we put out two albums of the Wesleyan musicians. We kept the numbering of the International series, 17 and 18, but these were the first of the Explorer series. *Real Bahamas* was in the International Series, number 13 or 14.

E♯: Were they promoted?

PS: Yes! Jac was running a damn record company! There may have been guys who ran record companies even if they didn't make money, but Jac was not one of them. He was a record man, like Ahmet Ertegun; he dreamed of selling. He finally got his wish when he got The Doors. That's what he wanted to do. I don't think I personally had developed any sense of marketing at that time; I just wanted to make records. So the first two records initiated the whole package idea. We did it in a great acoustical environment with a great engineer, great notes by Robert Brown, who took the time to explain the scales and the *ragas*, then we had these covers *plus* we got to master it in a good studio and approve the test pressings, which you never got to do at Folkways, so we had a really high-quality product.

E♯: What else was recorded in those days?

PS: Now I was connected to Robert Brown at Wesleyan, so if anything interesting came along he'd tell me about it. I got introduced to Goro Yamaguchi; I recorded the first *shakuhachi* record that was ever made in the United States called *A Bell Ringing in the Empty Sky*. I used that same formula. Then Robert Brown turned me on to a guy named Ramnad Krishnan, one of the greatest Carnatic singers. I recorded enough from him to eventually make three albums. He passed away and he had only recorded for me, kind of a sobering thought, because if he hadn't recorded for me, he never would have recorded. Those were great albums. We recorded a bunch. Izzy Young told me about these two great Swedish fiddlers who were in town, conventional violins, they had a style of playing that was just stunning. I made a lot of records! One of the things about those Indian musicians particularly is, they balance themselves, they had a tradition of playing together, you didn't have to—when they performed, they sat on a rug and played, they didn't have monitors, they usually work without microphones, they were master musicians who balanced themselves. When you've got great musicians who balance themselves and a great classical recording engineer, you're going to come out with a good sound. David Jones had a wonderful thing, he had a half-inch two-track running at 30 ips and what we would do is basically, with a razor blade, put the albums together, leave ambient sound and go right into the next piece and for the most part, there's only two or three pieces on a side anyway. We had this original master tape running at 30 ips and we'd give it Bob Ludwig and that was it! What more could you do! We might have told him, "raise track 2 2 dB," but that was the extent. We didn't do anything else. We'd be really picky on the test pressings; I'd rejected a lot of test pressings. With Ludwig, I was also working with him on pop records, folk rock, we knew about him. He'd come out of Eastman School of Music, he was a trumpet player, he had great ears, and he had good equipment, Ortofon, we knew he wasn't going to butcher the music, and he would give us a reference disc. I don't recall any problems with the references; getting good pressings was harder. I made a lot of records, at a certain time.

I want to get to David Lewiston! David Lewiston called up cold and somehow got me or Tracey on the phone—she was very fastidious. There's a million little tiny things you need to do so it will be clear and full, no cringe-able moments—Tracey was really on top of all that stuff. Lewiston said he had just come back from Bali and he had recorded gamelan music, and I said, "What's gamelan music?" He came over and it was on 7½-inch quarter-track going in both directions, which meant you couldn't play it on a half-track deck. We had these Studer tape recorders; I was able to get a quarter-track head, and it was completely mind-blowing. David Lewiston and I sat down in the Elektra studio. We had moved to 1855 Broadway at 61st Street, and we had a mixing room and a very small overdubbing room—the mixing room would be up to here and the overdub room would continue as far as that banjo . . . but anyway, we sat down for several days and played all the tapes and eventually put together an album that was called *Music from the Morning of the World*. He also said, "There's this other thing that I recorded on an Uher tape recorder, 3¾, you probably don't want it anyway . . . " which turned out to be the "Frog Song!" We listened to it, we found some way to play it back, we made that record, it was really exciting. I listened to it for about ten minutes and said, "We're doing it!" The other thing about Jac, he gave me signing authority for the Explorer Series, which was easy to do because they were real cheap to make. I never would have had signing authority for signing some rock band which was going to cost $10,000. He allowed me to sign anyone I want to the Explorer Series and pay them a $500 advance and make a cheap recording, David Jones was like $20 an hour, the hall cost like $50 for the afternoon. Because it was low budget, he said, "Do it," and I was able to do a lot of great stuff that way. I personally produced fifteen or twenty albums, but then after I left, they continued.

E♯: The folk-rock stuff you were producing, was that for Elektra or after you left?

PS: For Elektra—one of my favorite records that I made was by Paul Siebel. That record has stood up. *Woodsmoke and Oranges*. I made a lot of people's first records. I made an album of Dave Ray. One of the first things was a record of Mark Spoelstra called *State of Mind*. It was half-finished; there was a number of things recorded half by me, half by Paul. Koerner, Ray, and Glover were Elektra artists, and it was time for Ray to make a solo record and he was without a producer. So Paul Nelson, who was from Minnesota and knew David Ray, Jac got him to produce the album of Ray, and I was the engineer and the associate producer, which worked very well—Paul knew the songs that worked well, but I knew how to make a record.

E♯: I was curious, you had mentioned that a lot of people had played your D-28 guitar. Did you bring it to recording sessions?

PS: No, Spence played it at my parents' home.

E♯: Fred McDowell?

PS: I recorded Fred McDowell as part of FOTM concerts, but I never got to know him. I actually recorded some great tracks of his. I recorded everything from the third FOTM concert on, but we still don't know who recorded the first two. That's an album of three CDs out of a dozen concerts, and I was extremely picky about finding good stuff. I wanted to find really prime stuff. It's not that these people didn't play great stuff, but there were technical issues, mic stands falling over, people coughing, there's this "Going Down to The River" by Fred McDowell that really blows me away. I wrote the notes, a sixty-page book, so a lot of the answers are there. There was an interesting book that Steven Petrus put together about Folk City, that came out of an exhibition. There's an Alton Delmore book, *Truth is Stranger Than Publicity*, about the country music business in the '30s and '40s.

E#: Mississippi John Hurt—you recorded him?

PS: I recorded him a couple of times but never got to know him. At the Gaslight, him and Rev. Gary Davis, pretty amazing. Here's what happened: this was during the time of FOTM producing concerts, we got the idea, John, Mike, and Ralph ran it, but with input; I was part of the family, I'd go to meetings.

E#: Was there any discussion or awareness of it being a Jewish thing, a bunch of Bohemian yids in the Village playing this Appalachian music?

PS: No, but there was one joke that John Cohen told. We were planning this record of NYC folklore, a concert too, fun, partly a response to being in New York and not doing anything about local folklore. We'd have an Irish street musician, some Spanish musicians who played in a club in the Bronx, we got a bunch of people, but John's joke was, "I know a lot of Jewish guys who play banjo." By the way, at that last Charlie Poole banjo gathering they had a whole thing of Jewish guys who played banjo, which included Henry Supoznik, Eli Smith, but also Jerron Paxton who is converted to Judaism, he's the only observant Jew in the bunch—you know Jerron? Of young people doing traditional music, he's the best thing happening! Back to Mississippi: on the FOTM album which you have there, there are a few cuts by Mississippi John Hurt—there was a time during the run we decided it would be great to put out an album. We weren't thinking of preserving for posterity or for scholarship, we were thinking of promoting the organization and getting people to come to the concerts. I had at that time recorded a concert of Hurt and Doc Boggs, portions of which are on the FOTM album. At that time audio restoration technology was not what it is now. Some of the recordings I made with cheap equipment and funny halls . . . the recordings of John Hurt did not come out as I had hoped. I considered them unusable. Years later, having learned a lot about restoration myself, having more technology available, I went back to them, and they turned out to be fine. When we were going to make this record, we recorded Hurt but it didn't "come out," so since he was going to be playing at the Gaslight, Stefan Grossman arranged for me to go to the Gaslight to record him to use on the FOTM album. We didn't care that it wasn't recorded in our concerts. So I got to record several sets of Mississippi John Hurt but never got to know him, I just showed up like an engineer. It was a thrill to watch him play and sing.

E♯: Did he sing "to the audience"? Did he think of himself as an entertainer?

PS: All these guys were professional entertainers at one time; they made records in the '20s and '30s. During the Depression they all went back to working on farms, Doc Boggs in the mines, Clarence Ashley had a trucking company that hauled fruit around. They were all professionals, so when they were performing again, they were still professionals!

E♯: Was there any thought to get Doc Boggs and Mississippi John Hurt to play together?

PS: On that concert, they did one thing together. Doc Boggs played an instrumental solo on the banjo called "Banjo Clog," and MJH came out and clogged to it. Actually, there were two attempts — first, he played the song and Hurt forgot to come out, so he played it again and someone pushed him out on stage. There are a lot of amazing similarities and contrasts between them, but they have stories that intertwine. There is a great story that I have not independently confirmed, and you might not want to say this unless it's confirmed: Tom Hoskins went down and found Mississippi John Hurt in Avalon, Mississippi, and they brought a guitar — he [MJH] had not been playing for a long time, he didn't have a guitar. They found him, went into the house and gave him a guitar, and he was playing, and Hoskins says, "Do you know how good you are?" and Hurt says, "Yes, and I've been knowin'."

Roy Buchanan

PS: Around 1971, I got hired as the actual director of A&R of Polydor. At that time, somehow they had signed Roy Buchanan, maybe around the time of that PBS special about him, *World's Greatest Unknown Guitarist*. There were two albums produced of Roy Buchanan, neither of which was deemed worthy of coming out, I heard them both. One was produced by Charlie Daniels; one was produced by a *Washington Post* writer, Tom Zito. When I arrived there, the relationship with Roy had deteriorated to not actual litigation, but a number of lawyers' letters back and forth. Probably because he had been there a couple of years and nothing had happened. I had been at Elektra for five years and decided to become an independent producer. I didn't have a good idea of what was good for me. The idea of being director of A&R for Polydor seemed attractive, and it did give me the opportunity to make some records. But eventually I had several jobs in the record industry, executive positions—it took me away from the music. I was not getting anything out of it. So at a certain time, by the late 1970s, I just wanted to get back and record fiddle music . . . and I did! Made a label deal with Rounder, recorded all kinds of things.

When I got to Polydor, there was a very bad situation going on with Roy Buchanan. He had a couple of guys who were representing him as managers who were never going to get along with Polydor and let Roy talk to me. So, I found out that Roy was playing at a club in Dupont Circle in DC so I decided I would just go down and talk to him. Took a plane to DC, caught his show, and went up to talk to him. After, there was nobody around, and I said, "Man, Peter Siegel, record producer from Polydor, can I talk with you?" We went back into this room, covered with beer bottles and overflowing ashtrays. So I talked to him about music, we were able to talk about music. What had been going on was a war between managers and lawyers. I had been coming out of music, and he had some favorite musicians that I could really talk about. One of his big influences was Gatemouth Brown, who he called "Gatormouth Brown." He loved Hank Williams; I could talk about any Hank Williams song. So we spent the evening talking about music. Now at that time, Roy had a band, which in my opinion was not a studio-quality band. He had one musician who was, named Dick Heintze, who played piano and organ, B3. And Roy was incredible, of course. The bass player, drummer, and stand-up singer I would not call studio-quality. You know, you record five studio musicians and it's easy to get a full, rich, bitchin' sound. You record two studio musicians and the rest bar band musicians, especially if two are bass and drums, and it's a different sound. I went back to NY and I told Jerry Schoenbaum and some other people dealing with the fiasco, "I think if you talk to him now and tell him I'll produce the record myself,

I'll take care of the music, he might agree to do it." So they talked to the manager and the manager talked to Roy, and they came back with one of the most bizarre counter-offers that I've ever heard (which we accepted). The counter-offer was that it has to be with his band and you only get three four-hour sessions.

So we said okay. That was the only way we were going to do this, so we arranged for his band to show up at The Record Plant, Studio B, which was not my favorite, I really loved Studio C, it was not available, it was all short notice — so we arranged for Roy to show up with his band. Let me tell you, Roy Buchanan, he spoke through his music. He didn't speak a lot himself. But in blues especially, I can hear the words that go with the notes. And there was this little "school" of Telecaster players in DC, [which included] Danny Gatton. So he shows up, and I worked with an engineer who could do this on the fly. Roy's show at that time, and his sets and his band, had an issue which I imagine you've seen with bands, where he was not central to his own performance. It was like a rock band — the singer would sing, he plays a killer solo, but it wasn't really so much about him. However, he also played a few guitar solos, instrumentals. In the next couple of nights, we recorded the first album, and he was powerful enough to make up for the fact that some of the musicians didn't have a lot of studio experience. And actually, people who were outside the studio who heard him were saying, "What the fuck is that?!" They did a number of their show tunes, things they'd do on the road, and I pushed them to do more blues songs where he plays his ass off, and at the end, I said, "You got any more things we could try out?" and one of them was this country one called "Sweet Dreams." And he played that, and it killed me. And I think that, in a way, the band really worked on that one, and it became a minor hit in England. But that "Sweet Dreams" track still floors me. And as I listen to that band the way they recorded on that first album, I can think of it, even though they weren't super powerful studio players like Roy or Heintze, you know the way you hear old 45s, different rockabilly bands, they were that! They were okay. Now that record came out and it sold a lot of records, successful enough — I don't know how many, hundreds of thousands, somewhere in the mid-charts of Billboard, maybe thirty-two, but it really did the job for Roy. I stayed in touch with Roy, and we talked about music a lot.

And so they wanted to do another record. Basically, I wanted it to be more about Roy. We had more time to plan this one. I wanted to make an instrumental record. There was this thing going on at Polydor, all record companies have this thing, "He's the next something-or-other," and Roy was going to be the next Jimi Hendrix. Now, Roy had nothing to do with Jimi Hendrix, at all. Roy was not a great singer; he could sing a song. What I wanted to do was have Roy playing the music he played, mostly blues, Chicago-style blues, and BB King–style blues, some country stuff. I'd arranged for him and Heintze to record at Record Plant Studio C and I got some actual musicians: bass player Don Payne, he was great, he sounded like a studio musician. Boom! I got a rhythm guitar player named Teddy Irwin — he could actually play rhythm guitar! I got a drummer who was not a studio musician but I heard at the Record Plant with some band he was in, a guy from Canada named Jerry Mercer, just a really great rock drummer. We got this group together in Studio C and encouraged them to play the blues. And he played some well-known blues numbers like "After Hours" and I also encouraged him to play in different styles of blues like, "Hey, you ever listen to Elmore James?" And he would say yeah, and we did this thing, "Tribute to Elmore James." We were trying to find things he could play in his native style. There's a great take where he broke a string in the middle and kept going and going: "Five-String Blues." To me, it wasn't a perfect album; we called it *Second Album* 'cause we'd been calling it that for so long, you know how that happens with a working title. That was the one that got a gold record. The sound was great, we worked on that with an engineer named Shelly Yakus, I sat next to Shelly Yakus for so many thousands of hours that we like, it was like ESP, he knew what I wanted, he knew how to get it, to do stuff that I didn't know how to get it.

E♯: Did you have a sound in mind when you were recording, or did that come after?

PS: My whole philosophy about mixing is that tracks are mixed the way they want to be mixed. You could have a preconceived idea of the sound, but it very rarely turns out that way. In this case, Roy was clearly the voice of the band, and he was out in a certain place. I think the sound was really good. He had a little old brown Fender, don't remember what model it was, and he used it! He had this sound that he really liked. He was not a screaming loud guitar player — one of the things you may have noticed, stuff that's played really loud is not always the best way to get it to sound loud. We got it to sound big. Years later, last time I actually saw Roy, he said, "How did you get that sound on 'After Hours'? That sounds good!"

All the records I made on Elektra, we had an old EMT Plate Reverb — it had a wheel on the top that you would adjust to change the reverb time, where the returns were inside — actually do it physically and go back and listen to it. We were definitely at the Record Plant, we might have used some Eventide things. I trusted Shelly Yakus to take care of that. Basically, the job was to record this band and make it sound powerful. We had a lot of conversations as we were doing it. There's a whole philosophy question as to, what is your relationship as a listener to the sound. But I just wanted it to sound strong and good. I don't want to say that I wasn't involved in the sound, because I was; we talked about it constantly. But I didn't get down to try these four different types of echo and see which we like best. And a lot of that stuff is done in mixing. Working with Shelly, he actually had his hands on his board, which was fine with me. Sometimes we had to get extra people in there to do the moves. Part of the problem, though, is when someone from the record company says, "Can you do the same thing with just a little more guitar?" We spent twelve hours sometimes getting a sound.

E♯: After Polydor?

PS: By the mid-1970s, there were all these little labels like Rounder around; I started making records for Rounder. I'm making an album now of Doc Watson and Gaither Carlton. I don't have permission to make this, the way I've made all of the other records like this: I put the record together to see if it's really there, and then work on getting permission — if it's that good, you'll probably get permission. Doc's daughter Nancy is still there. Gaither Carlton was Doc Watson's father-in-law, and he was a traditional fiddle and banjo player, Rosalie's father [Rosalie, Doc's wife]. He was so great, and the two of them together made this incredible true old-time music, fiddle and guitar, fiddle and banjo, fiddle and singing. I actually recorded a lot of it, never thought too much about it. Meanwhile, Doc becomes a big star. So I found these tapes of Doc and Gaither and they're so amazing that I'm working with them. It's really some of the best old-time music you'll ever want to hear.

First I'm trying to figure out what songs should be on the record, out of a couple of hours of material. My idea of how long a record should be is about forty-five minutes. Maybe I have a short attention span, but I grew up on LPs; after about forty-five minutes, I'm getting tired. So I'm shooting for about forty-five minutes out of two hours. I will make internal edits if it doesn't damage the spirit of the music. What I mean is, if everything is going great and a waitress drops a plate on the floor, I'm not above finding that passage from another verse in the song and sticking that in there. What I'm also saying is that I used to make a lot of money at this—you sell several hundred thousand records, you get good checks! You could actually make a living—this is not off the record, I don't care, I gotta do something I really love. It's such a monumental job producing an album and an artist; I don't want to do that and get $29. Look at that Clarence Ashley record, I spent a ridiculous amount of time making it sound good. I'm never going to make any money off that. I was always in a niche market anyway, but I don't want to know what I'll get. I have no idea what I'll get off of Spotify, it's not even worth talking about. In a way, I'm back to "If I'm not going to make any money, then I really have to be in love with this" . . . and I'm really in love with the Doc Watson and Gaither Carlton. I've produced a whole album of Doc in the past.

Doc Watson

PS: So Doc Watson had this concert at FOTM with the Watson family: Doc, his brother Arnold, and Gaither Carlton. A week later, Arnold had gone back to North Carolina, but Gaither was still around. So there was this club on Sullivan Street between Washington Square and 3rd Street called Blind Lemons that was open for like two weeks. It came and went very fast, about as big as this room. Ralph Rinzler was friends with whoever had it, and they set up for Doc and Gaither Carlton to play this gig for one night—that's the one I recorded. They were so wonderful, it still sounds great, I can't believe it!

E♯: Did Gaither sing too?

PS: No. Doc singing beautifully, a different Doc in those days. He hadn't really toured . . . especially with his father-in-law, he's doing music from down home. Anyway, the next thing that happened was Ralph got him a gig at Gerde's Folk City, which I eventually put out as an album as *Doc Watson at Gerde's Folk City*.

E♯: How old was Doc then?

PS: He was about forty. So I basically was given the job of helping Doc. He was staying at Ralph's apartment on Christopher Street, a sixth-floor walkup, and Doc was blind. So about a six-, seven-, eight-block walk from Christopher to Gerde's Folk City, which was at the corner of 4th and Mercer. Now I got the job of taking him over there—Ralph would also do it. Gerde's was like a two-week gig. They don't have those anymore. One dark night, then a hootenanny night, but the artist would perform five nights and two sets, then three sets on Friday and Saturday. Doc never had a dog, never had a cane. You just put your arm out and he'd hold on to it and walk . . . and we talked a lot. It was very cold at that time. So we'd talk a lot and on the nights that Richard would take him over, I'd bring my tape recorder and record this. I started sending Doc tapes and he'd say which ones he liked, and we eventually put that out on Sugar Hill, that was his first solo appearance anywhere. By this time, he's more into show-biz than when he was working with Gaither.

E♯: By showbiz, do you mean doing popular songs? Or growing into the entertainer role?

PS: Yeah. You have no idea how surprised Doc was that people went for this. Doc wasn't like Clarence Ashley; he'd never been a professional musician. He was very good at playing the guitar, and he played in a rockabilly band and dance bands.

E♯: Playing electric guitar?

PS: Yeah! He didn't have an acoustic guitar—he had to borrow an acoustic guitar. He had genuinely grown up in a musical family in rural western North Carolina where his family, his father—the guy's name was General Watson, that was his name—mother, they all sang, [his] mother sang "The House Carpenter," he learned all those songs, he could play them. Being blind, he went to North Carolina School for the Blind over in Raleigh, which he did not like very much at all. Being blind in those days, especially in rural North Carolina, there were not a lot of job opportunities and it was one of the reasons that people played music. So he got really good. He was doing a lot of what we now call busking, but also, when he got married and had to try and make a living, he worked in a rockabilly band for Jack Williams and they played dances, lots of terrible gigs. The way I understand it is they would sometimes do square dances and they didn't have a fiddle player and Doc was like, "I think I can play that stuff on guitar," which is how he developed his playing, I believe it was on a goldtop but not a Les Paul. [It was indeed a Gibson Les Paul goldtop—there are pictures!—E♯]

There's this whole story about how Ralph Rinzler came to record Clarence Ashley. He'd met Clarence at the Union Grove Fiddle Convention in 1960, and he realizes that this is THE Clarence Ashley who recorded these great sides on Columbia with the Carolina Tar Heels. He finds that Clarence Ashley can still sing, and he makes an arrangement to come back and make an album, to record him. So he comes back a few months later with recording equipment, and Clarence Ashley has this electric guitar player accompanying him who was Doc Watson. Now Ralph is like, "No, we want to get the real folk music, we don't want this electric music, this is on Folkways records," and he asks Doc Watson, "Could you maybe play that stuff on acoustic?" And Doc says, "Quite honestly, I haven't played an acoustic in so long that if I try to play this stuff on acoustic, it wouldn't be very good." And Ralph says, "We can't use that, we'll go look for someone else." So then, Ralph goes to visit some cousins of Clarence Ashley looking for guitar players, he comes back the next day, and he's surprised to see that Doc Watson is still there, still playing the damn electric guitar. So, somehow they're all going on some journey to find some banjo player, I think Willard Watson, I don't know who was driving, maybe Clint Howard—they had this band, they're driving in a pickup truck and Ralph is in the back, open-air part of the truck, playing a banjo. And they stop at a light and Doc jumps out and jumps in the back of the truck and says, "Let me see that, son," and he starts playing on the banjo and blows Ralph's mind. That's when he realized what was going on here. So by the time I meet Doc, he has become acquainted with the idea that people would like to hear his traditional music, which he would never get paid for in North Carolina—like, he couldn't get people to sit still for it. And when he played at Gerde's, he said he couldn't believe that people would sit quietly and listen to these old ballads. So it really blew his mind.

E♯: Was there ever a discussion that "folk music" was played on *these* instruments and never on electric guitar?

PS: Ralph had a lot to do with guiding Doc Watson's musical career. And part of Ralph's plan, his big life mission, was to get folk music to be recognized as part of our national heritage, which he really did! It made sense to him that it would be acoustic. So I'm sure that Ralph had lots of conversations with Doc about what he should and shouldn't play.

E♯: How about when Dylan went electric at Newport, was there a lot of discussion at FOTM?

PS: There was a lot of controversy. No, nobody ever really showed up with an electric guitar, except for Jesse Fuller who was a one-man band; he had a Dearmond pickup on his twelve-string. Nobody cared.

Anyway, I always stayed in touch with Doc and I always loved his music, and he's much featured on that FOTM compilation. He was a special, special musician.

E♯: Did he ever express an interest in picking up an electric guitar again?

PS: He made one rockabilly record on which he plays some electric guitar. He made so many albums, and they were always looking for something new. That one was for Sugar Hill, started by Barry Poss in North Carolina who basically retired. One of these things that happens, it happened with Elektra in a way, the guy who founded it retires, sells it, and the company loses a lot of its identity. And Sugar Hill had a real identity, but they sold it to Welk Group, which owns Vanguard, and it stopped being Sugar Hill. He had recorded for them for many years and made many great records. Now, with artists who become big artists, you don't have any consciousness of them being on a particular label. You used to know, "he's on Atlantic!" Labels like Elektra, for better or worse, had a sound—Atlantic had a sound, Stax had a sound. First of all, there aren't a lot of labels now, not in the older sense, three maybe. You don't have that kind of identity, it's too bad. Now Gaither's record is going to be on Jalopy Records, and it's one that will sell 500 to 1,000 records. So far, Jalopy is not doing downloads. I actually didn't give them that because they didn't want the CD—LP only.

E♯: Do you have a feeling about whether or not the things you produce should be on Spotify or whatever streaming services?

PS: What I do think, I'm sorry that it's harder to make albums that really bring forth the essence of a musician today. You look at old Blue Note records, they have liner notes by someone who actually knew about the music, they had great photography.

E♯: For me, with the great musicians you hear one note and you know who it is, Sonny Rollins, Roy Buchanan . . .

PS: There's a few guitarists, Josh White, you hear one note and you know it's Josh White. Part of the thing is that a lot of those musicians came of age at an earlier time before there was such a mass homogenization of music . . . I never recorded Josh White, but I loved listening to him. He was one of those artists that my parents had 78s of. That guy plays one note, you know who it is. Lightnin' Hopkins plays one note and you know who it is. Just amazing, electric or acoustic. There used to be a time—that's one of the reasons I love the record I'm working on, if it is indeed a record, Doc and Gaither—before radio, before records were a big thing, there could be a style of fiddle playing and you go over to the next valley and it's completely different, and talk about richness! It's very hard today, everybody gets to hear everything, so in a way you lose something. Miles Davis recorded with Charlie Parker . . . if you think of Charlie Parker, it gives you a different time frame. Musicians used to make records after they'd become established, a record contract after touring for years; it made a difference. There's this other thing, which for better or worse is true in producing records, which is that record companies in effect were a kind of gatekeeper, because they had the technology to put out a record. You need a record company to put out a record, you needed the infrastructure. You don't need that anymore, and in a way, producing records would be harder today. When I was doing it with artists, the record company would say, "Artist: here's your producer; Peter's going to produce your album." Now what would happen would be . . . it gave you a lot of decision-making authority, like if you really hated that song, you just wouldn't do that song. Today it's not quite clear who producers work for.

E♯: Did you have an identity as a producer across the various records, or would you keep your own personality out of it?

PS: It depends on what kind of record you're talking about. I kept my personality out of the Nonesuch recordings, but if you listen to some of the rock records I made: Roy, Elliott Murphy, Paul Siebel, Ellen McIlwaine (I made her first two albums), Earth Opera, Mark Spoelstra, David Peel . . . his first album, I got it right! *Have a Marijuana!* Danny Fields at Elektra saw him and had this concept of the album. And I recorded it as a "field recording." I recorded it in Washington Square with remote equipment, which was the only way I could see doing it, like "indigenous music of the Lower East Side." It was never incredible music, but it was what it was.

E♯: Did you have anything to do with punk bands in those years?

PS: I knew Seymour Stein. He used to work for Sid Nathan at King. He was a promotion man, some kind of record man.

E♯: Neil Young! Did you mix it?

PS: I recorded it! Paul Rothchild made a deal—he was independent at the time—he made a deal to make a live record of Neil Young with Crazy Horse for Warner Bros or Reprise and then he couldn't make it, so he called me and asked me to do the gig, so I went over there and recorded it. It came out really good. I was the engineer. I did some on-the-fly mixes the next day, and they came out really good. Paul never did anything further and by the time that record came out, he was no longer with us. What that record is is a combination of stuff that I engineered and mixed with other stuff that I engineered that someone else mixed. But that was a really good-sounding gig. I got really excited. That was one of the reasons I quit my job at Elektra, if I could do things like this. That was a very simple setup, I hung two mics over the drum set and one on the kick and mics on everything else. They were good. They had Jack Nitzsche. It came out a few years ago, some of Neil Young's people found some of the tapes and they got in touch with me; I had the rest of the tapes, we worked it out. They mixed stuff out there, except there were some that they couldn't find the 8-tracks of, so I gave them my mixes, which were pretty good. I mixed them at a studio called Century Sound, which was owned by Brooks Arthur. They were almost . . . they *were* rough mixes. Something about rough mixes can be really good . . . you haven't had time to fuck them up.

E♯: The union songs?

PS: I didn't know how bad things were going to get in this country! I got the idea to do that right after Scott Walker in Wisconsin was trying to shut down the unions. And I thought it would be good to, one thing that was missing, there was a lot of national conversation about unions—were they good? Bad? But the reasons those unions were formed was not part of that conversation. But I knew all those songs. Eli and I had made a double banjo record; we made it for ourselves for Jalopy, came out good. So I call everyone and say, for our next record, how about we do these union songs? And it turns out he comes from this family of radical lawyers, and he was into it. His father was Michael Steven Smith, who had a show on WBAI called "Law and Disorder," a radical law program. So we made that record, here in this apartment; there's only a couple of songs made in a studio in Brooklyn because we got Andy Statman to play mandolin, an old friend, a friend forever—he was apparently very allergic to dogs, and there's never been a time in this apartment when there wasn't a dog in it. You couldn't just board the dog for the night, so the stuff with Andy we did at Wombat, I don't know . . . so we did that record. And one thing about the way I produced that record, there's a kind of lost genre of folk music records, which is a thematic genre: *Songs of the Gold Rush*, *Songs of the Sea*. So I wanted to make union songs . . . We did a song by Joe Hill called "There's Power in a Union," but Billy Bragg did a different song called "There's Power in a Union," which was great.

One of things that I always felt as a record producer that my job was, was to figure out what the essence of this artist is, and how to get it on a record. And it's not as easy as you think . . . But I like old craggy musicians, old banjo players, old fiddle players, that stuff speaks to me.

E#: Frank Wakefield!

PS: You know who Red Allen was? I recorded those two together on Folkways, and David Grisman and I had a little record company when we were kids called Silver Bell Records, named after a banjo. We recorded a session in New York of Red Allen and Frank Wakefield. We put out only one 45. This was in the '60s before I went to work at Elektra. We considered ourselves a record company—we had no office or anything, just two kids. But we went to a real studio and recorded it, and we put together a session with great musicians. We got Chubby Wise, great fiddler who played with Bill Monroe, to come up; he was my favorite fiddle player. We got a guy named Winnie Winston on banjo. We made some great records. Frank was like, there was a handful of great mandolin players around and he was definitely one of them. He was crazy . . . We arranged for him to come up and join the Greenbriar Boys after Ralph left, except that night he was in a car accident, a question of whether he was going to live or die, and a few months later he recovered and came up and played with the Greenbriar Boys.

Chess Records, amazing. Howlin' Wolf, Muddy Waters, Chuck Berry, hello! . . . They didn't make that many records, but so classic. I mean Chuck Berry invented a whole new kind of music. You could say Muddy Waters invented a whole new kind of music. This thing of homogenization we were talking about—one of the most disappointing aspects of blues today is these blues bands all sound the same. One of the things about the old music is that if you listen to the Stanley Brothers, if you listen to the old bluegrass musicians, Bill Monroe, that was music. There was a time when farm boys from Kentucky or Tennessee had to leave their homes and go to Ohio or Chicago and Detroit to make a living. And bluegrass at its inception was music that [brought] them back to their old roots. The Osborne Brothers or Red Allen would go and play in Akron where there'd be knife fights and whatever. They were all playing for people who had been technologically displaced. The Stanley Brothers, Bill Monroe wrote songs like "I'm on my way to the old home, there's no light in the window . . . " The Stanley Brothers: "I long to see the old folks back home." That's what that music was. Like what Chicago blues did . . . someone working in a steel mill in Chicago: "This is your music."

E#: Do you think there's any young people writing songs like these?

PS: Jerron Paxton! One of the reasons that bluegrass music as well as blues appealed so much to people of my generation is that we were technologically displaced! We were like, what the fuck is this? Vietnam . . . A lot of people grew up saying they couldn't relate to what they see right in front of them. But for me, I heard bluegrass and old-time music, and I said, "This is my stuff!" Mississippi John Hurt, where was this all my life? A lot of music originally functioned as a way to connect people to the earth, and they still work that way. If you listen, my personal favorite bluegrass band is the Stanley Brothers. If you listen to them, it has all the right instruments playing all the parts same as you can find today, but the message of that music is something completely different. Here's the problem, you can't find a singer who's the product of whatever Mississippi John Hurt was the product of. They know too much now. They're coming from a different place. When I think of someone singing the blues today, you can't get that back, that comes from a certain time. You know, if you listen to old blues recordings, old piano recordings, like Bessie Smith, it floats in a way that newer things don't float. It floats in the sense of being looser, sometimes behind or ahead of the beat, and also it's a twelve-bar but maybe there's a couple of extra bars in there . . . I do not follow all these new musicians, I can't even keep up on the stuff I love. But I am not going to say they don't speak for anybody, but I am going to say if I hear you play the blues and you don't know what you're doing, then you don't have the blues! I mean someone like Leadbelly that came from a place and a time, and even if you could sound like Leadbelly, you wouldn't be sounding like Leadbelly!

20

John Fahey on the Decline of the Western World

Many of our weekend suburban high-school soirees during the late 1960s would be winding down just as the sun was winding up. Ears and synapses blistered by a mix of Hendrix, the Dead, Charles Lloyd, Velvet Underground, John Coltrane, Big Brother and the Holding Company, Morton Subotnick, Paul Butterfield, and Quicksilver, we often sought sonic balm in the form of the acoustic guitar solos of John Fahey. Born in 1939, Fahey called his music "American Primitive," a name which belies the thought, erudition, guitar skills, sophisticated compositional strategies, humor, and passion that Fahey channeled. A deep-rooted scholar of the blues, Fahey's voracious listening encompassed (but was not limited to) gamelan, Béla Bartók, and Gregorian chants, as well as Brazilian and Indian music. These sounds might turn up in his compositions for guitar, in his sound collages, even in his paintings. He was also principally responsible for the rediscovery and revitalization of Delta blues genius Skip James. On June 3, 2000, I had the pleasure of interviewing John Fahey via phone for *Knotes*, a publication from NYC's Knitting Factory, in advance of his concert there in July 2000. This is the complete unedited text—a greatly edited version was published by the Knitting Factory. John's voice was weak, but his wit was honed and powerful. It was a deep shock to learn of his death on February 22, 2001, after undergoing sextuple coronary bypass surgery.

E♯: I'm sure you get a lot of redundancy when you do interviews, so I'm going to hopefully avoid that. First, what are you working on now, and what will you be bringing to the Knitting Factory in July—what kind of setup will you have?

JF: Oh, I'm bringing an electric guitar and a couple of pre-amps.

E♯: Do you continue to perform on acoustic guitar, or are you solely electric now?

JF: I'm just doing solo electric. One gets old and then the fingers hurt . . .

E♯: Oh yeah, that's true.

JF: Oh, God—I mean I've got an acoustic guitar, but Jesus, it kills me. The left hand—and then I can't practice very much. Like razor blades cutting into my left fingers. Then I can't practice the next day. I tend to do very long practicing, like for hours, and I just can't do it . . . electric guitar. Life is so tough.

E♯: Do you ever do your sound collage work live in some form now, or is it pretty much solo guitar?

JF: Well, I did a collage at the beginning and the end of my newest record, *Hitomi*. But I used an echo pedal, and I recorded it; first I recorded the "riiiing riiiing riiiing riiiiing," then I recorded over it, so I did it all by myself. I did most of this by myself. With maybe one helper.

E♯: Do you have your own personal studio setup at home of some sort, or do you go in to a studio to do it?

JF: I've been recording mostly in the motel I was living in, or right here in the house. Yeah, I don't have a big studio; I have very little equipment.

E♯: Do you like spending time with it, getting into the technical aspects of the recording, or do you use it just as a way to document what you're hearing?

JF: No, I enjoy innovations. It's boring playing the same old stuff. I keep reaching out for new sounds and new harmonies and new electronic devices. I don't think a big studio would . . . [laughs].

E♯: That stuff sometimes gets in the way more than anything else.

JF: Yeah, it takes longer and longer and longer, and the more people you work with, the longer it takes, you know. So I tend to be a rugged individualist.

E♯: That's true, that's why we listen to you! When you did the project with Cul de Sac, did you spend a lot of time rehearsing with them, or did you just go into the studio and lay that down?

JF: Well, we didn't get along too well. [laughs] They kept trying to play jungle music.

E♯: Jungle music meaning . . .

JF: Oh, you know, like neo–Les Baxter . . .

E♯: Oh, okay, got it, neo-exotica, that's their thing . . .

JF: I didn't like it, and I didn't want my name associated with it. So I called up the money man and said that I thought: this record is going to be a disaster. I don't want my name on it. And we had several days left and I said, if you put me in charge of this, we'll come out with a good record. And I said as it is now, it's going to be awful.

E♯: This is a new one with them?

JF: No.

E♯: Oh, *The Epiphany of Glenn Jones.*

JF: Yeah.

E♯: And they finally let you control it . . .

JF: Oh yeah, right away. We did what came out in three, four days. But we spent many, many days trying to get along with each other musically. And so most of that is really a John Fahey, or John Fahey–produced.

E♯: As it should be . . . Collaborations are sometimes funny.

JF: I never thought I could get along with them too well musically. But they did, and their record company did. So without very intelligent planning, they put us together to make a record. So, it turned out pretty good, but most of it's me.

E♯: What do you feel was the easiest collaboration project for you? Or do you really prefer to work on your own?

JF: The easiest one?

E♯: In terms of personalities and music. You know how sometimes you get into the studio with somebody, and you don't even have to say a word.

JF: Yeah, right, right. Well, I have to say some words. I have to give an indication of what we're going to play and give them chord charts. One of the easiest ones were those two Warner Bros. records, *After the Ball* and the other one, *Of Rivers and Religion*, where I had a much more sophisticated and knowledgeable music producer, Denny Bruce, and he wrote out all the parts. I sang him or played him the parts I wanted, and he faithfully got them down. That was the easiest one. Although it was the most frightening one, because we had all these great, sophisticated New Orleans musicians and Hollywood musicians.

E♯: I remember that was quite orchestrated. In a beautiful way. So he had done all the charting himself?

JF: He's really good. We always cooperated with each other every way. Of course, that was twelve million years ago.

E♯: Do you think things have changed radically in the way records are made? Do you think you could make a record in that way these days?

JF: Sure I could, if I could find the right musicians and a good musical director.

E♯: And the time, of course, and the studio, that's often a problem, I find.

JF: We cut those records really fast. Everybody really knew what they were doing except me. We brought those in under budget.

E♯: What kind of stuff are you listening to these days for your own enjoyment?

JF: Mostly to my own records.

E♯: Can you enjoy them, or do you listen very critically?

JF: Well, the ones I don't hear critically I enjoy a lot. I'm listening to *Hitomi* a lot lately, to try to figure out what the hell I did.

E♯: Often I'll not listen to a record once it comes out, for a long time, even though I'm listening to it over and over and over again while I'm mixing. And sometimes I just can't listen, because I just hear every warped . . . or they become magnified and then with some distance I can go back and say, "That's why that happened."

JF: That happens.

E♯: Are you coming out to the Knitting Factory as a part of a tour, or just flying out for the one thing?

JF: There's one in North Carolina, one in New York, and one in Chicago.

E♯: Do you like touring still?

JF: Love it. Especially going overseas.

E♯: Are you going to be coming to Europe or Japan any time soon?

JF: I don't have the dates.

E♯: Do you think audiences are different overseas?

JF: Yeah, I think they're much more appreciative, especially in Japan.

E♯: Oh yeah, they go crazy there. Do you feel like they listen in a different way?

JF: No, I think they hear the same stuff, they're just polite when they applaud, they don't yell and scream. I'm used to yelling and screaming. That's just my impression. I mean, you play a great song and you play it well and they go clapclapclap. They consider it rude to go hooray, scream, yell! You kind of have to adapt to Japanese audiences. They really like it, but they don't want to be rude.

E♯: They're very careful about that. One thing I felt about Japanese and German and Austrian audiences, I feel like they know history much better than American audiences.

JF: Oh, they do, they do. Holland, too.

E♯: Do you think that affects how they perceive you as an artist?

JF: Well, the American perception of the artist is, "You are going to please me right away in the first few minutes, or we're going to be rude to you." And over there, they listen better. They concentrate better because you might have something to say. Or they figure well, this introductory section is going to turn into something more exciting, and you're playing dialectically, kind of quiet and slightly boring on purpose so you can contrast—the exciting parts sound even more exciting. Over here, they want to hear an exciting part right away.

E♯: Do you think it's gotten worse, or has it always been that way?

JF: I think it's gotten worse and is getting worse. People are getting dumber and dumber here.

E♯: Can we point to a prime cause of that?

JF: I'm trying to figure it out. It's not just in music. People can't speak anymore, the English language. Like in Oregon, they can't pronounce *etcetera*, they call it *ekcetera*, with a k. I'm afraid to go out of the house because people can't speak English. Where are you, New York?

E♯: In New York. Here it's a real polyglot.

JF: I just can't imagine being in New York and hearing somebody say, "blah blah ekcetera."

E♯: We have our own New York-isms, such as "Howaya?!" I wonder, I find myself trying to decide if it's good that the language is changing to reflect different populations and different priorities, or if it's bad and we're losing things that are really valuable.

JF: I don't know if people are getting dumb in New York and on the East Coast, but they sure as hell are in the Midwest and out here. In California, it's due to the school system. I never have liked teachers, and I never liked school. But where I grew up in Maryland and DC, I didn't like them, but still I learned something. I learned how to pronounce *etcetera*.

E♯: I don't think people read anymore either.

JF: They don't. Bookstores are closing all over the place.

E♯: It's a new kind of literacy. The Web seems to have created a different kind of intelligence, and sometimes I'm very optimistic about that.

JF: Yeah, I am too. I think in order to use the Web you must be able to speak correctly and think correctly. I think when people don't speak correctly, it indicates that they can't think correctly; that's why I say people are getting dumber and dumber. Yesterday I ran into a really funny example. It had a colon after the word *your*. I mean you just don't do that.

E♯: Do you run across any things that make you optimistic or excited—music, or cultural events?

JF: Not recently. Music is getting dumber and dumber.

E♯: We have the accountants and lawyers to thank for that.

JF: How's that?

E♯: Well, they run the record companies, it seems. I find people have their listening context shaped by very genrefied programming and very genrefied marketing. It comes down to the lowest common denominator factor. Do you know Douglas Hofstadter's concept of the meme, the idea that sometimes all we can do is put a meme back into the system, like a little virus? [In this part of the twenty-first century, the original meme has been transmuted into a single image transmitted over social media.] Pop culture is a really fast-acting meme. But some of the other things that we'll create are much more slow. Maybe we dump this back into the system and, like any organism, sometimes it reproduces and is able to grow as an idea that gets people excited, and it begins reproducing itself as an idea. For those of us who make music, that's somewhere on the fringe; I feel like sometimes all we can do is keep pumping these memes into the system and hope they take root.

JF: That's a good idea, but it seems to be working less. I think culture's gone downhill; it has been for a long time. You can use the name of that book by Spengler, *The Decline of the Western World*.

E♯: Indeed. But don't you think your audiences are getting bigger? Wouldn't that be some sort of enhancement of Western culture?

JF: Oh yeah. I consider myself apart from it. I can't take the decline. It's very disturbing, I mean frightening. What's it going to be like in forty-five years? A nation of cretins.

E♯: Do you find you are reacting to this trend in the music you're making?

JF: Yeah, it's getting more and more "alternative," is what they call it. Actually, I consider it more and more advanced.

E♯: I think *alternative* was always a bad term.

JF: People like Thurston Moore and so forth, his coterie . . . I mean you can't even say a word like *coterie* anymore. Nobody knows what it means. People can't read anymore. There are some people who are trying to inject intelligent ideas into music. And Sonic Youth seems to have done a lot of good and succeeded. But of course now they're Sonic Middle Age. They're still doing neat stuff. But I don't know to what extent it's penetrating.

E♯: I think they will always have a core audience, and it also grows sideways. Listening to you throughout my tortured youth, I also enjoyed the music of Robbie Basho. And I always wondered what happened to him.

JF: I knew him pretty well. He died, maybe twenty years ago.

E♯: I had no idea—from my perception, he disappeared.

JF: He didn't disappear at all. He was a chiropractor. Chiropracty is an indication of the spread of stupidity. I mean, I've been to chiropractors when I have a backache, and I . . . Anyway, he was a chiropractor, and he had a stroke and a heart attack. He was dead immediately. I don't blame it on the chiropracty. He was affiliated with the New Age a lot.

E♯: There was a spiritual bent to his music, but the music itself was great.

JF: Some of the music was really good.

E♯: I didn't associate it with the New Age music, because a lot of musics in the early '60s, even stuff in the hippie vein, were kind of outside. They seemed to touch on more timeless things than just whatever the trendoids at the moment were going for.

JF: I never got into New Age music myself.

E♯: Oh no, there's nothing to get into.

JF: [laughs] Basho was a little previous to that, and he was coming up with some neat stuff now and then. And he was also coming up with a lot of schmaltz, and he couldn't tell the difference. I'd talk to him about it a lot, and he just couldn't get it. And then these people like Will Ackerman and so forth would name him as a predecessor to what they were doing, and they never sounded like him, and they didn't understand what he was doing.

E♯: They reduced it to the lowest common denominator and walked away with the cash.

JF: Because the music was so innocuous. Basho had some intellectual stuff.

E♯: It had bite.

JF: And it worked. I don't know what to tell you about what's happening. The music's getting worse and worse, and the literature's getting worse and worse. I'm really worried about the progress of this country.

E♯: Is there anything you've read recently that's excited you?

JF: Excited me. About what?

E♯: Do you know Jack Womack's writing? He's a fiction writer. His books are very sardonic views of American culture. Loosely science fiction. You can't just easily say it's sci-fi. They take place in the very near future in New York City and America, Elvis cults, minor apocalypses. Very funny, very dark.

JF: I think we're in an apocalypse and it's pretty bad and getting worse. However, my views might be extreme. I've been alive a long time and I don't know, when I was a kid we had responsibilities and we would enjoy doing them, and there was also a decline happening after the war and the government got more involved in what we were doing and passing laws and teachers weren't allowed to teach anything too difficult. Take the California school system, they don't teach anybody anything. They have kids down there who can barely talk when they're twenty-six.

E♯: There's a lot of parallels to the post-WWII era, this kind of mindless prosperity.

JF: Yeah, and it's getting worse. I'm amazed it's working as well as it does.

E♯: House of cards. The internet economy, the emptiness, the huge investment structures may just collapse. Do you think that's gonna be good for music?

JF: I don't know what's gonna be good for music. I know one thing that would be good for music would be an across-the-board elimination of all these communication devices and fast transportation. People would be forced to sit at home and try to come up with something different on their own. One of the things people do today is, they want to get into music and so the first thing they do is listen to what other people are doing, and they all play the same damn thing. Now, if you have an isolated guy out in the country [laughs] who didn't know anybody who plays the guitar, he would probably come up with something different. What happened is, as soon as they invented phonograph records and everybody could buy them all over the country, everybody started to sound like Blind Lemon Jefferson. And record companies looked for other people who sounded like Blind Lemon Jefferson and Charley Patton or whoever, and the weirdos, the innovators, nobody heard them.

E♯: I feel like people are rediscovering the wheel continuously because of the conservatism of the times.

JF: Now, they can't even discover it.

E♯: They can buy it, though.

JF: You can buy it at all kinds of places. But have somebody try to build a wheel from scratch who doesn't know anything about mechanics, and I don't think you get much of a wheel. We've been talking about all kinds of things, and I think the decline of music is just a symptom, which is part of the decline of the West, and that's a great title, *Decline of the West*. I tried to read Spengler . . . and I'm not intelligent enough to read Spengler! I mean, I'm part of the process too, going down. But I'm old enough, and I got educated better than anybody is now, grade school, junior high school, where innovation was not encouraged—in fact, it was punished. The only really good teacher I had was in seventh and eighth grade, an art teacher. And I said I didn't want to draw things that looked like what they looked like. I wanted to do abstracts and so I did, and I was really good at it. I'm still good. I didn't do any for a long time, but now I've been doing abstracts and some of them are beautiful.

E♯: Are they displayed anywhere?

JF: In Japan. And I sold some in London. I sent them to a girl in New York who runs an art gallery, I don't know if she displayed them or not. Her name is Maryanne Fahey and she works in a gallery, I can't remember the name. One of my most exciting, rewarding experiences was when I went to Dublin and played. I'd never been to Dublin before and unlike anywhere else I ever was, I had an emotional response from the audience—they were crying. Really. And I haven't quite figured why that's true. I think that maybe they haven't heard so much of the mediocre middlebrow music.

E♯: My girlfriend who is half-Irish has a little sticker on our refrigerator that says, "Being Irish means knowing that the world is going to break your heart."

JF: Being Irish is very sad, and to counteract the sadness, they play this stupid (ba da da da) commercial Irish music, which is real fast, up-tempo, and it's a tourist thing and they export it, but it's really sort of silly music. And you go over there and play some sad music like I always play, because everything is always sad. And man, they knew what I was talking about. And they wouldn't let me go. So I hope to go back there sometime because they seem to understand.

E♯: Is your family Irish?

JF: My father was. And my mother was Jewish-English. I'm not really sure about that. I was playing a lot of really depressing blues, which is Negro of course.

E#: A friend of mine, Charles Keil, has traced the typical blues progression to Elizabethan sixteenth- and seventeenth-century forms, this twelve-bar structure with the I and IV and V chord movement and many of the lyrical elements of the blues. And it's funny how it got re-synthesized in the US by the slaves into something else.

JF: Well, they had the tripartite form too, but they didn't have any guitars in Africa, they had banjos. There's something mysterious about where that form of music comes from. I haven't studied that much. But I wouldn't be surprised if there was what they call a "polygenesis" that started in different places and different times with the same structure.

E#: I've always wondered about regionalism. Because now we're seeing regionalism disappear, and my favorite musics were always those that could be tied to a small population with a very specific form of expression. And maybe there is some other kind of regionalism. I fight against this growing depression about the world just becoming one giant McDonalds, and sometimes I think as the possibility opens up for some sort of interplanetary meeting or communication that this world becomes integrated into one thing that is just a region called "Earth," as opposed to a region called "the Mississippi Delta" or "New Jersey" or whatever.

JF: I believe I think I understand what you're saying. There are fewer and fewer regionalisms every year. And the world is turning into a homogeneous place. And the only place we're going to get an infusion of newness is from another planet. And that may be what all these UFOs are about. They're trying to teach.

E#: People are lazy, they have to try to find the creativity within, they feel like they're at a wall. So they're looking for salvation from the UFOs—it takes someone else to give us a monolith to touch, like in the film *2001: A Space Odyssey*.

JF: Oh, I study UFOs a lot. I've seen a couple. Two, three, possibly four, but they weren't real big ones. They were little light balls in my backyard.

E#: How long ago was that?

JF: I had two sightings in 1948, '49, maybe it was '47, and I had another one in '61 or '62. The first ones were quite parallel. Across my backyard, as if they had been projectiles or something that were crashed into the ground. About six feet high. They were real small.

E#: Do you know about plasma? I've heard some theories that say you could have literally a small ball of super-heated plasma floating in the sky. Like a micro-environment of super-heated gas that could just arise from various atmospheric and electrical conditions in the atmosphere.

JF: Oh yeah, they call it swamp gas where I live. But swamp gas can't float about ten miles, parallel to the ground. I mean, it was not a natural phenomenon. And I saw it in my backyard and there was a fence in back of them. So they weren't on the other side of the fence and I couldn't see where they came from, and then they disappeared half to my left. No, they weren't a natural phenomenon. I don't think any natural phenomenon can be that slow without falling into the ground, unless it had reverse magnetism holding it up. And then later, in '62, I saw some. And a friend was with me, and he saw them. Way up in the sky shooting across. Same size, same color. They were really quite fast, but they were parallel—they weren't declining, and they were flying in formation. That's all the UFOs I've ever seen. So I've been reading a lot lately and listening to radio programs at night on unexplained appearances. It goes from crop circles to alien abductions and chem trails, that stuff.

E♯: Are you skeptical of these things, or a believer?

JF: I'm an empiricist. And we have no way of examining them by scientific method. The truth is, nobody knows what the hell they are, so it's all speculation. But within the speculatory range, there are people who say I'm cuckoo and scientists who don't say I'm cuckoo. I'm not interested in ghosts or psychic healing and that crap. That never gets on the radio anyway. So I'm very skeptical. But I've seen minor examples of this, and I hear people like Richard Hoagland, and these guys just don't sound like nuts.

E♯: If you listen to a quantum physicist talk, a lot of it sounds like gibberish unless you have the background to map concepts and terms to things explainable in everyday language. I just feel like we know so little. We're always being told that everything has been discovered, and yet there are continually new ways of defining things that change our perception, that allow us to do things in a way that has never been done before. Technology does continue to evolve.

JF: Have you seen the face on Mars, the photographs NASA took? This is clearly a face, a human face, and it looks kind of like, Egyptian, because it has ear muffs on it, and they've examined it geometrically and it's real big and exactly the proportions. For example, the distance from the tip of the nose to, say, the left to right eyes, are exactly the proportions and angles of the human face.

E♯: This is something seen in the actual landscape?

JF: And it must have been built to communicate something with us or with other planets. There are photographs in a book called *Alien Architecture* with NASA photographs, and the first time I looked at it, I thought that couldn't possibly be the case. But then I measured the distances and it's definitely bilaterally symmetrical. You just wouldn't get that. Get *Alien Architecture* and you'll have your mind blown—there's pyramids there, all kinds of stuff up there. I think it's by Richard Hoagland. NASA is holding up photographs. When space exploration started and the Brookings Institute said we're not ready for this information and we would all go crazy . . . I don't think that was true at the time, and it's certainly not true now. But that's what's running the policy at NASA, and the government has thousands of files and they're classified because of this damn Brookings Institute report, and there are various lobbies and lawsuits against the government to release this stuff, because hell, we're paying for it. Then they have these secret things we're paying for, and we don't even know what they are. It's in the Constitution and we're supposed to know what the hell our tax money goes for and we don't. That's not a joke, I'm really pissed off about it. There are activist groups now suing the government and it's got to come out sooner or later. And who knows, these aliens or whatever you call it might have interesting forms of music.

E♯: I would hope so.

JF: I would love to hear it.

E♯: Unless they've been listening to our broadcasts for the last ten years and are really into alternative rock. Or maybe the McDonaldization of the Earth is just a giant plot to make the aliens feel welcome when they come.

JF: Next they're going to try to McDonaldize the Universe.

E♯: Unless the McDonalds itself is an alien exploratory.

JF: You can't tell.

21

Hubert Sumlin Speaks

In *IrRational Music*, I wrote extensively about time spent working and touring with Hubert Sumlin, one of the most original and influential electric blues guitarists. His uniquely angular and vocal-sounding guitar licks with Howlin' Wolf inspired many, and one can hear his sonic DNA in the playing of Jimi Hendrix, Jeff Beck, Eric Clapton, Robbie Robertson, and Jimmy Page. This interview was recorded in 1993 at a tiny pizzeria on 8th Street in the West Village, just before Hubert's solo show at Terra Blues.

E♯: You've put out a number of records in recent years—what's your favorite? Your favorite playing?

HS: I tell you what, it seems to me that *Heart & Soul* with Little Mike on Blind Pig, it ain't stopped yet, I still get a little money. The last one was *Healing Feeling*. About the playing, I don't know, I don't know, what it is about the engineer's got to do with the sound, but, I believe it's something about me that they end up pushin', got to just comes out, act like they knowing me for years, all my life.

E♯: Do you like recording in general?

HS: I do, I really do now. I start to play, hey, I found me a style. By listening and looking I said hey, so, "This is me." You know 'cause I'm so used to, a man been called so many things by Leonard Chess, Phil Chess, it got old, he stopped it. From then on, I did what I want to do with the music. By my own sound, I came by all of it after all this happened, after this incident with the Chess brothers. [Hubert declined to explain the incident.]

E♯: Did your style start to develop when you worked with Wolf in 1953?

HS: I think that's what happened, with him and Muddy. When I first started he didn't like what I was doing. I knew it wasn't right 'cause it didn't sound like I was playing with him. So he fired me, kept on firing me . . . and hiring me. He called me on a date, a date of need, he called me, said, "Let's try it tonight."

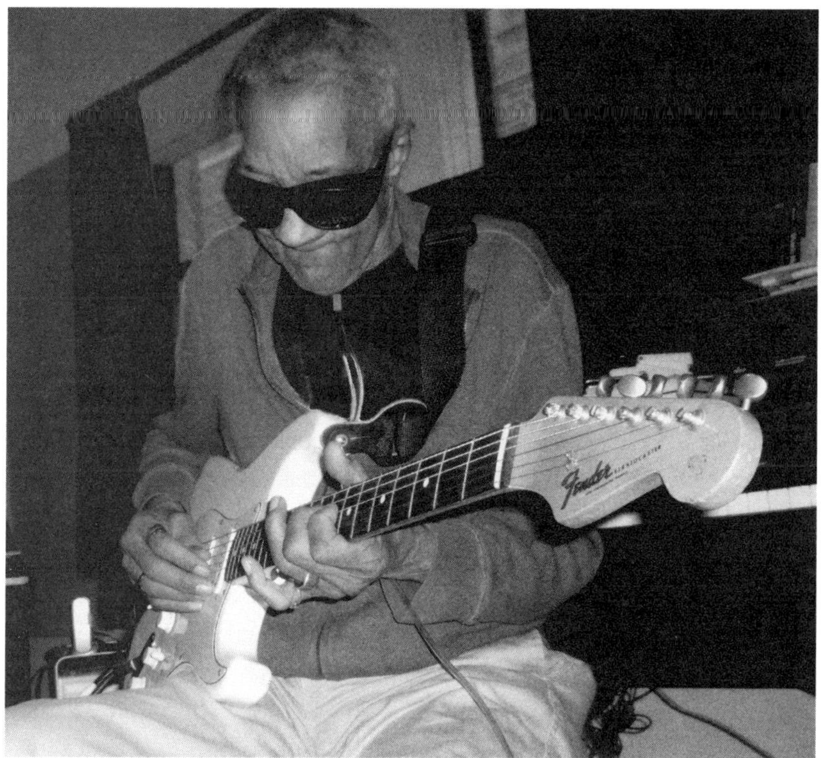

Figure 12 Hubert Sumlin recording for *Sky Road Songs* at NuNoise Studio, NYC

E♯: What kind of guitars were you playing?

HS: We had Kays, we had Silvertones, me and Jody Williams. I don't know how many guitars Wolf had. They were Wolf's guitars.

E♯: When you came back to the band, did your style change the way the band sounded? Would you come up with parts, shape the songs? Your guitar parts define the songs in so many ways.

HS: I came up with the parts, the songs. I got together with the horn blowers, baritone and tenor, and we made "300 Pounds." When those horns came in, it was the greatest feeling. It's finally happening, he's doing his *own* thing. So I put the music to this thing—arrangements in the studio right there before—there was no time—we had a few rehearsals, but the horns were always "no show." So it was no problem in the studio, I just told them what parts have to be played: bup bup bup . . . heh heh. I didn't get credit for it. At least seeing my name somewhere, that makes me feel good.

E♯: It seems like your playing has really influenced all the great players in the world, a fount of inspiration. How does that feel to you, do you reflect on that?

HS: You know, I'm glad to hear that, I'm glad to know that if I touch anybody, even touched one, you get feelings of a million, you'd be surprised how they come. If you ever heard of hypnotizing, I know you have, this music, sometimes puts you in a state of hypnosis. Well, this is what it will do you. Sometime, you hear things, hear things coming through and you know it seems that everybody's hearing them. When I'm reaching an audience, I feel it, I feel it before I'm knowing it. I feel things that you don't want anyone to know at any particular time. I think about this, I think about that, not about notes, but I'm going to make it sound right. From now on, I promise me, I want to feel the best, do the best. It's not that I feel I haven't paid my dues; I believe you don't get through paying these things, not until you die. Just like you can't get out of this business—you may get out one year, two years or five years, but you coming back, brother, somewhere down the line, like starting to walking, it's something that helps. Then you going to find that your playing is going places, it starts to help. I feel proud, you feel like you can do anything you want sometimes. It's a high mountain to climb, this business, sometimes too high, but we got to get over it. I believe I can go anywhere in the world and communicate.

I've seen a gang of worlds since I've been born—we survive—I sit back sometimes and think of Lightning Hopkins and Son House, Bukka White, all these guys—the kind of music they were playing, you still hear it today. It may be scattered, you may not hear it in everybody's home, but it's there, it should have gone to the moon. It's management—they could have pushed it.

E♯: Are there singers you'd like to record with or play with?

HS: There was this girl, she sung with me once, long time ago, like Dinah Washington, fourteen years old, can't keep up, don't know where. Maybe one night I'll be playing somewhere and she'll walk in.

E♯: When you were young, did other guitarists show you things?

HS: On the Delta wasn't too many people that was interested in showing you too much, 'cause they were trying to work themselves. At that time you had to be good, if you just listened. I tell you I was playing wrong all the time! [laughs] But I tell you I can't be too bad, you know what I'm talking bad, I got with [James] Cotton when I had my first guitar, the one my mama bought. Cotton went and got this guitar. I saw pictures of Cotton with the clamp on the guitar. I clamped that guitar! My first clamp was a pencil with string wrapped around. I went with Cotton. Cotton said, "I'll use you!" Me, Pat Hare, Cotton, piano player, drummer. Then I left Cotton, went with Wolf 'cause Wolf paid more money. Sometimes we'd make fifty cents, sometimes we'd make a dollar for a Saturday night. The whole piece! Things was back then, things were good, things were bad.

E♯: Your sound is so unique — so completely your own. What would you say to young guitarists just starting out?

HS: Define yourself, find yourself! Just like you'd get an answer from a dictionary. Find out what you want to do! I knew at eight years old what I wanted to do, I figured I'd be the best guitar player. I wanted to be the best at everything I did.

22

Pete Cosey

Bridging Sonic Realities

The search for hot guitar and cool licks took up an inordinate part of my teen listening years. An incendiary break with that elusive WTF!?! factor might be found on odd sides and save an utterly banal song from banishment to the audio scrapheap. When Jimi Hendrix and The Yardbirds were inhabiting the Top 40, the quest became easier with the Isley Brothers, Mitch Ryder, The Temptations, and Rotary Connection joining them on the air. The Connection was an industry construction featuring the singing of diva Minnie Riperton and a cast of outstanding studio players, including the great Phil Upchurch on bass and guitar. Their main attraction for me, though, was Pete Cosey's massive guitar sound. He played searing blues licks with a psychedelic dimension. Pete's lines were unpredictable and larger than terrestrial life, clearly aligned with the Jimi Hendrix wing of the Futurist Blues party but with a unique personal twist.

Howlin' Wolf and Muddy Waters were perennial favorites, and when Chess released the notorious *This Is Howlin' Wolf's New Album* and *Electric Mud*, I immediately ran out to get them. The purist in me hated the "groovy" veneer, but that part of my soul that craved sonic extremes was thrilled at the wah-wah vocalizations and sneering fuzz of Cosey's leads, not to mention his sitar obligati. The Wolf record provided one of my favorite quotes of the era, too, also courtesy of Cosey: "Howlin' Wolf looked at me and he said, 'Why don't you take them wah-wahs and all that other shit and go throw it off in the lake?—on your way to the barber shop!"

I began to search for Cosey's playing and found it in such unlikely places as John Klemmer's *Blowin' Gold*, the soft-lite saxman's funkiest album. Cosey played many sessions but was often uncredited. When Cosey surfaced with Miles Davis in 1975 on *Agharta*, it promised apocalyptic joy and delivered. The expectations were more than met with his combination of bebop phrasing and ripping blues licks twisted, filtered, and vocalized with fuzz, wah, echo, ring modulation, and blasts of feedback—keening and wailing, ebbing but then always rising like an exhortation. Pete could be heard not only on guitar but with an EMS VCS3 synthesizer to further mangle his guitar or add atmospheric textures to an already exotic soundscape. Later in the 1970s, my friends and I eagerly sought out samizdat copies of the impossible to obtain (in Buffalo anyway) *Pangaea* or *Dark Magus* and cassettes were passed hand to hand.

I felt that Cosey was bridging two seemingly mutually exclusive worlds: the rarefied laboratories of European composers Karlheinz Stockhausen and Iannis Xenakis and the Southside Chicago blues of Muddy and Wolf. In his hands, there was no gulf between these realms: Cosey translated all of his sounds through his own sonic vision, one with the times and filled with the rhythm of the streets. One may see the parallel with such a visionary artist as Sun Ra: earthy and out of the blues, but at home in the cosmos, conversing freely in alien languages, an avatar of Afrofuturism at its best.

I met Pete Cosey only once, briefly. In 1989 he joined Power Tools with Melvin Gibbs and Ronald Shannon Jackson and performed at the old Knitting Factory. Between sets I encountered Pete on the stairs, and we spoke for a second about the Casio guitar synthesizer that he was using. He said it was "his orchestra." He exuded intelligence and warmth—both qualities in abundance in his playing. Certainly he produced symphonic textures that night, but I can't say that I wasn't disappointed not to hear him shred a corner of the universe on a fuzzed-out Strat or Morris Mando Mania guitar.

The news of his passing caught me by surprise, even though I had heard that he had been ailing. I had been recording that day and was caught in the doldrums, unable to find a suitable strategy for completing a solo pass on a track I had built up for the *Haptikon* album. Calling a halt to work and holding a private memorial meditation for Pete Cosey, I searched for and watched a number of clips on the web. A stunner was Pete with Miles in Vienna, 1973, playing one of his uniquely tuned Vox twelve-strings and making a music so brilliant and incandescent that I was floored. Inspired, I was able to return to my task having asked the musical question, "What would Pete Cosey do?" and receiving a wealth of answers to choose from.

23

Bekerey

Pastry and Politics on the Lower East Side

With Janene quite pregnant with our twins, it was the highest priority for us to quickly find an affordable apartment with an elevator that could accommodate the SUV-size stroller we would soon be using to transport our offspring until they could walk on their own four feet. Janene had done her homework meticulously, and we now found ourselves on our way to view an apartment situated on Corlears Hook in the Lower East Side, one of Manhattan's last frontiers, the easternmost point of the island. Because the shape of the shore jutting into the East River was supposedly reminiscent of the nose of General Corlear, one of George Washington's Revolutionary Army staff, "the Hook" was named after him. With an active waterfront until the late nineteenth century, the workers of Corlears Hook were serviced by the many local taverns, not to mention the accompanying professional women. Perhaps apocryphal, but it's said that the women who worked the Hook became known as "hookers."

J and I walked down Avenue C, which magically became Pitt Street as we crossed Houston Street. There was an increasing amount of uncontained trash on the sidewalks as we approached the demarcation point of our departure from the East Village. Traversing Delancey Street under the Williamsburg Bridge, we entered alien territory, neither the metastasizing gentrification of the East Village or the now ultra-trendy and expensive Lower East Side, but an area of faceless brick apartment buildings, taller than the surrounding low-income housing projects along the East River, but not really high-rise either. Very New York, but not the Manhattan I knew and sometimes still loved (but that's another story that could lead to an epic *kvetch* about how the inexorable tide turned into a rogue wave, with 9/11 resulting in the American military occupation of NYC . . . but I digress). Wait, have we been transported to Queens? Reaching Grand Street, there were the predictable establishments found in every neighborhood in the five boroughs: drugstore, bank, pizza, Chinese takeout, supermarket, ninety-nine-cent store. There was also Frank's Bicycles, a venerable institution where Janene had purchased her first Manhattan bicycle some years before, plus a Kosher market and, lo and behold, a bakery.

I habitually require a carbo in the afternoon washed down with a double espresso as the minimum to propel my work past that time of circadian depression and into the evening hours. Life has taught me that a Jewish bakery is always a good source for a tasty nosh, so as we passed, I suggested to J that we stop in for a quick reconnaissance. Perusing the cases, my eyes roved past the pies, marble cakes, and black-and-white cookies (known in Germany as "Amerikaners"—is that name a comment on American diversity?) and spotted a classic cheese danish nearly hidden by its abundant dark chocolate topping. The elderly woman behind the counter gave us both the once-over and paused to glare at Janene while she handed me my change. Janene said the "*shiksa* radar" must have been beeping hard.

It's now June, and we've completed all of the paperwork and are in possession of our keys, not to mention a hefty mortgage. The apartment had been the residence of a woman who had moved in "from blueprints" when the buildings were first constructed in the 1950s, a project of various unions including the ILGWU. Italian, Jewish, Irish, Chinese, African American: the Lower East Side in all its demographic glory. By July, our simple renovations are complete and I'm painting the apartment by myself to stretch our meager budget. An electric kettle has been given a place of honor so that I can make filter coffee when needed or desired.

On my way to the apartment to work, my daily itinerary includes, besides the hardware store, a stop at the bakery to pick up fuel for my labors. The old lady on the bakery's morning shift, Mrs. S, begins to interrogate me after my second visit. "Are you Jewish? Married? Kids? Where are you living? What do you do?" A typical *schtick*. I don't mind the nosiness because Mrs. S has a lightness about her, a sparkle in her eye, and I know that I'll be visiting the bakery regularly. She seems to be about eighty but very quick, adds up all of the receipts in her head and is always correct. She tells me on the third visit that she sat out the Holocaust in Russia but her husband had survived internment in Auschwitz, and that one of the owners of the bakery also was a survivor of the infamous death camp. I imagined a festively decorated plaque over the door: "We know ovens inside and out."

The twins are born the following September. I continue to make my near-daily pilgrimage to the *bekerey* for bread for our home and for my afternoon sugar buzz. When I take the twins down to the East River at sunrise in their oversized stroller, the bakery is often our last stop before returning home. When Lila and Kai begin to teethe, Mrs. S smilingly begins handing them a hard cookie or a slice of pumpernickel. As I begin to vary the timing of my morning routine, I start to make sense of the rhythms of the bakery and its clientele: workers heading to their labors, children on their way to school, *rebbes* and members of the various local synagogues post-*shul*, Hatzoloh EMT crews, *bubbe* and *balabusta*. A sprinkling of tourists and the curious stop in as well, asking endless questions about the pastries in the cases, mispronouncing *bulka*, *kichel*, and *rugelach* and slowing down the process for everyone else. Finally, there's the gang of regulars installed on boxes or stools around the bakery, killing time, *kibitzing*, gossiping, dozing: *schnorrers* and snorers. There might as well be an additional sign at the entrance bearing the legend: "casting and dialogue by Harvey Pekar."

We've been living on the Hook for less than six months now, but Mrs. S and I have become very friendly and we've spoken enough that she feels she has a handle on my beliefs. Nothing too serious is discussed, mostly the weather. Occasionally she'll refer to an illness suffered by someone I don't know or she'll offer a mild *kvetch* about an ache or pain that she's experiencing. If she hasn't seen me for more than a few days because I've been out on tour, she'll always ask for a full account of my travels with a complete list of countries visited. Politics will come up now and then, and when it does, she prefaces any remarks with her characterization of me as "an ultra-liberal Jew." One morning late in 2005 she announces, "You ultra-liberal Jews don't believe in the Holocaust!" I'm taken aback at this determined statement of fact and ask, "Mrs. S, you know that my mother is a Survivor. What Jew doesn't believe in the Holocaust?" to which she nearly jumps in the air shouting, "Steven Spielberg!" This really floors me, and I answer: "Steven Spielberg!? Didn't you see *Schindler's List*?" Now she yells: "His new film [*Munich*] has the Jews very angry!" I tell her that many Arabs are angry about it as well, and perhaps he's getting something right. Her face red, Mrs. S waves her hands to dismiss me and says angrily, "You! Your wife isn't Jewish." End of discussion.

The morning of September 10, 2006 was filled with commotion as President George W. Bush was scheduled to visit the Ground Zero site. The FDR Drive was closed to traffic, and there were helicopters filling the sky and police cruisers on the streets. Unfortunately, East River Park was also rendered inaccessible, but I wasn't going to let this completely derail my morning routine. Twins in the stroller, we head up Grand to the bakery. While I'm completing our purchase I hear sirens and see police motorcycles chug past the open bakery door. I step over to the entrance just as the first of a series of big black cars pass slowly by. As the third one comes into view, I see W himself framed in the car window. He looks out at me and reflex takes over. I flip him the bird and the car moves on. Though I'm a bit embarrassed at my childish reaction, I also have an incredible sense of satisfaction: a nano-blow against the empire. There's a flash of worry that the Secret Service will now storm the bakery and grab me for a Guantanamo vacation, thereby rendering the twins fatherless and Janene a political widow. But no, the motorcade completes its run, and everything returns to normal. I push the SUV out the door and we head home.

One morning during the 2008 presidential election campaign, Mrs. S declares to me her love for Sarah Palin. She tells me this with glee after I've made my purchase. She smiles, waiting for my response. I have an urge to say something nasty and cutting but restrain myself. She digs in and tells me that Obama hates Jews and wants to kill them, and that only the Republicans can save "us" and that Sarah Palin is "a genius, the greatest." Though I'm continually frustrated and disgusted at the Dems ineffectual governance and cowardly far-too-moderate stance when some courage and wisdom are needed ("the meanies vs. the weenies"), I've reached my limit. I'm seething and a bit frayed after a night working too late and rising too early. There's a distinct edge in my voice when I say, "If the Republicans take over, the Jews will be the first to be in the new concentration camps, so get ready!" I exit quickly, furious but also sorry to have snapped. I return the next morning and tell Mrs. S that I'd like to apologize for getting angry with her. She laughs and says that at her age she never remembers anything that's happened the day before.

While I'm waiting for change from a purchase, an elderly gentleman comes in and asks for a rye bread, proffering three dollar bills. Mrs. S stops rummaging in the cash register, takes the man's money, and quickly bags a loaf and hands it to him. After he leaves, she turns to me and says, "He's a Democrat, I shouldn't give him nothing."

It's 2014, and I head to the bakery late on a rainy Sunday morning. Usually, this is a time to avoid the bakery, because this is when the tourists pack in to bring edible souvenirs back to the 'burbs. Because of the weather, the place is unusually empty, except for two men in *yarmulkes* looking to be in their sixties. One is proclaiming loudly, " . . . the world is so screwed up these days because of that Obama. Hey, Mrs. S, I hear Obama is your cousin!" Mrs. S looks up and says, "Obama is my cousin, Hitler, too!" Oy . . .

The chocolate babka sold by the bakery is fantastic, and we've decided that it will be the perfect way to cap off a festive dinner with friends. As I'm waiting for the woman behind the counter to wrap it up (Mrs. S is not there in the afternoon), Y, a youngish Chasid who often works mornings, enters bearing on his shoulders one of the largest challah breads I've ever seen. The domed top crust's crenellations have a sublime glow in the store's fluorescent lighting. The thing must weigh fifteen pounds, if not more. I express marvel at the challah and ask the clerk if it's a special order. She tells me that they can make as large a challah as anyone can order, especially for a *bris*. At this, she grins, spreads her arms wide, then makes a chopping motion over the loaf. Slicing bread . . . ?

As I'm just about to enter the bakery one morning, I'm frozen outside by the sound of a rich tenor voice singing a *nigun*, a wordless spiritual song. The name itself means "melody" in Hebrew, and *niggunim* can have the intensity of the greatest gospel or free jazz. The singing is sublime, and I'm transfixed standing outside the door. When the music finishes I enter, and Y looks up at me with a sheepish smile. I compliment him on his singing, and we speak a bit about music, with Y asking me about the instruments and music that I play. On a number of occasions after this, Y writes down for me the name of a singer of *niggunim* who is trending on YouTube and that I should check out. One time, Y tells me that a particular singer is so good "he's like a needle," and he mimes shooting up.

Mrs. S thinks that NYC's banning of plastic and paper bags is ridiculous. When I tell her that I don't need a bag for my purchase, she grins and says, "Then you pay double!"

24

On the Journey That Wasn't

In August of 2005, I was visited by Joshua Cody and Kirk Noreen, the co-leaders of Ensemble Sospeso. They brought with them an offer to take part in an intriguing project, a collaboration with French conceptual and multimedia artist Pierre Huyghe. Huyghe's works never pandered to the obvious, but required engagement, extrapolation, and associative thinking to apprehend all of their facets. They're all different enough from each other that to define his stylistic identity one must dig deeper than the surface manifestations of the works. There's a strong component of criticism of public media and its manipulation both in meaning and in value, but also subtle humor to underscore the concepts.

The New York City Public Art Fund and the Whitney Museum of American Art commissioned *A Journey That Wasn't* in 2005, to be presented on October 14 of that year. The work included a large-scale installation at the Wollman Ice Rink in Central Park, along with a projected film and live performance, plus a full multi-camera filming of the event itself which would then be incorporated into the final document of the work. The projected component of *A Journey That Wasn't* presents the story of a sailing expedition from Tierra del Fuego to the coast of Antarctica, where a rare and reclusive albino penguin lives on a small island. The film documents the actual voyage taken by Huyghe and companions on a research vessel from Tierra del Fuego to Antarctica in February of 2005.

The design of both Josh Cody's symphonic score and the sound and light installations was based on the physical shape of this island. The intention was for the sound to summon the elusive penguin with its sympathetic vibrations. The score paid homage to music of Varèse and Xenakis with its sweeping glissandi and massive chords. My role as soloist was to provide a continuous obligato that would emerge from the orchestral texture, not oppose or overwhelm it. For this event, I brought the Saul Koll eight-string electric guitarbass that I had just picked up in July, as well a small collection of slides, springs, an EBow, and a processor for overdrive.

Because of the enormity of the forces to be assembled for this event, it would only be possible to have one full rehearsal, which would take place immediately before the performance. We converged in the hall adjacent to the ice rink, the orchestra's musicians jammed into every possible space, while the rest of the support and film crews worked around us. I was happy to see many of my longtime compatriots in the orchestra, and also to be working with multi-reedist Scott Robinson for the first time. The music was about twenty minutes in length and, though sectional, it was performed in one long movement. My strategy was to use my objects and extended techniques to create slow glissandi, deep sustained feedback, coruscating noise, and fibrillated rhythms—essentially, a textural approach.

In terms of vibe and atmosphere, and given the subject matter, a better day could not have been chosen for this performance. It was dripping wet when we arrived for the afternoon rehearsal, with rain and wind only getting more intense as daylight shifted to dusk. The orchestra was assembled on wooden platforms with an open-sided tent erected to provide some measure of protection from the elements. I was situated on a small wooden platform that held the guitar amplifier and a compact pedalboard, with just enough room left for me to stand.

The Wollman Rink had been absolutely transformed into an Antarctic landscape of the type seen in John Carpenter's *The Thing* using black plastic tarpaulins, dry ice, blocks of foam, and stage lighting. Nature added the final topping of reality with mists, real fog, and blowing rain. As we approached the zero hour, I noticed with apprehension that the water level around the platforms was slowly rising. The twins had been born less than one month before, and the fear that Janene might become a single parent due to my imminent electrocution seemed very real. The orchestra's musicians were all playing acoustically. Of course, their extremely valuable instruments were in danger of being harmed by the weather, but at least their lives were not at stake!

With the downbeat, we swung into action, although the sounds we produced were not exactly swinging. It was indeed exciting to perform Cody's powerful score, especially with the underlying *frisson* of possible doom. At the climax, the adorable little albino penguin rolled out on a mechanical contraption to make his solitary appearance in the middle of the dramatic icy gloom.

25

Migration and Sanctuary in Bochum

Living and touring in Berlin, Germany between January 2015 and July 2016 provided ample opportunities to see how war and turmoil in the Middle East led to turmoil of a different kind: a massive refugee crisis with hundreds of thousands of displaced persons from Syria, Iraq, and Afghanistan in need of housing, employment, and medical care, not to mention education for the children. To their credit, the government of then–Prime Minister Angela Merkel did a decent job resettling refugees in various places throughout Germany, but not without obstacles: xenophobic propaganda from right-wing political groups such as the AfD (Alternative für Deutschland) tried to balance a climate of caring and tolerance with racial hatred and fearful rants reminiscent of the Hitler era. In February of 2016 with the sounds of this domestic conflict as underscore, I was contacted by Matthias Osterwold and Stefanie Carp of the Ruhrtriennale festival and asked to think about creating a work for the 2018 festival. They expressed the desire for the work to somehow address the most cogent issue in Germany at that moment: the influx of refugees and what it meant in the larger scheme of things. There were a number of possible venues where the performance could take place, all repurposed industrial sites that had formerly been the locations for power plants, coal mines, refineries, and factories in the Ruhr Valley. I was taken on a wonderful tour of locations and marveled at the gargantuan size and decayed beauty of these facilities.

The resultant work, *Filiseti Mekidesi*, was designed to be both an opera and an installation. It would be an abstract narrative with a libretto and orchestrated parts, but presented in such a way that the audience members could freely move through the space to take in varying sonic and visual perspectives. My proposal was accepted, and I was offered the Türbinenhalle of the Jahrhunderthalle in Bochum for performances in September 2018.

The words *filiseti* and *mekidesi* are derived from words meaning "migration" and "shelter" in languages spoken in Ethiopia and Eritrea—the region

Figure 13 Janene Higgins and E#, Bochum, Germany (2018).

where humanity is supposed to have originated. Migration and the search for places of shelter are integral aspects not only of human existence since its very beginnings, but for all creatures who share these experiences. They all seek a safe place where they may find food and where they may reproduce and raise offspring without danger. The migration of populations is a regularly repeated process that is part of the make-up not just of humans, but of all creatures. Migration allows cultures to spread and develop, evolve and thrive. Unfortunately, the origins of migration are rarely benign: it is usually the result of danger, expulsion, suffering, or poverty. Immigrants are seldom welcomed and given a friendly reception; they may be repelled or even killed, but they can also put established populations under pressure and thus be forced to move on.

Filiseti Mekidesi is a meditation on the universal search for a safe, neutral place free from danger. It does not tell a linear narrative, but uses musical and poetic means to reflect moments and situations in cosmic and human history in particular resonance with the critical events taking place at that time. *Filiseti Mekidesi* offers neither analysis nor solutions: it is audiovisual reflection and psychoacoustic observation, both an opera and an installation. Though there was some seating available, the audience was invited to wander around the spacious Türbinenhalle to allow focus on particular performers and to hear electronically produced sound "shadows" of both the

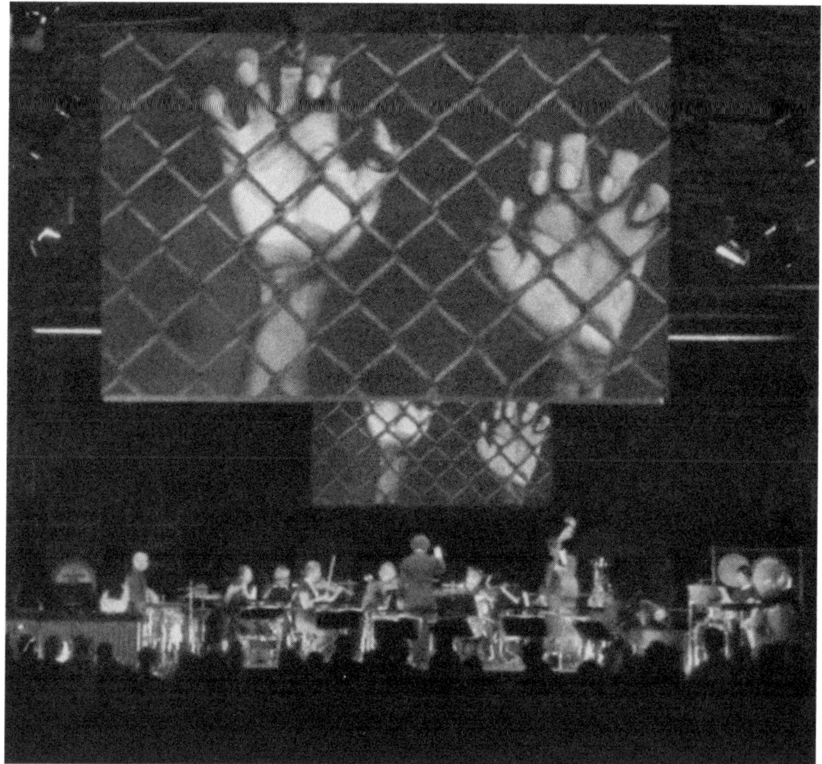

Figure 14 *Filiseti Mekidesi*, performed by Musikfabrik in Bochum, Germany (2018).

live performers and the prerecorded electroacoustic tracks drift around the space, augmenting the live sounds or standing alone.

Brilliant poets both, my longtime friends and collaborators Tracie Morris and Edwin Torres were invited to write texts on migration and sanctuary and given the freedom to take any approach they desired, as long as there were rhythmic elements that I could amplify with the music. I also wrote texts, and all were combined to form the libretto.

The performers included Palestinian singer Kamilya Jubran, the vocal ensemble VoxNova Italia (led by Nicholas Isherwood), and the ensemble Musikfabrik from Cologne. Janene Higgins created set, setting, and abstracted commentary on video synchronized to the music. The video displayed images keyed to vocal or instrumental phrases and designed to amplify their meaning as well as present emotional counterpoint. The final element in this work was a set of electroacoustic soundfiles, also synchronized. This audio provided "sound shadows" of elements in the score in the

Figure 15 Palestinian vocalist Kamilya Jubran performing *Filiseti Mekidesi*, Bochum, Germany (2018).

form of prerecorded processed phrases appearing in performance. Another function of the audio was to provide textural underscoring which both exaggerated and spatialized key segments of the work.

To create the soundfiles, it was necessary to compose sampling scores for both Musikfabrik and VoxNova Italia in addition to the full performance score. *Filiseti Mekidesi* was composed between January and March of 2018 and the sampling score during April. During the first part of June, I had a series of solo concerts booked in Europe, which was to be combined with the sampling sessions. Musikfabrik has an incredible facility in Köln. There is a well-equipped and modern multitrack recording studio, rehearsal and performance spaces, and storage for an orchestral range of instruments, including many non-Western ones, modern electronic, even a complete set of reproductions of Harry Partch's microtonal instruments. We conducted the recording session in Köln very much like a film-scoring session, with each segment recorded separately—some quite simple and direct, others requiring open-ended interpretation of given materials with instruction sets. The percussionists willingly indulged my desire for multiple variations of the written cues.

Recording the vocalists for the samples was a bit more complicated, as they did not all live in the same place. The organization Tempo Reale in Firenze generously donated a day in their studio, during which I was able to record four of the singers. The baritone singer came to my hotel in Torino, and we recorded him separately. Finally, I recorded Nicholas remotely over Zoom. A metronome and my conducting was used to synchronize all of the vocal parts.

The recordings of Musikfabrik and VoxNova were all brought into ProTools and edited to tighten the unisons and prepare all of the files for processing. Strategies for processing included filtering, spatialization, and reverberation. In some cases, more radical transformations were effected using extreme gain-staging to create feedback, ring modulation, digital delays, and time stretching. The finished samples were catalogued and referenced in the master performance score using measure numbers, as were the video clips. For the performances, all media was loaded into the Q Lab software, which allowed us to easily launch lights, sound, and video with great accuracy. The sound desk also possessed memory to create preprogrammed scenes, also synchronized, which included full mapping of all of the microphone and sound input levels, equalization, panning, and effects.

It's now necessary to zoom away from the details of the construction of *Filiseti Mekidesi* and examine the controversial events surrounding the Ruhrtriennale during July and August of 2018. Stefanie Carp, from Vienna, was chosen to be the artistic director of this edition of the Triennale, covering 2018, 2019, and 2020. Stefanie's work as a curator has always displayed the deepest integrity and sensitivity to sometimes conflicting schools of political and social philosophy while also fiercely defending artistic freedom. Her motto for the festival was *Zwischenzeit* (English: "Interregnum"), defined as the duration between two events in a series. Ms. Carp explained, "It's the short span of time that we still have to make adjustments as to how we want to live as an international community. With societies in great economic, ecological, and social upheaval and a growing potential for violence, people are fleeing and being excluded from societies. The current time of transition is an opportunity to sketch models for a different kind of life in freedom and equality."

Other bookings for the 2018 Triennale included *The Factory*, a play by Mohammad Al Attar; Christoph Marthaler's *Universe, Incomplete*, a theatrical remix of composer Charles Ives's never-completed "Universe Symphony"; performance artist Laurie Anderson; the dance-theater work "Kirina," a collaboration between Serge Aimé Coulibaly, a choreographer from Burkina Faso, the Malian composer and songwriter Rokia Traoré, and the Senegalese writer Felwine Sarr; choreographer Sasha Waltz; and the source of the turmoil, The Young Fathers, a Scottish hip-hop group.

At that time, on the webpage for The Young Fathers was a collection of links, including one for the BDS movement. "Boycott, Divestment, and Sanctions" was and is a collection of strategies that was a major force in the elimination of the official policy of apartheid in South Africa. Many people see parallels between South African apartheid and Israel's dismantling of the West Bank territories of the Palestinians while practicing a form of ethnic cleansing. The cynical Israeli forces of Netanyahu and his coalition with extreme right-wing nationalist forces have supported the terrorist organization Hamas that governs Gaza, with the end of undermining any future legitimate Palestinian state. Updating this chapter in November 2024, we have seen Hamas launch a major terrorist attack on Israel on October 7, 2023, sparking a huge conflict with Israel brutally attacking Gaza, the West Bank, Lebanon, and Iran with a concomitant catastrophic loss of civilian life in the Palestinian and Arab territories; at this date over 70,000 civilians killed, predominantly women and children, with military attacks on Lebanon and Syria following. Devoid of logic, the German government has ruled that the BDS movement is antisemitic and therefore outlawed.

Stefanie Carp was the recipient of great pressure from local and national German politicians. In bowing to this pressure, she reached an agreement with the Young Fathers to cancel their appearance at the festival for the 2018 season in exchange for a later booking. When it was announced by the festival that the Young Fathers would not be appearing this season, they in turn announced that they had been the victims of censorship. As a result, there was a growing sentiment that artists should cancel their bookings with the festival.

From Stefanie Carp's letter to the artists participating in the Triennale:

> The Ruhrtriennale did not cancel the Young Fathers. When the social media shit storm about Ruhrtriennale being anti-Semitic etc. had started, we asked the management of the Young Fathers, whether they could do us the favour and write a text with which they would say that they are not part of the BDS campaign. We described our difficulty especially as German[s] and as a German institution, but also generally. (I don't generally want that art is functioning as part of a campaign and I don't want to have anything to do with the BDS because I don't have enough knowledge about it.)
>
> We talked five days with the Young Fathers about our point. They decided not to make such a statement. We said that we have a problem now, which they fully understood. Then we agreed with the management of the Young Fathers to cancel the concert from both sides. We wrote the text for the press word by word together. They wanted to use the word cancellation because of their Fans. A day later they made another proclamation and blamed us for censorship.
>
> As I said, I see now, it was not a good decision. But we did never say, that we cancel the Young Fathers because they would support the Palestinian[s]. We said, we have a problem with the band being used by a campaign which they cannot control.

Huge counter-pressures appeared, including threats of boycotts of the festival, and it was now deemed best to restore the group's concert. With this latest development, the anti–Stefanie Carp forces reached for the big guns. The Israeli embassy purportedly demanded that she be fired as artistic director of the Ruhrtriennale, and this was supported by some in the national arts bureaucracy as well as officials from North Rhine-Westphalia, where the festival is based.

As is very typical in Europe when a controversy arises, a conference was called for an open discussion on both the nature of this specific conflict and the general topic of artistic censorship. As a festival artist, I was invited to be a panelist and was flown to Germany to take part in this August 18 event. On the panel were Stefanie Carp; Isabel Pfeiffer-Poensgen, minister for culture and science for the State of North Rhine-Westphalia and chairwoman of the supervisory board of the Ruhrtriennale; Michael Vesper, a Green Party founder and politician of North Rhine-Westphalia, former minister of culture, and chairman of the Friends and Supporters of the Ruhrtriennale;

Alain Platel, Belgian choreographer and filmmaker and Ruhrtriennale artist; theater director Schorsch Kamerun, a founding member and singer of the Hamburg band Die Goldenen Zitronen; and Norbert Lammert, politician of the Christian Democratic Union and former president of the German Bundestag.

A few days before my departure to the conference, participants received this email:

> Safety precaution:
>
> Separate driveway for the participants to the turbine hall secured by building fences and guarded by a security;
>
> The area around the Turbine Hall is closed off by construction fences. These are guarded towards the west park by a security from inside;
>
> The inlet area is blocked by grid. Here two security persons will guard the passage;
>
> The grid will be opened at the beginning of the event, about 30 minutes before the beginning of the event and the audience will be guided in to the hall under the supervision of the security;
>
> Admission will be only for persons who have registered in advance;
>
> Should escalations occur, these persons will be kept away from the event;
>
> Security check for all visitors;
>
> Security will be also inside the hall;
>
> Should it come to riots during the discussion they will be stopped first politely. Otherwise, the appropriate persons will be asked to leave the event;
>
> There will be no serving of glass bottles and alcohol;

It was quite reassuring to know that any riots would be "politely" stopped. If there's one thing I can't tolerate, it's for rioters to be ejected without a "please" or "thank you."

The United States Department of State Office of International Religious Freedom offered this report on the conference:

> In June, Ruhrtriennale, a cultural festival receiving state financial support in NRW, invited the Scottish band Young Fathers to play a concert. The private company Kultur Ruhr GmbH organizing the festival said it cancelled the appearance when it learned the band supported the BDS

movement. The organizers stated they later reversed their decision and reinvited the band so they could publicly explain their views, but the band declined. State Minister of Culture and Science Isabel Pfeiffer-Poensgen criticized the organizer's reinvitation of the band in a press statement, and the minister-president cancelled his attendance. Jewish organizations criticized the scheduling of a panel discussion at the festival about the BDS debate because it took place on the Sabbath and featured Jewish artists who supported BDS. A Jewish activist, Malca Goldstein-Wolf, organized a demonstration headlined "No support for BDS with taxpayers' money." The demonstration took place in Bochum on August 18, and there were approximately 250 participants.

This report gave a one-sided and overly simplified version of the events of the conference, in keeping with the biased weighting of the opinion of the anti-Stefanie forces who tried to present the controversy as one between groups of "anti-Israel" and antisemitic artists and defenders of Israel. This could not be further from the truth.

Approximately ninety minutes before the start of the conference, Alain Platel and I were driven from the hotel to the festival site, which was located at the end of a long uphill driveway. Outside the entrance of the driveway, and thus completely off festival grounds, was a small folding table staffed by what appeared to be a pair of university students and an elderly gentleman in a *kaffiyeh*. The table had some photocopied information sheets about conditions in Gaza and the West Bank under Israeli occupation. Very low key and low budget. Arriving up at the plaza outside the Türbinenhalle was a professional stage approximately twenty feet in width with imposing sets of public address loudspeakers on either side which I was told was brought in by the Israeli government. There were dozens of large Israeli flags on mounts surrounding the stage and the perimeter of the plaza, which was filled with people carrying Israeli flags. I watched and listened for half an hour as a series of speakers gave short angry speeches condemning Stefanie Carp as antisemitic and anti-Israel and demanding that not only should she be fired from the Ruhrtriennale but prosecuted as well for her crimes. Most of the people in the plaza cheered each of the speakers.

To enter the hall, one had to pass through a high-tech security checkpoint very much like one might find at an airport. Jackets and bags were emptied out and the contents closely examined. While I normally resent this type of intrusive examination, I must say that in this context I welcomed it. Still fresh in my mind were the death threats left on my answering machine when I was involved in organizing anti-Occupation benefit concerts in 2003 in New York City, not to mention finding my picture in an online "rogue's gallery" of so-called "self-hating Jewish antisemites" by a now-defunct organization calling itself Masada 3000. I do not relish the thought of having my existence terminated by one of these fanatics!

The format of the conference called for each panelist to be introduced with a short bio and then to read a statement. We would then be presented with questions by the moderator to be discussed between us.

My statement was this:

> I speak here as a human and an artist. It's not my favorite situation when I have to describe my positions as coming from any more than that, but given the nature of this discussion I must add that I am Jewish and the son of a Holocaust survivor. These factors have contributed to my views as much as anything else, whether situational, cultural, or esthetic. I am grateful to the progressive artistic vision of Stefanie Carp that has brought us all here, both in this edition of the Ruhrtriennale and in our discussion. The artist is an antenna and transmitter, sensitive to signals and open to frequencies that are not within the bandwidth of many citizens or typical politicians. The artist is also a translator, taking their internal images, thoughts, feelings, and sounds, and transposing them to that part of the spectrum where those elements may be received and processed. These signals allow the artists (unless they've tuned their receivers to only resonate with the frequencies of money and power) to understand and even predict trends, to empathize, to highlight the wrong directions a society may take, and to point the way to positive solutions. A key to both the creation and reception of art is empathy, to place yourself within the eyes, ears, brains, and shoes of another. Art and society function best when empathy is recognized as an essential part of the system. The creator of art is part of a feedback loop between all external factors and their own output. When restrictions are placed on how the artist may express themselves, on what topics are allowed, then the artist responds in kind: provocation yields provocation, negativity breeds negativity. We cannot be bullied by self-righteous organizations that claim to speak for entire populations, that falsely try to foist a simplified view of a complex situation on artistic

expression. The badges on the sleeves may change, a swastika, a hammer and sickle, a star of David, but autocratic suppression of the arts must not stand. The arts may be the first victims of punishment by censorship and beyond but rest assured that those who unleash this Pandora's Box may well be next. Some place artistic expression in the same corner of "freedom of speech" that posits that all speech, even "hate speech" calling for harm to a particular group, should be allowed. With this I strongly disagree. One must look at the dynamics of power and how "hate speech" is used to incite fear and antipathy: the opposite of empathy. Those in positions of power claim their own victimhood, usually imagined, as the rationale for their strategies. One sees this in force at the moment in the USA with the current Trump Administration aided and abetted by white nationalists, neo-Nazis, and pseudo-Christian theofascists all striving to suppress actual free expression, twisting laws and even election procedures to benefit themselves and give themselves license to discriminate against the powerless.

There are many counter-strategies that progressive artists may use to work against these forces. They may include their own personal esthetic output, the spreading of information, and the formation of alliances with like-minded individuals to create organized structures, perhaps even on an international scale. No single strategy is appropriate for all situations, they must grow from the ground up. No single strategy is perfect: there must be discussion, fluidity. We live in a universe of links and pointers. The manifestation of these external connections are very much a part of one's artistic identity and one might say, even part of the responsibility of the artist to the world at large. If one is open to the artist, then one must be open to their web of thoughts and processes, even if one has disagreements. Attacks on artistic expression are of a piece with attacks on race, immigration, refugees, gender, and truth and transparency in the media—all part of an ongoing campaign of distraction and suppression to keep peoples who should be acting in cooperation at each other's throats while the wealth of the world is looted by the plutocracy.

The audience was mostly quiet during initial statements by the panelists, but as the discussion proceeded, decorum evaporated (at least when the speakers questioned or opposed the official view that any and all speech directed against the actions of Israel regarding the Palestinian population was by definition antisemitic). When any of us expressed these positions, dozens of audience members would stand and shout over the speaker while waving large Israeli flags. I compared the conditions in Gaza (this was in 2018) to that of the Warsaw Ghetto under the Nazis and was loudly booed and jeered. For myself and the others, when this would happen the moderator would call for quiet and things would settle down until the next such statement. The bureaucrats on the panel staunchly held to the notion that fealty to a non-critical view of Israel was one of the prime requirements for an artist in Germany at this time. This may be seen as a function of *Staatsräson*, or "reason of state," whereby Germany, because of its history of genocide and antisemitism, is atoning by inextricably linking the fate of Israel with the core purpose of modern Germany. It's an irrational position that leads to German organizations defining Jews who criticize Israel as being "antisemitic," even arresting Jewish Israelis who criticize their government, an ironic state of things.

A surprise guest appeared, Israeli-American filmmaker and author Udi Aloni. An energized presence, Udi made a strong case for unfettered artistic expression and cooperation across what many define as unbreachable barricades. His 2006 film *Forgiveness* made that expression concrete—in the film, a young Israeli-American who has moved back to Israel is committed to a mental hospital built over the ruins of the Arab village of Deir Yassin, in which 117 of its inhabitants were murdered by Jewish paramilitary groups Irgun and Lehi on April 9, 1948. Aloni's contribution to the discussion was, of course, met with hooting and shouting.

When the discussion was finished, I don't believe anyone could say that anyone's mind had been changed. One observation is that it was difficult to maintain focus on the discussion of artistic freedom itself, as there was a tendency from all to emphasize criticism of current Israeli policies as a higher priority.

Just after, we milled about to the side of the stage, where we were met by journalists as well as friends and colleagues who were able to negotiate the "velvet rope" of armed guards. I appreciated that most of the questions we fielded here were not tainted by a predetermined judgement. The real question was how our answers would appear once they were edited. One man who was allowed entry was self-identifying as a Serbian white supremacist and wanted us to endorse an alliance between all who opposed Muslim terrorism. We called for his removal. There was a general feeling among those of us with a progressive point of view that we could be subjected to violence at any time. The tension was sustained as we were escorted by guards to waiting cars to return us to the hotel. It did not subside for me until my return flight to NYC reached an altitude of ten thousand feet.

In a post-conference online interview, I wrote:

> There's no doubt that the Arab world suffers from terrible autocratic governments. The worst of the Arab governments have been willingly aided and abetted in the oppression of the Palestinians and their own people by the United States and the international arms cartels. Armaments are happily traded for oil and influence. The Israeli government plays a big role in this and one should be alarmed at the military relationships growing between them and the Saudis. The refugee crisis is a direct result of Western intervention (not to mention the Russians, Iranians, Saudis, et al.). Remember, Al Qaeda is a direct outgrowth of the US arming and training mujahideen against the Russians in Afghanistan. BDS does not address Israeli internal policies so much as it does the human rights issues in Gaza and the Occupied Territories. The two-state solution, in my opinion, the only way for the Palestinians to have any future, has been torpedoed by the current administrations in the US and Israel. I believe the new laws in Israel making the Arabs second-class citizens are designed to make them leave, a not-so-subtle form of ethnic cleansing.

The practices of Hamas are horrible and clearly terrorism — but they were actively enabled by the Israelis to strategically undercut such secular political organizations as Fatah and the PLO while encouraging the Islamists' violent fantasies. Most people just want to live their lives — the politicians divide and conquer to keep people killing each other and never finding any degree of normalcy. Ultimately, I must say that I have no "position," just the desire that children will grow up with hope instead of hatred, with schools instead of weapons. No one side is completely right and there will never be a winner or loser in the long run of this game — but all have to look at the bigger (global) picture and look at what they are allowing in the name of winning their position.

I have previously stated that I am against the boycott of individual artists, scholars, and scientists, but "official" presentations are a different story. While I appreciate the goals of BDS, I am not a member, nor do I agree with everything they say or do. However, I do believe that they represent the greatest strategic hope for change in the Middle East. One has to be careful about absolutes, and in the Jewish tradition, I often voice my statements as questions: what about the case of the Israeli Philharmonic performing Richard Wagner's music? His music was boycotted since 1938, as Wagner was famously a vicious and virulent hater of Jews. (For any doubters, seek out Wagner's text on "Judaism in Music.") Do the same people who go after Stefanie Carp for the crime of booking a band that has a BDS link on their website also go after the director of the Israeli Philharmonic for playing the music of a known antisemite and inspiration for Hitler? A look at the new American embassy in Jerusalem reveals that the opening benedictions were made by two American Christian evangelical ministers, John Hagee and Robert Jeffress, both well-known Holocaust deniers and antisemites. Is anyone screaming for the removal of the American embassy? There are many instances, many ambiguities, many contradictions to consider.

We must pick and choose what we support in light of larger humanitarian goals. I certainly could never support the official Israeli government position on the West Bank and Gaza, especially when one sees how this position is putting ethnic cleansing into effect and aligns with the interests of the world's autocracies and their cohorts in the arms trade. I see BDS as one prong in a fight against an injustice that extends across national borders. Every country has issues to be examined in their histories, and if one traces the networks beneath surface appearances, one might be surprised at how the lines of power flow. It will be no surprise that they all conspire to maintain the control by the tiniest percentage of the wealthiest people, determined to keep people alienated and mutually hostile. Zero-sum games are never won.

26

Wholly Land

Poet extraordinaire Ronny Someck and I first met through Ze'ev Schlik, Ronny's brother-in-law and manager. At Austria's Saalfelden Jazz Festival in 1997, Ze'ev gave me a book of Ronny's poems translated into English and asked if I would consider a collaboration. The poems were powerful, dark but occasionally humorous, and filled with linguistic and emotional twists and turns and wry commentary on the state of being of a Jewish Iraqi living in Israel. Ronny and Ze'ev came to NYC a few months later, and I recorded Ronny reading a number of his poems in Hebrew, then created settings for two of them using overdubbed guitars and electronics to see how a collaboration might sound.

John Zorn had been bugging me to do a recording for his "Radical Jewish Culture" series on his Tzadik label. I was completely uninterested. I didn't find the framing appealing, mostly because I felt that Jewish culture had always been considered radical and I was also wary of marketing that might be seen as part of a Zionist or otherwise Jewish nationalist movement. Still, as the music in this project with Ronny began to develop, I thought that it might actually be appropriate and suggested it to John. His reply was that Hebrew sounded like people clearing their throats and that he wasn't interested. I countered that he should listen to our two completed tracks before he made a final decision. Ronny's voice is rich and mellifluous, subtle and rhythmic. John listened and agreed to release the CD. I spent the next couple of months composing the underscore to the rest of Ronny's recitations using a variety of instruments including mandolin, analog synthesizer, eight-string bass, B♭ and bass clarinets, hand percussion, drum machine, and various guitars. Recording and mixing all took place at my humble Studio zOaR, and a number of guests added their talents, including Zeena Parkins on accordion, Margaret Parkins on cello, Anthony Coleman on piano, Seido Salifoski on dumbek, and Ahmed El-Motassem with Arabic reading.

The CD would be called *Revenge of the Stuttering Child*, and the title poem refers to words like "flames on the tongue." For the cover, I asked Eric Drooker, a talented NYC artist whose work resembles woodcuts and pays tribute to the essential and pioneering graphic novels of Belgian artist Frans Masereel, one of my longtime favorites. I asked Eric to create an image to illustrate this, but not to make the flames look too much like actual Hebrew letters, only a suggestion. On my way to Foothill Productions for the mastering session for the record, I met Eric, who gave me a striking and beautiful piece of art, hand-painted on a small board. I did notice that the flames looked to be very obviously Hebrew and wondered at the meaning. Eric didn't know; he didn't speak or read Hebrew and had just looked at some Hebrew letters. It had been decades since my childhood Hebrew School studies and I was pretty rusty, so I only had a vague sense of what was spelled out on the cover. But at Foothill, Allan Tucker told me that his wife was an expert in Hebrew, and we faxed the cover image to her. She called a minute later, and Allan was beside himself with laughter: Eric had unknowingly spelled out *Jeshua*, the Hebrew name of Jesus. I have no problem with Jesus's philosophy, but still didn't deem his name appropriate for this cover, nor did I think Ronny would be happy with it. Eric changed it the next day, and the CD went into production and was released in the fall of 1997. We played a number of concerts in Germany and Austria from 1998–1999 and began to discuss presenting the project in Israel.

Despite my initial reluctance to visit this country, the political policies of which, both international and internal, I found quite offensive, I was overcome by curiosity, plus I greatly enjoyed working with Ronny. Negotiations for the Israeli concerts were completed on my behalf by Ze'ev, and the contract was then faxed to me. A minute after receiving the contracts, the presenter called me from Jerusalem and asked if I would lower the fee that had been agreed upon. I refused, saying, "Forget the whole thing." The next day, Ze'ev called me to apologize and said that he would straighten it out, and soon enough, the contracts were signed with the originally agreed-upon terms. In May of 2000, I was in the air and on my way.

The presenter had suggested to Ze'ev that I should be lodged in the Scottish Hotel in Jerusalem. My friend Renata Schmidtkunz, a producer and director for the ORF Austrian Television, was a frequent visitor to Israel, so I asked her advice on the hotel. She was enthusiastic: "It's a wonderful place, very quiet and tranquil, no distractions, no internet or television, small rooms without private baths, simple breakfast . . . " I quickly wrote to Ze'ev saying, "No Scottish hotel—give me a modern hotel right in Tel Aviv with all of the amenities . . . "

Landing in Tel Aviv, the vibe in the airport made JFK's always-hectic International Terminal 4 at its most frantic seem positively tranquil. There was a manic energy in the air, flavored with more than a touch of free-floating paranoia plus a generous dose of *tsuris* for good measure. Soldiers with automatic weapons at the ready stood at attention around the hall, eyes darting around. There was a Russian string orchestra in line waiting to clear customs, not unusual I imagine. Lots of "black hats" as Michael Chabon refers to the Haredim in his fantastic novel *The Yiddish Policemen's Union*. I passed easily through immigration and customs and met Ze'ev and Ronny, waiting just outside. Within thirty minutes, I was happily ensconced in my hotel room, windows overlooking the city on one side and the Mediterranean on the other. I watched military transport planes and helicopters head up the coast to Lebanon to take part in their own little version of Vietnam. The show was mesmerizing but, exhausted from a very turbulent transatlantic crossing to Frankfurt plus an additional four-hour flight, I put on some blindfolds and fell immediately into a deep sleep. That evening Ze'ev and Ronny picked me up for coffee then brought me to a wonderful Lebanese restaurant in nearby Jaffa, followed by a walk on the cliffs in the chilly night air, looking at stars and sea.

Back at the hotel, I received a call from the promoter asking, "Do you really need an amplifier? It's impossible to find one in Israel." I told him that I absolutely needed an amp and without one, there could be no concert. End of conversation. After breakfast, I headed out for a walk and found two blocks from the hotel a huge music store. It was a little surprising to have my bag searched to be allowed to enter, but that was the way it was here. The store had an incredible display of instruments and accessories, including an imposing "tower of Fender" consisting of amplifiers, basses, and guitars. I found a salesman and asked if he knew of any place that rented amps. "Of course, we can rent you anything!" Ronny and Ze'ev picked me up to drive to Jerusalem to do a radio interview, and I filled them in on the amplifier situation.

Driving on the highway, one saw burnt-out skeletons of tanks and other military hardware, a reminder of local stories and myths. Walking around Jerusalem, there's no shortage of fanciful and historic architecture, but there was more than a little feeling for me of "holyland theme park," negatively enhanced by the hordes of tourists and gangs of young Haredim. Ronny and Ze'ev brought me to the Wailing Wall with its surfeit of surly old Orthodox men glaring at anyone they deem unworthy of being there (and needless to say women are kept *very* separate). Ronny and Ze'ev both wanted me to touch the Wall. "Why?" They urged me on and waited with expectant smiles. "Just do it!" I reached out and touched . . . nothing. I certainly am fond of contemplating history in all its glorious fables and contradictions, but any feelings I might have had for religious Judaism left me as soon as I was conscious enough to understand it. At age eleven, an introduction to the visionary philosophy of Baruch Spinoza by a Hebrew School teacher as "one of the heretics trying to destroy Judaism" certainly helped my direction in that regard. Spinoza's struggles and writings as the first modern philosopher became an important influence for me. After the interview on Radio Jerusalem, there was a sublime moment watching sunset from a high hill over the city with *muezzins* from three large mosques calling the evening prayer—gorgeous phasing and blending with the ambient sounds emanating up from the city below. As night fell we drove back to Tel Aviv.

The next morning, Ze'ev and Ronny picked me up for our drive back to Jerusalem for this night's concert. An amplifier had been found in Tel Aviv. There it was, sitting in the back seat of Ze'ev's car, a 1970s vintage silver-face Twin Reverb, looking a little beaten down. I found out after some discussion that the promoter didn't mean that there were no amps in Israel; he just wanted to find one for free. He was not interested in paying for a rental, and somehow had found a loaner. We set up quickly and broke for coffee. When we returned, the hall was crowded but the audience was subdued. Perhaps the uncomfortably bright fluorescent lighting was a factor. The vibe was stiff and formal, and we ended up treating the concert like a recital, playing the pieces beautifully though keeping each of them discrete and within their originally defined parameters, nearly clinical. Still, there was a little wildfire in places to give hints of where and how this might expand. We were invited by the promoter to a post-concert dinner at the restaurant of the hall but were told we could have something from a certain part of the menu: some soup or sandwiches, but not from the main part. I was now quite hungry but there was nothing I wanted on this little snack menu, so I suggested to Ronny and Ze'ev that we go elsewhere to eat. Ze'ev informed the presenter who, now acting embarrassed, mustered up a simulacrum of hospitality and told us to order what we wanted. We dined quickly then drove back to Tel Aviv.

I spent the next two days walking around Tel Aviv, very different from Jerusalem in look and feel. Modern and wired, the streets were teeming, people were animated, stylish, and there seemed to be fewer obvious tourists. A camera store and photo-processing place on the main drag liked to display provocative pictures with the sole purpose of enraging religious zealots of all stripes. Ronny told me that Tel Aviv is NYC to Jerusalem's Washington, DC, and the comparison seems apt.

For my final evening in Israel, we had a show at the Felicja Blumental Center and Library, a community hall in Tel Aviv. Our soundcheck was quick, after which we headed out for espresso at an outdoor stand. When we returned, the room was absolutely packed with a huge crowd gathered out front hoping to get in, as the concert was sold out. The venue crackled with a carnival-like energy and this inspired us: our performance was more fluid, less controlled, and we allowed the work to change substantially from the recorded versions and made spontaneous suites of a few pieces strung together with sometimes smooth, sometimes jagged transitions. After the show there were many well-wishers, plus CDs to sign. We finally packed and headed out to what I was told was the "bad part of town" near the bus station, where we hit a funky grill-bar for humus, kebabs, and beer. At one point a motorcycle backfired. It was a familiar sound but all of the Israelis were under the long and solid table in the blink of an eye, just in case. I remained in my chair, slow to react. They all returned to their seats, and I was a little stunned, a little amused. The meal over, I was dropped off at the hotel to pack as I had a taxi pickup in two hours for the airport and a flight at 4:00 a.m. for Frankfurt.

At the security checkpoint, the agent, a young male Israeli, heavily armed, was extremely hostile. He gave me the once-over, clearly not liking what he was seeing, and asked why I was in Israel. I told him, "to perform concerts" and, thinking that I could forestall any extended interrogation, gave him the current issue of *Ha'aretz* with a big picture of Ronny and me on the front page and a long article about our concert and the CD. He took it away and asked me again with even more hostility, "Why were you in Israel?" This type of behavior just brings out the contrarian in me, and I felt like goading him but restrained myself as I did not want to do anything that might cause me to miss my flight home. Very softly, I told him, "You can ask me the same question for the next two hours and the answer will be the same, so don't waste both of our time." He made it clear that he didn't like this response, but after a few more desultory questions finally moved on from the purpose of my trip to the actual flight. "You are flying on Lufthansa . . . why?" "I like their service." "You are going to Frankfurt, why?" "Because that's where I catch the flight to New York." "Do you know anyone in Germany?" "Yes, I have many friends there." He was completely flummoxed at that one and I wanted to smile but, again, felt it was necessary to keep the poker face. After another twenty minutes going over the same questions again and again, I finally said to him, "You know, my mother didn't survive the Holocaust so her son could be harassed by some schmuck." He left to speak to someone and returned: I was cleared to fly. I then ran to the gate with just enough time to board a flight to Frankfurt packed with American evangelicals there to celebrate the Jubilee of something or other and no doubt looking forward to the return of Jesus when they, as part of the 144,000, would ascend to Heaven while the Jews and the rest of the unsaved would rot in Hell for Eternity. Soon enough, I was home to the relative sanity of NYC.

Ronny and Ze'ev were very pleased overall with our Israeli concerts and asked that I return. After the difficulties of that first trip to Israel, I hoped that careful attention to details would make my second visit more pleasant by removing some of the more annoying aspects. The first step was clarifying that I did not wish to work with that same presenter again. I would also send a detailed and mandatory tech rider well in advance. Instead of performing in Jerusalem, we would have one concert only at the Anbal Folk Arts Center on the border between Tel Aviv and Jaffa. Ze'ev was enthusiastic about Anbal as they presented a wide spectrum of artists, both Arab and Jewish.

I arrived in the late afternoon from Frankfurt after finishing other concerts in Europe. Early that evening I met Ronny and Ze'ev for another fantastic dinner, this time at an Iraqi restaurant. They told me that everything was in place for our concert and that the next morning we would meet with Nili, the director of Anbal. She was incredibly charming and also assured me that everything in my rider had been confirmed and that I should arrive for soundcheck at 6:00 p.m. My needs were simple: just an amp, a microphone for the horn, and two direct boxes for my computer. From past experience, I knew that nothing would be ready so thought to get there at 6:30, still allowing plenty of time for a show at 8:00 even with problems.

Arriving at Anbal precisely at 6:30, I found the theater, a lovely room for about three hundred people with proscenium seating, completely deserted. There was no PA in evidence and no amplifier on stage. I shouted hello and, receiving no response, climbed the stage and began assembling my equipment. After a few minutes, a gray-haired gentleman emerged from the wings, exuding bad vibes. "What do you want?" he barked at me in heavily accented English. "I have a concert with Ronny Someck and need to do the soundcheck." "So make soundcheck, why are you bothering me?" I answered that we needed the guitar amplifier; it was on the tech rider along with the PA system. "Well, we have no guitar amplifier, why didn't you bring an amplifier?" Irritated, I asked him if he brings his own seat when he takes a plane. He didn't appreciate this and told me again that there was no amplifier. I said, fine, tell Nili the concert is cancelled and that I'm going back to the hotel. Knowing that we had two sold-out shows that night, I believed that this might cause some positive action to take place. Indeed, he said, "Wait," got on the phone, and after a few minutes of heated discussion in Hebrew with the party on the other end, told me that an amp would come. He dragged out a modest sound system and set it up and then I waited and waited. Ze'ev and Ronny finally arrived, and we tested the underpowered little PA with microphone and laptop. The amp made its entrance just a few minutes before doors opened: a crappy little solid-state combo bass amp with a blown speaker, a far cry from the Fender Twin Reverb I requested. It sounded like shit. We played the concert anyway to great response, the music transcending the obstacles. After the concert we headed to an outdoor restaurant for food, then around 2:00 a.m., Ze'ev drove me back to the hotel to pick up my baggage and we went to the airport. After my last experience with airport security in Tel Aviv, I insisted that Ze'ev accompany me to security. He greeted the agent, and they had a smiling chat in Hebrew. I was quickly waved through security and headed right to the gate for my flight to Frankfurt and from there back to NYC.

The events of September 11, 2001, led to a cornucopia of events with arts organizations everywhere trying to ask the right questions and give the right answers, even if they had no idea what these were. On November 24, 2001, Ronny and I were brought to Vienna to participate in a festival with a focus on the Middle East plus a panel discussion at the Schausspiel Theatre about "the arts and Israel in the current crisis." The panel was moderated by Renata Schmidtkunz and also included the wonderful Arab-Israeli actor Mohammad Bakry; Marwan Abado, a Palestinian Maronite-Christian virtuoso oudist and composer; and Vera Goldman, an eighty-year-old Jewish Israeli choreographer. These were my notes after returning from Vienna:

We were to give brief opening statements outlining our own personal history and views. Goldman begins: she is an old-school Zionist and a hippie, good-hearted but in denial about current events and oblivious to history. In her overly-long monologue, she merely explains that she just can't seem to understand why Arab Palestinians that she has known over the years would become hostile. Bakry gives a calm but impassioned account of his life and work in Israel, displaying his warm humanistic spirit and clear analysis. He points out that there are no Palestinian artists from the Occupied Territories represented in the festival. Abado was born in a refugee camp in Lebanon and his family suffered humiliation and death at the hands of the Israelis. He lives in Vienna now for some years and focuses his energy and feeling on his music, refraining from bitterness. Ronny talked about how his Jewish parents, born and raised in Baghdad, still thought of themselves as Iraqis. He read a few poems that illustrated the shared love and pain of Arabs and Jews in the region. In my portion, I talk about my analysis of historical issues and how I, as a Jew and son of a Holocaust survivor, came to be anti-Zionist, finding ways in my art to allow audiences to focus in some way on the current state of things, not in a journalistic sense but in the form of "pointers" or "signposts."

I believe that the artist has a responsibility to devote some of their esthetic energy to this task. The issues around the Israeli actions especially pain me—Jews have traditionally fought against injustice and their historical role as "victims" has caused them to "fight the good fight" at least until the rise of Israel, an end-product of the British Mandate of 1917. At the behest of Zionists, the departing imperialists divided Palestine and armed both sides. Before this act, during the Ottoman rule of the region Moslems, Jews, Christians, atheists, socialists, anarchists, and more all lived in relative mutual peace and friendship—ALL were Palestinians. Herzl's own diaries as he was developing Zionism reveal his strategy for "ethnic cleansing" and desire to eliminate the Arab populations from "Jewish regions" of Palestine. I believe that when Jews say "Never again!" it should apply to everybody. The collective world guilt after the Holocaust allowed the Zionist agenda to be advanced, with deeper and deeper shockwaves resounding throughout recent years. As the panel discussion advanced, Goldman slept (thankfully without snoring) and we spoke among ourselves about possible strategies for artists and what role Americans can have. Now, especially after 9/11, I believe Americans must act as part of the solution rather than continuing as comfortable and detached observers.

The panel opened to questions from the audience, sparking a maelstrom of shouting and accusations between different factions—very revealing and very depressing as we watched it unfold. The moderator correctly let the storm burst and subside, then outlined an orderly approach. I felt that most questions were more the audience members venting their own feelings rather than asking us for our responses. After the discussion, we received much direct feedback from the audience—some *very* positive (especially an American woman, Jewish and married to a Palestinian, who leads a local chapter of the organization Women in Black, opposed to current Israeli policies) and some *very* negative. A few of us retired to a local cafe for continued discussion, coffee, and beer. I met a local Palestinian organizer: intelligent, warm, objective, hopeful, not hateful—but willing to dig in and struggle. That evening, Mohammad Bakry performed Emile Habibi's play *The Peptimist*. It was an astounding act to witness: Bakry ranges from Chaplinesque humor to the darkest of rages and sorrow—he is physical and soulful. The play was performed in Arabic with German supertitles, so I could only understand about thirty percent—still, so much came through.

27

On the Road and in New York with Bachir Attar

Bachir Attar is from the village of Jajouka in the Atlas Mountains of Morocco and plays the double reed *rhaita*, the goat-skinned lute *guimbri*, and *lira* flute. After his father's death, Bachir became the leader of the Jajouka musicians, a group that was brought to international attention with the album *Brian Jones Presents: The Pipes of Pan at Jajouka* released by Rolling Stones Records in 1971. They have toured internationally as a group, and Bachir has appeared as a soloist with various musicians, including the Rolling Stones on their *Steel Wheels* album.

With Bachir joining Carbon on tour, we were often presented with special challenges, thanks to the white European's generally negative attitudes toward people of color and especially to those from Arabic-speaking countries. Before the relaxation of border control within the European Union, musicians in general would regularly be challenged and searched as part of standard operating procedures. Adding a Moroccan to the mix would up the ante by many degrees, with extra scrutiny paid to all documents and baggage. Even though Bachir had a US green card, he was still subject to arbitrary and unkind treatment. In *IrRational Music*, I chronicled our encounter with security at Frankfurt Airport in 1990 at the end of a tour, when the entire band was to be denied our return to the US until I invoked Bachir's connection to the Rolling Stones, which magically caused all problems to disappear.

During this tour, after a gig in Wels, Austria we were heading to Stuttgart by train, as we had a concert that night at a culture center in one of its suburbs. With a little foresight, our agent might have booked us on an international train where the border controls took place in the train itself, thus avoiding the complications of a border transfer. But because he didn't, we would have to disembark from the train with all of our gear at a little Bavarian town on the border of Austria and Germany, go through immigration and customs control, and then catch a German train to our destination.

This transfer would have to be accomplished in fifteen minutes for all of the passengers on the train. Because of our equipment, we were among the last to enter the customs queue as our connecting train was already being boarded. As we stepped up to the counter for our turn, the officer—tall, blond, uniform crisply pressed, mean eyes—scanned us and said loudly, "Ve are looking for drugzzz," the final consonant stretched out for emphasis. The proper response from us should have been "So are we . . . " but that might have been counterproductive.

Instead, I told him that we are a professional musical group on tour and that we cannot miss our waiting train as we have a concert that evening and that, needless to say, we had no drugs. He held his hand up to stop my spiel, and he and two khaki-clad minions began to tear through our equipment cases and backpacks. We watched our train roll off as their work continued. After about forty minutes, they stopped and the kommandante said, "I did not find anything so you may go." Bachir couldn't resist a parting message: "When I come to your country, I do NOT smoke hashish. But when you come to my country, you WILL smoke hashish." The look on the officer's face (accompanied by a red flush of anger) was one of abject horror, and it was difficult but necessary to keep from laughing. Now we had two more hours to kill until the next train on a freezing platform at a station with absolutely nothing but the customs office. We did make the gig that night, but just barely.

At the end of January 1991 we returned to Europe for a much more compact tour, beginning with the Rive-de-Gier Festival near Montpellier, France. Our flight to Paris and TGV train to the gig were both uneventful, as they should be. After the festival, we had a concert in Fribourg in Switzerland. Little did we know that in the previous week, entry requirements had changed for Moroccans wishing to enter Switzerland because of the impending Gulf War. Bachir would have had to apply for a special visa which could not be granted at the border, so he had to return to Paris where his brother Mustapha was living. While the Swiss police were engaged for about twenty minutes with Bachir, the border was left completely unattended. We watched, amused, as various passengers passed through, confused looks on their faces. The guards returned and there was some quiet discussion among themselves when they realized their error. We were quickly sent on our way.

Bachir was able to rendezvous with us in Munich, after which we headed to Nickelsdorf, an Austrian village near the Hungarian border and the site of Cafe Falb, hosts of a summer festival of jazz and improvised music, but also weekly concerts. After the show, we returned to the hotel. Bachir was not seen at breakfast, a matter of some concern as we would soon be picked up for a van ride to Vienna, about ninety minutes away, where we would catch a train back to Germany for our next concert in Munich. Neither calling Bachir's room phone nor knocking on his door yielded any results, and we began to worry that he had decided to take a walk and run into an overly enthusiastic border guard. Hans Falb called the local police, but they had not seen Bachir. Our driver cruised around the area, even going over the border into Hungary. We had reached a critical threshold—if we didn't leave immediately we would miss our train and subsequent connections. Finally, the hotel owner arrived and took his master key and opened Bachir's door to reveal him snoozing deeply and peacefully, head under the hood of his *djellaba*. We got him up and out the door and into the waiting van.

The day after returning from a European tour that included the premiere of my orchestral work *Calling* at the Darmstadt Festival in July 2002, I jumped right into preparations for the July 20 concert of the Al-Mashreq All-Stars. This event was part of the Lincoln Center Summer Festival and was one of a spate of post-9/11 concerts in the US and Europe designed to provide token recognition of the music of the Arab world after too much neglect. Because of my past activities collaborating with Arab and Middle Eastern musicians, I was asked to be music director, a job which included conceptualizing the project as well as composing and arranging music and coordinating the diverse talents that would make up the ensemble. The group was to include singer Natacha Atlas; Bachir Attar; Graham Haynes on cornet and flugelhorn; the Bedouin musicians of oudist Muhammad Abu-Ajaj with Musa Al Hajuj on vocals and Sultan Abu Takfa on *sumsumiya*; DJ Mutamassik with turntables and electronics; Palestinian oudist/vocalist Marwan Abado; Chicago drummers Michael Zerang and Hamid Drake; Zafer Tawil, the Brooklyn-based Palestinian virtuoso multi-instrumentalist who would play *q'anun*, violin, oud, and percussion; and me on eight-string guitarbass, bass clarinet, six-string bass, and electronics.

Our rehearsals were long and arduous, but not long enough! I wished that we had at least another day to work on the music. There was a wealth of material representing each player. One of the main issues was how to most efficiently communicate the musical ideas and structures, as some of the musicians read music and were familiar with a variety of styles, others were not. I was able to compile a set of cues in text form for each piece, with accompanying notation for those players who could make use of it. Openness abounded and all put forth great effort into making the pieces work. By the final hours of the last rehearsal, I felt that we were indeed becoming an ensemble.

The concert was at the LaGuardia High School auditorium—in my opinion the best room in the Lincoln Center complex for electrified music. We had a beautifully spacious stage, great equipment, and a fine crew, plus a sold-out house of over 1,200 people. The concert commenced with a free-time intro, with Zafer soloing on *q'anun* over a slow ensemble unison melody that I had composed. Next, Abu-Ajaj and his musicians performed one song as a trio, with the rest of the ensemble joining them for a second song. Their music had a lilting quality with the sweet drone of the *sumsumiya* providing both harmonic underpinning and rhythm. Next was Bachir Attar's song "In New York," a version of which we had recorded for our eponymous duo CD in 1989. I set up a shifting and harmonized drone with EBow and electronics on the eight-string, with Bachir improvising an intense *maqam* on *rhaita*. Hamid, Michael, and Zafer kicked the drums in with a deep groove, and we were off. Graham Haynes's composition *The Griot's Footsteps* was the next piece and was based on Gnawa music. The odd-meter bassline with its wide intervals gave my fingers quite a stretch. The piece builds over its ten-minute span with four different ostinati, over which the trumpet and violin improvise. Marwan Abado next sang an incredibly moving song accompanied by his own oud-playing. The audience was hushed and then exploded in applause. We continued as an ensemble with his piece *Do You Do How!* which begins with unison lines then finishes with a collective improv which melded into DJ Mutamassik's solo, which was then transformed by the entrance of Bachir's *rhaita*. Gradually, the entire ensemble joined in for an indefinable mix of hip-hop, Middle Eastern sounds, and NY noise. Zafer next played a solo oud piece that displayed the connection between *maqam* and the flamenco styles of Andalucia. The whole group joined in for his piece *Bela* (named for his young daughter), which built intensity on an ostinato. After *Bela* we performed Natacha Atlas's feature, a song called "Rah" from her CD *Ayeshtemi*. She sang a beautiful *maqam* over a bass drone followed by the intro on cornet and violin by Graham and Zafer. The song has a deep dub funk groove, and there was a percussion break in the middle with ensemble members contributing sounds. "Rah" was followed by a percussion duo

Figure 16 Bachir Attar and Mustapha Attar, Le Poisson Rouge, NYC (2014).

from Hamid and Michael, beginning abstract and displaying the incredible interaction they've perfected in years of playing together. It morphed into a 6/8 rhythm over which Bachir played a slow, twangy melody on *guimbri*, with Graham playing a gorgeous flugelhorn solo on top. The ensemble played a slow unison melody to bring the segment to an end for my solo, which was played on the eight-string and laptop—I used the EBow to play a winding melody which triggered dumbek samples as accompaniment. This kicked us into my composition *Al-Mashreq*, written to be a finale for the concert and ranging from stop-time melodies to a heavy ostinato over which Natacha improvised, as did Bachir on *rhaita*. This brought the concert to an end.

Throughout, we could feel the intense attention of the audience, so we were not too surprised by the strong response. Still, we were truly excited and amazed by the sustained applause and standing ovation. We returned to play one more of the Bedouin songs led by Abu-Ajaj, and the evening was complete (except for the late, late after-party at the Moroccan restaurant Souk in the East Village).

Jump to January 2004, and the next Iraq War is in full swing. Flying to Frankfurt to begin a Terraplane tour, we noticed that our flight had a fair number of American soldiers on it, no doubt heading to one of the large military bases near the city. We're at the baggage claim waiting for our equipment and one soldier stands out, as he's a skinny white dude wearing an Australian bush–style hat with a Confederate flag on it and a flight jacket emblazoned on the back with a slogan in lurid colors: "Kill 'em all and let God sort it out." We were sufficiently disgusted by this display, but what could we do? Fortunately, an American military officer also noticed this soldier and headed over to him. She was African American and large and took no shit from this cracker as she led him away while he whined about his rights.

28

Tarab and Beyond

Beirut, New York, Sharjah, Berlin

A commission from the Performa Festival in NYC to take part in Tarek Atoui's project *Visiting Tarab* brought me to Beirut in August of 2011 to do research at a private archive of Arab classical music run by Kamal Kassar. This coming right in the middle of the overdubbing sessions for the new Terraplane CD for Enja Records, *Sky Road Songs*, presented a challenge, but this incredible opportunity was not to be missed. I took off for Frankfurt from JFK with my first flight on the new super-jumbo Airbus A380 (smooth and quiet and uneventful as it should be), three hours of layover in Frankfurt, then another three-and-a-half-hour segment to Beirut, the plane passing over the city on its approach. I was surprised to see rustic makeshift housing built right along the runway—apparently a national scandal. Guitarist Sharif Sehnaoui picked me up at the airport, and as we drove into town, he set my mind spinning with two little factoids: 1. The currency in use in daily life in Beirut is the US dollar. 2. Contrary to the prevailing public story of mutual diplomatic alienation, officials of the US and Iran met almost daily at a building pointed out to me by Sharif.

After checking in at the hotel, Sharif, Tarek, and I had a fine lunch at a streetside cafe before heading up to the archive for the first session. The foods were all familiar to me, but what was especially thrilling was the vividness of the flavors. We took a taxi to Kamal's house on the Christian side of the city, it being divided by the Green Line into Muslim and Christian sections.

Over the next three days, we had long sessions with Kamal, who presented us with a concise overview of the evolution of Arab classical music, starting with its "Golden Age" in the 1920s and its roots in the Syrian city of Aleppo. Needless to say, the musical traditions extended back hundreds and even thousands of years, but their codification and refinement began in the twentieth century. Besides lectures and discussion, Kamal presented to us well-organized listening sessions with each focusing on a specific topic: singers, small heterophonic ensembles, larger orchestras, and numerous examples of solo *taqsim* played on violin, oud, and *q'anun*. *Taqsim* are improvised, unmetered solos performed as introductions or transitions. The music was all extraordinary, but the vocalists and the oud players stood out for sheer inventiveness and outrageous technique, displaying both virtuosity and passion in equal parts. At the end, we each took back huge files of music to be used for further listening and as source material for sampling and remixing for the *Visiting Tarab* concerts.

Sharif also arranged a concert at an old silk factory, then owned by a longtime theater director, Mounir Abou Debs, who sadly passed away a couple of years after this visit. In Sharif's words: "He was the essential figure of Lebanese pre-war theater, the leading figure of a movement to modernize this art form and challenge its norms." A barn-like building made of stone, the space had wonderful acoustics and a fantastic aura. There was a garden outside for sitting, and benches and chairs inside for the audience.

Soundcheck was complicated by intermittent power outages, not unlikely in Beirut, but this had stabilized by the time of the concert. First up was the trio of Lukas Ligeti, Tarek, and myself. Lukas played drums using a trap set, Tarek used many homebuilt controllers as well as the Lemur tablet to manipulate samples on a laptop, and I had brought the solid-body eight-string processed through my laptop in Ableton Live and amplified with a silver-face Twin Reverb. We played an intense twenty-minute improvisation with kaleidoscopically shifting textures plus layered rhythms and noise. After the break, I joined The Johnny Kafta's Anti-Vegetarian Orchestra, which included Mazen Kerbaj on trumpet and objects; Charbel Haber on electric guitar; Sharif Sehnaoui on electric guitar; Raed Yassin on keyboard and electronics; Tony Elieh on electric bass; and Malek Rizkallah on drums. Charbel had a Fender Jaguar and a magic carpet covered with pedals. Sharif used a fine-sounding archtop electric and just a few effects. The music was drone-oriented and completely improvised, with lots of noise disruptions and microtonal Arabic-scale synthesizer filigree from Raed over a very heavy groove that positively glowed with a sense of location, of being Beirut in all its tragedy and beauty, exciting and hypnotic. For an encore, we played a two-chord punk song about a giant robot from manga cartoons. This song had special significance for those whose childhood coincided with the Lebanese Civil War, as the character was one of the only cartoons that was on during the limited time of electricity and even-more-limited time of broadcasts. The audience was all invited guests and friends, and extremely enthusiastic. After, Kamal hosted a gathering where the fun continued until late with delicious homemade food, wine from the B'Kaa Valley, and spontaneous performances on oud by some local masters. My last day in Beirut was spent at the archive for final talks, walking around town with Tarek, then with a final dinner with Tarek, Sharif, and Lukas at an Armenian restaurant before heading back to the airport for a flight at 3:00 a.m. to Frankfurt, a layover of a few hours, then finally a return to NYC.

Visiting Tarab continued in New York in November 2012 with a gathering of the various musicians who had either gone to Beirut to study *tarab* or received the information and soundfiles secondhand. The manifestation of our research in Beirut and Tarek's vision for an interface of Arab classical music and contemporary Western improvisation was presented in a marathon five-hour concert as part of the Performa Festival, a biennial of international performance art in many forms. Tarek organized the event in three suites, or *wasla*, with short small-group improvisations acting as segues between the longer featured segments. Underlying everything was the notion of *tarab*, which may be described as a longform development with the goal of producing ecstasy through sound. The evening opened with Tarek's high-speed, high-density piece using his self-constructed sensors and controllers to modulate a torrential flow of samples. Different artists formed a progressive transformation of sound onstage. At one point, saxophonist John Butcher, Tarek, vocalist/synthesist Robert Lowe, and I were improvising together. I'd brought my solid-body eight-string and a few pedals, with my Rat distortion and Boomerang III receiving special attention. Harpist Zeena Parkins led a group with her sister Sara on violin and Ikue Mori on electronics, which I joined for a few minutes before playing my solo piece. I performed *Ganging Tarab* on tenor sax and laptop. The acoustic sound of the horn was mic'd into the house with a send routed into the laptop, Ableton Live running a variation of the patch constructed for *Ganging the Hook* and used to convolve spatialized four-channel soundfiles prepared from samples of *taqsim* from the *Tarab* collection. In making my sound-beds, I'd concentrated on glissandi from oud and violin, often massively time-stretched or pitch-shifted down and then filtered. The saxophone envelope in the convolvers created a "ghost" of its sound in the prepared soundfiles. At the same time, I was processing the sound of the horn in real time in the patch using GRM Tools and other plug-ins, as well as allowing the acoustic sound of the horn in the room to remain in focus.

The third chapter of *Visiting Tarab* takes place in Sharjah in the United Arab Emirates, March 2012. In the afternoon on my departure day, I have a rehearsal with the ensemble Alarm Will Sound, as they will perform *Coriolis Effect* on March 19 in NYC, a process piece that transforms hocketed horizontal gestures into layered vertical drones. After the rehearsal, I have just a few minutes to do my idiot check then it's off to LGA to fly to DC to connect to my flight to Dubai. Before takeoff, the pilot of our tiny Embraer 140 jet tells us that because of weather conditions our flight will be at 6,000 feet, unusually low, and that it will be quite turbulent. There's a visible stir of consternation in the cabin as we start the trip, but the flight turns out to be quite tranquil, albeit extremely slow—nearly ninety minutes for a flight that usually takes forty. As we cross Delaware, there's an intense thunderstorm visible about ten miles to our west, with lightning flashes looking like globular thermonuclear explosions in the clouds below. The sky is clear as we approach IAD, and there's an incredible view of the planets Jupiter and Venus convergent in the evening sky. The flight to Dubai is over thirteen hours, but the time passes quickly for me in sleep, and I wake just as we're passing Turkey to continue along the Persian Gulf and catch views of the border between Iran and Iraq. I note with amusement that the plane's flight map omits any place names such as Tehran or Baghdad that might give discomfort to American travelers, only displaying small towns, obscure to those from the West. I have some apprehension about immigration and customs at Dubai airport, but except for one "steerer" who keeps asking/telling me, "Russian? Russian! Russian?" until I finally produce my US passport for his inspection, the process is fairly quick. There are many Russian visitors to the Emirates drawn by the gold markets, and there is an entire section of the airport devoted to processing their entrance. When I emerge from baggage, the driver for the festival meets me and I am soon in dense traffic heading to my hotel in Sharjah. The driver, Kutti, is from Kerala in India and has many critical observations about his hard working life in Sharjah, the emirate where many of the workers who tend to the wealthy in Dubai and Abu Dhabi and the lesser-known emirates reside. Many reunions take place that evening in the hotel lobby (location of the free wi-fi) and at breakfast the next morning: Tarek, Ikue Mori, Zeena and Sara Parkins, Defne Ayas, Lukas Ligeti, Robert Lowe, Susie Ibarra, and Roberto Rodriguez, with more to follow. We take a brief tour of the city by bus at noon on Saturday, and I go to the performance site at 6 p.m. to set up my rig and do a basic stage placement and soundcheck. Jupiter and Venus are glowing behind the stage, and the night has a damp chill with condensation rapidly appearing on any horizontal surface. For hardware I've brought a tenor sax with clip-on Beyer dynamic mic, one pedal serving as interface to the computer and preamp, and other pedals for distortion and pitch transformations. The festival has rented a new Fender Standard Stratocaster for my use in the concert, and it's quite a playable instrument though the pickups don't have much personality, vanilla-lite. Given how often baggage is delayed, if I have to play both tenor sax and guitar I'll take one as a carry-on on the plane and ask that the other be supplied by the local promoter. In this way, even if my electronics are waylaid, I can still perform a concert with what I have at hand.

The performance will be in a large enclosed courtyard in the Heritage Area near the shore of the Gulf, where wooden *dhows* and large cargo ships are docked. This was known as "the Pirate Coast" until the early twentieth century for many good reasons. For logistical purposes unknown to us, the soundchecks and rehearsal are two days in advance of the concert. A spacious stage and great crew make for a quick setup, though there's a fifteen-minute "prayer break," when the recordings of *muezzin* are played throughout the city (this begins at 5:00 a.m., making for an undesired wakeup call, and continues throughout the day). My patch is meant for a 5.1 sound system, which is not possible for this concert. Instead, I run two of the outputs into hi-fi keyboard amps onstage behind me and the other two to the house PA. The sound is not exactly as intended but still gives some of the spatiality that is an important part of the piece.

After soundcheck, I return to the hotel and run into Lukas and Robert, and we wander back toward the shore until we find Shiraz, a highly recommended Iranian restaurant where we have fantastic aubergine, kebabs, and flatbreads. An actual glass of Shiraz would have been most welcome, but Sharjah is completely dry (ironically, the Shiraz grapes originated in Iran, one of the first places where wine was produced). We cover quite a bit of territory in the town on our walk there and back. Passing through the *qasba*, I purchase a *dawa* and a package of Rio Black ground coffee so that I can cook up Turkish coffee in the kitchen of my suite, as the hotel coffee is weak in both flavor and caffeine content.

More reunions at Sunday's breakfast and a day free for working, writing, reading, and walking around Sharjah. A not-uncommon sight are huge and shiny American pickup trucks driven by men wearing *kaffiyeh* and *dishdash*. That evening, we all convene at the beach near the border with the Ajman emirate for a barbecue. Everyone is in attendance, including Raz Mesinai, KK Null, Joss Turnbull, Uriel Barthelemi, John Butcher, Takuro Mizuta, Mustafa Said, Ghassan Sahhab, Mohammed Antar, the members of Anti-Pop Consortium, Raed Yassin, filmmaker Fouad Khoury, and Kamal Kassar from the Tarab Archive in Beirut, plus our hosts and guides. The night is unseasonably cold, as there was a two-day sandstorm fueled by chilled winds from the north. Roiling waves and high wind do not at all diminish our enjoyment of this incredible Iraqi-style barbecue with huge river fish cleaned, splayed, and seasoned, then roasted directly on flat rocks placed over glowing coals. We eat the fish with flatbreads and various pickled vegetables and wash it down with hot tea. After dinner, we're told that we will "get a beer" and to get in the bus. We're driven to the emirate of Ajman, just a few kilometers up the road but a different planet. If Sharjah is Salt Lake City at its most sanctimonious, then Ajman is Sin City, Reno to the max. The bus pulls up to a high-walled compound topped by razor wire with a crimson neon sign, "Baywatch." It's a complex of bars, really brothels, the only nearby place to get a beer. The first bar, an Indian-themed place, is pathetic and depressing—three women with rigid smiles pretend to dance to ultra-loud *filmi* music on a small stage while being ogled by the men in the house. We leave quickly and head to the next joint, a Filipino bar. There's a mediocre band with four female singers in skimpy outfits playing covers by Adele and AC/DC. At least they give the appearance of having a good time playing. We're quite happy to drink a cold beer after dry Sharjah, but the bar is filled with "professional women" who are quite aggressive at soliciting overpriced beverages. We stay long enough to watch an acrobatic dance routine accompanied by the band, then return to the hotel. Nobody speaks in the bus heading back.

On concert day, we assemble in the late afternoon and are bussed to the venue to build up our equipment on the stage and do line checks. There's a prayer break to throw off the sked and then a brief reception with snacks and juice and speeches. At 2015 the marathon *wasla* begins with Tarek's manic solo performance, hands flying on his controllers and sensors as waves of sound fill the air. There's a huge range in concept to the sets, including prepared compositions by individuals and groups as well as ad hoc combinations programmed by Tarek. A notable trio is that of Mustafa Said, Ghassan Sahhab, and Mohammed Antar, who perform in the classical style on *ney*, oud, and *q'anun* but take the music *very* out into pure sound—truly exciting. I perform the twenty-minute *Ganging Tarab* on tenor sax convolving my collage of oud glissandi—it's dark and has a very slow buildup to the climax with altissimo saxophone overtones and high-density sonics from the computer. As it finishes, I'm joined by Tarek and percussionists Uriel, Raz, and Lukas for four additional minutes of orgiastic playing. Later, with guitar I join *q'anun* player Ghassan for a delicate duet and then improvise with Ikue, Zeena, and Sara. The *wasla* continues non-stop until 2 a.m., finishing with Anti-Pop Consortium's mix of hip-hop with Arab music and noise. We return to the hotel, where I change and pack then join a few of the others for a pickup at 5:30 for the Dubai airport. There I catch a six-hour flight to Munich and then a short one to Berlin.

Arriving at my hotel after the night's journey, I have time only for a quick shower and double espresso, then I'm picked up by Reinhold Friedl for rehearsal with Zeitkratzer of my composition *Oneirika* at a spacious studio in the Festspielhaus (site of previous Berlin Jazz Festival appearances). The ensemble had arrived earlier and set up exactly in the form of the performance, including the same mixing desk and monitors that would be used for our performance at the Berghain, a legendary and mammoth dance club. Having completed their soundcheck before I arrived, the ensemble goes out to smoke and drink coffee while I set up my horn and electronics, as well as tune up a Stratocaster belonging to Reinhold. Before we begin playing, we discuss various aspects of the 47'33" piece, especially how to approach the sections using graphic notation.

The composition's title refers to dream states, and the piece pays homage to that beautifully ambiguous state of unreality existing in the transition between sleeping and waking. MaerzMusik this particular year also honors the John Cage centenary, and when the piece was commissioned by Matthias Osterwold, he mentioned that somehow paying tribute to Cage would be most welcome. As a result, I'd made the opening section four minutes and thirty-three seconds in length, and the "thirty-three" duration recurs throughout. The score has through-composed elements that segue into sections that use graphics created by manipulating the score images in Photoshop using techniques developed in the creation of *Foliage*. These are the most Cagean elements in the piece—while the graphics supply a

Figure 17 Score excerpt, *Oneirika* (1998). Premiered by Zeitkratzer at Maerzmusik Berlin 2014.

certain degree of indeterminacy, they are not license for the players to do whatever they would like. Rather, they are to expand upon the composed elements that precede and follow them with the contours and sounds played in a manner defined by the shapes and textures of the images. This requires both great restraint and great abandon, and the Zeitkratzer players are all expert at this. There are also conducted portions within the sections where I can retrigger subgroups of the players in nested tempi, as well as cueing expansions, solos, and group dynamic changes. We make good progress over the three-hour session and then run through the piece again in the evening. Berlin is most definitely not a "dry" region, so Reinhold and I discuss the evening's rehearsal over a bottle of Bordeaux and dinner at an Italian restaurant in Kreuzberg. While the trip to Sharjah was a unique and valuable experience, I am quite happy to feel "at home" again in Berlin.

We convene in the afternoon the next day at the rehearsal room for a final run-through of the piece. I continue to refine various aspects of how the players approach the composed material, the graphics, and their personal sonic vocabulary, as well as the niceties of how I will conduct the various sections and deal with transitions. I welcome the manifestation of the players' individual personalities, though certain sections of the piece require specific approaches, especially the avoidance of "pure" musical tones—even when completely predetermined pitches are required, I prefer the players modulate them with noise from air, throat, bow, fingers. On occasion, a rare "pure" tone provides a contrast.

Setup and soundcheck and another run-through complete with additional tweaks take place at the Berghain on the next afternoon. The venue is a huge disco built in an old power plant and featuring techno and house music. It's notorious both for its state-of-the-art sound equipment and its omnisexual "dark rooms" in the basement, as well as facilities providing for all physical needs of its visitors. Sybarites from around the world are known to fly to Berlin and go directly to the Berghain for an entire weekend, where they indulge in relentless partying, sleeping wherever they drop, and never stepping outside until their departure. The "new music" audience for the MaerzMusik concerts is decidedly more staid than the usual Berghain crowd, and only the main room is in use on this evening (with the sold-out crowd seated in neat rows). The first set is Zeitkratzer's performance of a graphic score by Column One in which they simulate fully electronic sounds. After a brief intermission, we run *Oneirika* down, our best version yet. Drums, especially Maurice deMartin's two giant bass drums, sound absolutely monstrous when pumped through the Berghain sound system. The arc is completed in a flash, and the audience responds. Many friends in attendance to greet after the set and then a long and enjoyable post-toast'em at the bar. I'm back at the hotel around 3:00 a.m. to change and pack, and at 5:00 I head to TXL and my flights to Munich, then NYC.

In retrospect, I can't help but compare the impulses of *tarab* to that of the approach taken with a piece such as *Oneirika*. Aside from the explicit Arab influences in terms of techniques and microtonal scales used by many of the musicians in *Visiting Tarab*, the process of creating a sonic manifestation is not that different. There are many ways to define the goal of musicmaking, but I always return to the notion of psychoacoustic chemical change. With *tarab*, the goal is an ecstatic state. This is rarely considered to be what we are striving for in groups such as Zeitkratzer or in my various projects, but I would never say that this is *not* part of the reason why we make these sounds. Various states can coexist simultaneously, just as our minds continuously operate on a number of levels, defined not by separation but by porosity, continuous feedback and modulation.

29

Incident in Catania, 1999

It's already 10:30 in the morning and I've been waiting for C, the promoter, to pick me up at the hotel. I'm getting nervous, as he's already thirty minutes late—not unusual for Sicily, but still significant to an American mind installed in a body with a flight to catch.

We'd had a pretty heated argument before my set the night before. The agent in Rome who'd arranged this gig set the terms out to me very clearly: I was guaranteed a minimum fee for the performance against a percentage of the door, plus all travel costs and my hotel. I'd heard some stories from other musicians about C, so when we first met at the airport I requested that I get the guarantee and expenses before my performance, to which he said, "We'll see" while shaking his head "no." I was the headliner with the popular trumpeter Roy Paci opening with his band, so the place would be packed.

C had some very likable qualities, but I didn't necessarily trust him to come through to the letter of the agreement. On my arrival at Catania in Sicily, he had picked me up at the airport and brought me to his home for a delicious lunch of *triglia* (red mullet) cooked by his wife. They then drove me to Palermo for my concert that night, with C riding shotgun and complaining about his wife's driving the entire time. The next day we returned to Catania in time for a late lunch of more *triglia* and had a fine time discussing the music in various scenes around the world, about all of which C was quite knowledgeable.

After soundcheck, I again brought up my request for advance payment, and now we had a standoff: C would not give me the money, and I told him that I would not play unless I was paid the guarantee first. Back at the club, Roy's set had finished, and I quietly told C that without cash in hand, I would be returning to the hotel. This was a gamble as I had to rely on C to get me to the airport the next morning, because the hotel was quite a distance from town. All of a sudden, he stormed out of the dressing room with a scowl on his face—but soon returned with a grin and stuffed a wad in my shirt pocket. *Molto bene*. He told me that I was a "hard guy," which I took as a compliment. I played a long and fiery set, plus a generous encore. After, C handed me another wad of cash and brought me to the hotel, so all seemed good.

Standing in the parking lot, I'm a touch worried as I entertain the notion that C might be holding a grudge and stand me up, but he finally arrives twenty minutes later. As always, I've intentionally built in a significant margin for error, and soon enough I am at the check-in counter for Alpi Eagles in the Catania airport for my flight to Venezia. The agent's head is bowed into his terminal as he's typing in my ticket and passport information. He pauses and glances up at me. A moment later I'm distracted by a cloud of stink. The breath reaches me before any sound is uttered: an unholy mix of coffee, garlic, beer, and bad dental hygiene. This short, stout man in *carabinieri* uniform has his hand on my shoulder and is somehow both muttering and barking in my ear in dialect, with a few Italian words thrown in, a greeting that I instinctively understand to mean "come with us." He's accompanied by two others in airport police uniforms. I play the dumb American and say loudly in English, "I do not speak Italian." This time I'm told in Italian, "Come with us." I repeat my previous answer. Now, another gentleman wearing a badly fitted brown suit joins the party and says in English, "Come with us."

I ask what the problem is and am rejoindered once again with "Come with us." I refuse to budge and ask for the supervisor. Now a smiling man in a shiny polyester suit emerges from the airline office and says, "Please go with them, it will only be five minutes, there's a problem with your ticket." I ask what the problem is and am met with a sorry half-smile and a shake "no." Time for Plan B: make lots of noise: "I travel all over the world as a professional musician without any problems, Russia, Macedonia, Japan, Canada, fly on every airline, every country, no problems, I'm not going anywhere until I have some information—just tell me what is the problem." A crowd is gathering and people are staring . . . a scene (which is what I was hoping for). Now, yet another man with a brown suit—Mr. Good Cop, smiling, *sotto voce*. "PLEASE come with us—it is really no problem—just two minutes."

At this point, there is no choice, since the goons have already grabbed my cases from the belt and the suits have me surrounded and are holding my arms, gently but still insistent. Time to take the path of least resistance. I'm brought through the barriers into the sanctum sanctorum, the airport police station. Four youngish cops with pot bellies dressed in suits of various pastel shades lurk in the office, looking like *Miami Vice* wannabees. They're all quite surly and demand my passport, wallet, cell phone. One of them begins disparate questioning about what I am doing there, over and over, the same questions to no seeming end. They've opened all of my cases. One points to my guitar: "What is that? A guitar?" "Yes, that is a guitar." I bring out the concert posters, newspaper articles, and my ace-in-the-hole, this week's *Sicily* "culture" magazine, with the often-used picture by Andreas Sterzing on the cover of me in profile with my hand on my head. I show them the magazine: "See, this is who I am, and this is what I do." They take it from me, examine it for a minute and bark, "Take off your shirt!" What? "Take off your shirt!" I comply. "You have no tattoos!" "Yes, I have no tattoos," I answer as I wonder what they're hinting at. They point to the picture and have apparently interpreted the shadows on my neck from my upheld arm as tattoos. Now I'm barraged from all sides with questions: "Where do I live? Do I have friends at the airport? Where have I been in Sicily?" . . . Lots of typing into a teletype terminal.

After about thirty minutes of this, I'm left alone and told to sit. I ask if I can contact Massimo Ongaro in Venice, the promoter of this evening's concert who will be waiting for my arrival. This request is refused. Shortly after, a woman from the airline comes in and introduces herself to me as Linda and expresses concern. She's dignified and professional, speaks excellent English, is blonde and Swedish, and she's very tall. She has a dialogue in Italian with the cops, who seem somewhat intimidated by her, "What are you doing with my passenger?!?" and then turns to me: "They are very confused as to how you got here." Well, why didn't they ask? I give her my Alitalia ticket receipt for Roma-Catania. Rolling her eyes to me as she gives it to them, she turns back and whispers in my ear that they are very stupid and not to worry as my flight is delayed due to fog. She says she will return, which she does about thirty minutes later, thirty minutes spent in sheer silence—I'm not even allowed to take a book from my bag (plus my laptop has been confiscated).

Now she has another conference with the police, and she fills me in: "It seems that someone also on this flight has the same name as you, as it turns out, not really the same name, his surname is Ilio and yours is Sharp, but the police here will take no chances. This Ilio character may or may not have used a credit card (stolen? no, just not sure) to purchase a ticket, just like you did." In any case, it must be determined whether or not I am who I purport to be, passport and other ID be damned, otherwise I cannot leave Sicily. They still seem very interested in the question of the absent tattoos. She leaves again and there is dead silence in the little room, punctuated only with the sound of desultory tapping on the teletype keyboard.

This relative silence gives me the opportunity for a brief digression into the realm of contemporary noir literature and my most enthusiastic recommendation for the Aurelio Zen novels by the author Michael Dibdin (now tragically departed from our material plane). I give thanks to my old buddy David Torn for introducing me to Dibdin's writing. I have read them all and am devastated that there will not be another. Aurelio Zen is a high-ranking police detective from Venezia: intelligent but not necessarily smart, a little bumbling, world-weary, cynical. He's not really corrupt, but not really honest either, a harsh realist who has been somewhat beaten down by reality. Each book takes place in a different locale within the country and references local cuisine, wines, and practices. The stories are dark, hilarious, and sometimes horrifying. After spending a fair amount of time in Italy, they seem to smack of reality in the same way that, while riding on the train in 1983 during my first tour in Italy, I realized that Fellini was a documentarian, certainly not the surrealist that he was portrayed as in American media.

Reading the Aurelio Zen novels has perhaps prepared me for this little excursion into the labyrinthian world of the Italian police, devoid of logic. One must balance cooperation with a certain reserve, explore the possibility of floating above temporary irritations with a detached smile. Of course, one must also prepare for the possibility of spending an indeterminate length of time in a Sicilian jail until everything is clarified or, my first thought, being asked for a large amount of cash in whatever currency is available to expedite the clearing of my name. I was not planning to offer anything, but I would have been willing to pay a dear price for my immediate freedom.

Another forty minutes pass. Linda returns again to check on my progress and has told me that, fortunately, the flight will be delayed by yet another two hours thanks to the heavy fog in Venice. She asks the police a few questions, leaves, and time is suspended again as the teletype clicks away. Then something must have come in over the wire, because suddenly there are whispers, glances exchanged, papers passed hand to hand. The air has changed: light floods the room, birds are singing, everybody is friendly and joking. "You are *famoso*! Do you like Sicily? Do you like the food? Do you like

Italian girls? Do you sing?" Papers and forms come flying out of the printer. "You must sign, here, here, here, here, here . . . " Many copies all stamped with ornate and official-looking imprints. Linda from the airline returns. She must also sign everything. Now all is good in this corner of the world. "Please come visit us in the office next time. We will have a coffee. Do you like Italian coffee?" Linda bumps me up to First Class for the flight to Venezia and gives me vouchers for lunch in the airport and a very nice bottle of wine as a present. She apologizes for the boys, and we say *arrivederci*.

I've saved the foreshadowing for the end: When I arrived at Catania airport from Roma on the preceding Wednesday, we deplaned onto the tarmac where our baggage, removed from the plane, was placed in a row. We were to grab our things and walk to the terminal past a "receiving line." A swarthy and corpulent officer with mirror shades was standing near the entrance holding a German shepherd on a leash. He glanced up, stepped directly into the pathway, and thrust the dog at me. I ignored this obvious impugning of my character, as did the dog, and I passed into the terminal, amusing thoughts about stereotypes and airport police fleeting through my mind. "Glad I got that out of the way right at the beginning."

30

From the Italian Academy to Miami Beach

December 2004 begins with a sweep across the sonic spectrum, commencing December 1 at the Italian Academy in NYC near Columbia University with the world premiere by Jenny Lin of *Oligosono*, a piece for piano composed during a brief teaching residency at Dartmouth College earlier that year. The title means "a few sounds" and makes use of extended techniques, plus a limited palette of melodic cells that may be recombined in permutations inspired by genetic processes to create continuously shifting sequences.

Returning from a festival in Rome the previous day has given me only a little time to rest and to get re-acquainted with my Pavoni espresso machine. The three kilograms of espresso beans I purchased in Rome made it through the purgatory of checked baggage and has been put to good use in the relative paradise of my studio. A pre-concert talk is scheduled for 7 p.m., and we're introduced by the director of the Italian Academy, Rick Whitaker. The discussion ranges freely around the varied syntax and vocabulary of my compositions, Jenny's involvement with new music, and background material including my tortured relationship with the piano as a child. It turns out that the first public performances on piano for both Jenny and myself were at Carnegie Recital Hall—mine in 1958 as part of a group recital of the students of Ms. Joan Mayer in which I played Liszt's *Hungarian Rhapsody No. 2*. I can still remember the two mistakes I made, though the performance was exhilarating and much less traumatic than the pressure of preparing for it.

In discussing *Oligosono*, I refer to the processes at work in such compositions as *Tessalation Row*, *SyndaKit*, and *Quarks Swim Free*, all of which made use of modules ranging from one to four bars in length that are looped and recombined in a bio-morphological approach, but also allowing spontaneous disruptions, mutations, and extrapolations. Extended techniques in *Oligosono* include an overtone sweep created by sliding the index finger (or in the case of clusters, multiple fingers) pressed on the strings as a shifting mute while striking the keys for the chosen strings with the other hand to produce a cascade of harmonics. Another technique was having the pianist play the notes directly on the strings near the keyboard with the sustain pedal down. On which strings this would be played is dependent on the construction of the piano soundboard and where there is a gap between support struts. Finally, when there are repetitive ostinati with the sustain pedal, I've found that using alternating fingers produces more saturated overtones than playing the given riff with one hand.

The hall is opulent and ornate, with dry acoustics that reveal detail. I would have appreciated the benefits of a bit more room reverberation for *Oligosono* but still, the space did justice to the piece. Of course, the most important element was the musicianship of Jenny Lin. She's a phenomenal pianist in every way. Her incredible musicality and probing intellect are enhanced by her sheer technique and jaw-dropping endurance. At the end of the concert, I enjoyed the slight irony of playing in a very low-tech squat in Bologna on Sunday with rain dripping from the ceiling, a slick jazz club in Rome on Monday, and the luxurious Italian Academy at home in NYC on Wednesday.

Alanna Heiss is a vital creative force in New York City and was the visionary founder of the PS1 Contemporary Art Center in Long Island City and the Clocktower Gallery in lower Manhattan. One of her dreams was to create a radio station. This dovetailed nicely with the advent of faster internet service at the end of the last century, making web radio a reality. I was brought on as Curator for Contemporary Music to help make this happen, and eventually WPS1 Art Radio opened its studio in the Clocktower. WPS1 documented art happenings throughout the City and initiated various Clocktower events that could be live-streamed. For WPS1, I had curated and recorded a number of episodes of a show titled *Sonorama*. Now, they would be called podcasts. Some were playlists with specific themes, including Ethiopian music, noise, algorithmic processes, synthesizer pioneers; some were dedicated to specific composers such as James Tenney, Harry Partch, and Iannis Xenakis; and some were interviews. A highlight was watching Tenney prepare a piano brought into the MOMA for his performance of Cage's *Sonatas and Interludes for Prepared Piano*. As part of my role at WPS1, I would also join the crew at the Art Basel Miami Beach December 3–5, 2004, both to perform some of my own work and to do live *Sonorama* broadcasts.

I'm up at 4:00 to caffeinate and take care of correspondence then catch a car to LGA for my flight to Miami. Florida still weighs in my consciousness as that dreaded place responsible for the unholy collaboration of Supreme Court and "Brooks Brothers Rioters" resulting in the coup d'etat that ushered in the era of Bush 2. Writing this now in 2024, it's shocking to see how much influence Florida politics in all its reactionary glory has had on the American dialogue. Still, the whole country seems to have moved in a reactionary direction, with the faux populism of the Trump Republicans' victory in the 2024 election looking to end the democracy experiment and plunge the US into a disinformation-fueled fascism. I'm hoping to be proven wrong.

Our plane is second in line for take-off when we suddenly turn and head back to the gate, where two uniformed men enter the plane and escort off an unruly passenger. He was seated in the rear and I in the front so I didn't catch exactly what had transpired, but it was clear that the pilot wanted him off and the passengers in the rear applauded at his removal. Back in line and twenty-five minutes later we're in the air.

Art Basel Miami Beach is a giant schmooze-fest for artists, galleries, and collectors, but there are also alternative festivals and exhibitions operating in parallel including Scope, Position, and NADA for the many art world denizens operating outside of the mainstream. At the time of this trip, the Miami art scene is booming, with many young and enthusiastic practitioners and supportive collectors with money to burn. WPSI has set up a quick-and-dirty remote unit in a cabana poolside at the "fabulous" Delano Hotel designed by Phillip Starck. There's an Alice-in-Wonderland quality to the decor of the lobby and library with oversized chairs and couches and tall drapes. I find a certain absurdity in this whole scene, but I can also appreciate the ambience and enjoy being able to sit outside in the balmy Miami air when twenty-four hours before I was freezing in rainy NYC. One of the many contradictions of operating in the art world is finding a way to reconcile the necessity of acceding to the reality of both market forces and corporate largesse setting the deeper agenda. In that regard, the Delano has generously offered a complimentary bar tab to WPSI to keep its operations lubricated and to offer libations to the many art world luminaries who will visit the station for short interviews. Roy Lichtenstein arrived for an interview, gracious and warm.

In the pool itself, there is a powerful underwater audio system for which I've programmed an installation titled *Soundpool*, consisting of a selection of tracks all having titles associated with water.

The *Soundpool* Playlist

Genggong Batur Sari—"Frog Song," Alice Coltrane—"Blue Nile," Morton Feldman—*Atlantis*, John Barry—"Three Little Fishes," Richard Wagner—*Das Rheingold*, Wayne Shorter—*Water Babies*, Bun-Ching Lam—*Like Water*, Tod Dockstader—"Water Music, Part 3," Salim Al' Nur—"Inspired By The Two Rivers," Bernard Herrmann—"Beneath the 12-Mile Reef 3," Esquivel!—"*Surfboard*," Elliott Sharp—*Spring & Neap*, Dick Dale—"Tidal Wave," Sun Ra—"Atlantis," *Side* 2, Tod Dockstader—"Water Music, Part 6," John Lee Hooker—"The Waterfront," Iannis Xenakis—*Mists*, Tectonics—"Dadastream," Bernard Herrmann—"Beneath the 12-Mile Reef 1," Jimi Hendrix—"Moon, Turn The Tides," Blectum From Blechdom—"Sea Slurpent Sloop," Joe Meek—"Glob Waterfall," John Fahey—*The Mill Pond*, Jeff Greinke—"River Limba," Sun Ra—"Atlantis," *Side* 1, David Behrman—*On the Other Ocean*

I've been given two three-hour slots on each of the three days to present *Sonorama* as well as to perform my ambient microphone piece *Living Room*, plus some brief electric guitar/computer improvisations that I'm titling as installments of *Serf Music for the New Feudal Era*. *Living Room* is vastly different from its usual environment, the more sterile settings of gallery or theater. At the Delano pool, the microphone picks up splashing, shouting, laughter, and even some heckling, making for a much richer sound field that enters into the feedback system. The live improvisations under the *Serf Music* umbrella are abstractions with a beat, paying only oblique reference to surf music (but referential nonetheless). After my last set on the fifth, I pack up and head to the airport and home to NYC.

Sonorama Playlists

Dec. 3: Gordon Mumma—"Epifont," Robert Pete Williams—"Death Blues," Public Enemy—"Son of a Bush," James Tenney—"Collage #1 ('Blue Suede')," Skip James—"Hard Times Killing Floor Blues," Michiyo Yagi—"Talking Durian," Albert Ayler—"New Ghosts," Simon Shaheen—*Turath*, Hugo Chavez—"El Oraculo del Guerrero, Remix." Interspersed are three versions of *Living Room* and three of *Serf Music*.

Dec. 4: Willie Dixon—"Pie in the Sky," Banda Polyphony—"Linda Music

1," Othar Turner—"Late at Midnight, Just a Little 'fore Day," Karlheinz Stockhausen—"Studie Elektronische 1," Bernard Herrmann—"Klaatu," Tran Quang Hai—*Guimbardes du Monde*, "Tuva! Tuva!," Sun Ra—"Journey through Outer Darkness," Balinese Jawharp Orchestra—"Katak Ngongkek," Michiyo Yagi—"Seawall 1," Edgard Varèse—*Octandre*. Interspersed are three versions of *Living Room* (one of which is interrupted by a bizarre-sounding computer crash) and three of *Serf Music*.

Dec. 5: Bus Ratch—"Con," Robert Pete Williams—"A Thousand Miles From Nowhere," Neil Young—"Dead Man Theme," Gyorgi Ligeti—*Chamber Concerto*, "III. Movimento preciso e meccanico," Bernard Herrmann—"Fire Engine," from *Fahrenheit* 451, Willie Dixon—"Dead Presidents," John Fahey—"Desperate Man Blues," Miles Davis—"Black Satin," John Lee Hooker—"Misbelieving Baby," Bernard Herrmann—"Flamethrower," from *Fahrenheit* 451, Turgun Alimatov—*Ouzbekistan*, "Nawa," Willie Dixon—"It Don't Make Sense If You Can't Make Peace," Olivier Messiaen—"La grive des bois." Interspersed are three versions of *Living Room* and three of *Serf Music*.

31

Soviet Jazz

1982: a solo gig in Philadelphia and late return by train. It's 3 a.m. and I emerge from the filthy passages of Penn Station, at that time populated heavily by homeless people, to 7th Avenue to hail a taxi. Guitar and soprano sax cases are slung over my shoulder, bass clarinet is in one hand, and a bag of electronics in the other. A cab pulls over and I load everything in. As we roll out, the driver addresses me in a thick Russian accent: "You are musician. I, too, am musician. I play violin." " . . . and what music do you play?" I ask. "I play classic . . . but in Soviet Union, they FORCE me to play jazz."

1989: Mother Russia! Thanks to the organizational work of Artemy Troitsky, author of a history of the Soviet underground rock scene titled *Back in the* USSR, and Antanas Gustys, a Lithuanian music promoter, the opportunity appeared to make a brief tour in the Soviet Union in August of 1989. Our ad hoc group, Frame, would consist of Ned Rothenberg on reeds, Tom Cora on cello, Berlin-based drummer Peter Hollinger, and me on double-neck guitarbass, bass clarinet, and electronics. The idea was thrilling, as the ritual actions from the previous six years of intense touring had become somewhat predictable, and I was itching for something different. Not that I didn't love performing on the Wurst Circuit, but for an American improvising musician, the idea of touring Russia was filled with exciting mystery and many unknowns. Growing up during the Cold War, my daily life was filled with the threat of nuclear annihilation, with a hammer and sickle trademark plastered to the ICBMs that would vaporize us. They would "bury us," screamed the right wingers agreeing with Khrushchev's histrionic performative gesture. While I was skeptical of both American and Communist propaganda, I wanted to see it for myself. All four of my grandparents originated near Ukraine's Odessa, part of the Soviet empire, but departed at the threat of death in the pogroms of 1905 and 1917. A favored album during my senior year in high school was *Charles Lloyd in the Soviet Union*, in which the musically expansive quartet with Keith Jarrett, Ron McClure, and Jack deJohnette were greeted with an ecstatic response by the audience in Talinn, Estonia. European musician friends described touring in the Soviet Union in pretty much the same way we thought of touring everywhere: you might be pampered in a five-star hotel and performing on a grand stage on one day, and the next day the gig is in an unheated warehouse with a jerry-rigged sound system and, afterward, sleeping on the floor upstairs.

From a rendezvous near Peter Hollinger's apartment in Berlin's Kreuzberg quarter, we headed over to the legendary Checkpoint Charlie, where we presented our documents for cursory appraisal and then walked through to East Berlin, a surprisingly simple and efficient process. We were met on the other side of the Wall by a local colleague of Antanas's, who transported us in an ancient van to the East German airport, Schönefeld. There, we waited with our equipment in what seemed like a cattle pen in a cavernous hangar until released after showing documents, dragging our gear, to the next cattle pen. This process repeated itself multiple times until we eventually found ourselves at our penultimate goal, the check-in kiosk. Visas and passports demanded and examined, then we were cleared to board the plane. Visible through the hangar doors was our ride, a 1970s vintage Ilyushin IL86 looking like a Boeing 707 that had been overinflated until it formed a bloated caricature of a jetliner. We schlepped our baggage up the stairs and into the plane, where it was stowed by crew members in various cabinets. The aisles were filled with lounging dogs and television sets in cardboard boxes and the open overhead bins were packed to overflowing. We took off slowly but surely, the plane rattling along the runway until aloft. Once in the air, surly flight attendants hid in their rest areas and smoked, emerging only to pass out meals: plastic boxes with gray meat and gray cheese and gray bread accompanied by *limonata* of a sickly yellow color that hinted at an origin in the radioactive wilds of Chernobyl. The four-hour flight to Moscow's Sheremetyevo Airport seemed to take much longer, but finally, we arrived.

Our baggage was returned to us at the plane, and we dragged it into the receiving area. Passing through customs and immigration in Moscow was far easier and much more welcoming than entering Canada or even returning to our beloved Homeland. We were waved through with passports quickly stamped and then told to sit on nearby benches. The all-pervasive soundtrack to the airport was cheesy electronic disco with a relentless beat overlaid with synthesized minor-key arpeggios. The music conveyed a sense of nostalgia for something that had not yet arrived, a suitable accompaniment to the uncertain comings and goings in a Russian airport. After forty minutes or so, we were met by a group of three people, all widely grinning, one of whom was our host and tour manager, Antanas Gustys from Vilnius. He told us to wait while he ran off, returning thirty minutes later to shepherd us out to a paved area and into a parked yellow school bus that he had hired. We bounced over dirt roads, empty lots, and hard-crusted turf, a short cut (or perhaps the only route) to Moscow's domestic airport, Domodedovo. We had some time to kill and wandered about the hall with more of that same cheesy disco ambience coloring the air. An interesting attraction was a little booth with turntables and cassette decks where people could purchase made-to-order bootleg mix tapes of international pop and classical music. The proprietor had a huge library at his disposal, which sparked my curiosity as to how he obtained it and whether or not this was an "official" store or private enterprise. He spoke no English, or at least was not willing to share any information. We headed to the gate and soon boarded an iconic Tupelov 154 for the first stop on our itinerary: Vilnius, Lithuania. The Tupelov roared down the runway and, fortunately, skyward, sounding like a giant chest of loose iron chains as its monstrous turbofans belched dark smoke and shook the aged hardware.

That first evening in Vilnius was free, and we sampled some surprisingly tasty borscht and vegetables and enjoyed the sunset over the space-age brutalist architecture of the modern part of town, where we were ensconced in a poured-concrete hotel. The next day was spent strolling through the old and new parts of the city. A shop window caught my eye with its display of a gaudy four-pickup Jolana electric twelve-string guitar.

Finally, it was time to load in at the concert venue, a brightly lit town hall with a huge and elaborate crystal chandelier dominating the center. On stage were towering Tesla amplifiers—a promising sight, though the reality was quite disappointing. With all controls dimed and all of my effects at their peak output, the amp produced a sound not unlike an anemic table radio. Cellist Tom Cora was dragging along his own power amp, a weighty beast, but at least he could count on it for volume. A huge transformer was situated in the center of the stage to provide 110 volts for Tom's and Ned's equipment. I had brought my own transformer because of past touring experiences with questionable electricity. In this instance, as soon as the local iron was plugged in, it went up in a blast of noxious green smoke. We vacated the hall, and there was a lengthy wait while the air cleared and another transformer was found somewhere in town. With a huge cheer from the patient crowd, the concert was then able to proceed.

Our overriding esthetic was atonal rock and jazz with a fractured groove. No Wave could be considered a solid reference, but given Peter's Teutonic beat, its geographical center was situated closer to Berlin than the East Village. The quartet framed solos and duos in various permutations.

From Vilnius to Riga, Latvia, we boarded what should have been a short flight on an ancient Antonov prop plane that looked to be a hardy survivor of The Great War. The spartan interior held seats with threadbare cushions, and there were red curtains on elastic bands at the windows. As we made our takeoff run, the babushkas sitting in the rear crossing themselves fervently, I watched a man on a bicycle pedaling furiously next to us waving a red kerchief. The thought crossed my mind that this might have been a salute to the heroic pilots of Aeroflot, except for the white smoke that was pouring out of the right-hand engine. The plane stopped and returned to the terminal, but we did not disembark. Instead, we sat on the tarmac in the ninety-degree heat for nearly two hours while two men in overalls on a ladder poked at and around the engine, occasionally banging with a hammer. This did not inspire confidence. Finally, the pilot emerged from the cockpit, five feet tall and wearing an overcoat down to his ankles festooned with a grand selection of medals and ribbons. His Soviet aviator's cap had a brim nearly as wide as his shoulders. He looked directly at us and said with finality, "Kaput!" We exited the plane and returned to the terminal, which closely resembled a small-town bus station, and headed to the bar. Taking our cue from the various pilots and other representatives of the population one might find at an airport, we drank vodka and enjoyed another round of cheesy electronic disco. Finally, after about two hours, our flight was once again ready to depart. We were relieved to find that it was a different plane—our previous vessel now was decorated with red ribbons, which I assumed was to prevent another pilot from taking off in it and not a celebration. We were set to go. The babushkas resumed their gesticulations, we held our breath, and off we went to Riga.

Whether because of a lack of available hotel rooms or budget issues, we bivouacked at the spacious house of the organizers of our Riga concert. There was a continuously augmented pot of bread soup for our meals, with an occasional lonely bean floating tranquilly in the murk. The next day we wandered around this strikingly beautiful city, and at one point sampled *kvass*, a beverage made from slightly fermented bread. One metal cup suffices for all who will partake: the cup is rinsed in a pot of cold water between rounds. Walking in the market, we were surprised to find a political demonstration with perhaps thirty people carrying posters with portraits of Hitler and Stalin linked with an equal sign. Even though Stalin was long dead and out of favor, it was still extremely surprising to find such an overt counter-government expression.

That evening we went to visit the band Zga in their tiny rehearsal studio on the outskirts of town. Their homemade equipment took up most of the space, and it was like a recombinant genetics experiment—something between a plumbing supply warehouse, an Erector set, and a Heathkit radio lab. Metal tubes and rods had contact microphones affixed in various places and routed to a primitive mixer. For their rehearsals, everything played was monitored exclusively in headphones. This provided sonic intimacy as well as preventing any curious neighbors from overhearing potentially subversive sonics. We donned headphones and listened to their fantastic music: organic, bubbly, chunky, jagged, metallic. To return to the hotel, Antanas attempted to hail a taxi, speaking in the "official" language of Russian, with no success—nobody would take us. Finally, he switched to Lithuanian, and we immediately found a willing driver.

Our concert the next evening, as in Vilnius, was held in an extravagant and decadently decorated town hall with good acoustics. It seemed as if the same weak Tesla amps had followed us from Vilnius. No, they were local, but sounded equally wretched. Still, we played with fervor, and the audience demanded more. The next day we returned to Vilnius in a train built neither for comfort nor speed. There were no seats, just berths, essentially shelves. The six-hour trip took the same length of time as our flight to Riga, given the complications that we had encountered, but this journey was fortunately uneventful.

After a free day, we found ourselves taking a midnight flight from Vilnius to Kyiv on another well-worn propellor plane that had managed to survive the events of the 1940s. We made sure to prepare ourselves with proper lubrication at dinner, then made our way, again via rented school bus, to the airport where Antanas supervised our check-in, cheesy electronic disco music, as always, providing the soundtrack. The Aeroflot representative, a woman with a grim countenance and the air of one who had been a victorious commander at the battle of Stalingrad, sported a permanent sneer and the hostile demeanor to accompany it. She was Russian, Antanas was Lithuanian, and an antagonistic relationship was automatically assured. They began arguing over our checked baggage, the discussion at top volume and lasting over thirty minutes. It was first determined that we had too much baggage and we would not be permitted to take it all. In the final installment of the argument, the baggage would be allowed, but there would be a charge. Defeated, Antanas turned to us and said that he was sorry but we would have to pay, there was nothing more to be done, we would have to eat the loss. The total cost in US currency: $4.00. Lasting nearly three hours, the flight was deafeningly loud and persistently shaky. We landed in Kyiv at 3 a.m. and rolled up to the darkened terminal, no lights visible outside either. Our equipment was pushed out of the cargo door of the plane, falling ten feet down to the dark tarmac in a magnificent symphony of clunks and crashes. Arriving by taxi at the similarly unlit Inter Hotel, we were forced to bang on the front doors for fifteen minutes before we were finally let in. The walls of the stifling rooms were crawling with thumb-sized dark roaches and there was no hot water.

The next morning we met our smiling hosts, Alexander and Katja, both fluent in English. Antanas leaned in close to me and whispered with a smile, "KGB." They were to stick close by us during our entire time in Kyiv. Katja took us on a tour of the city, reciting a memorized spiel with all of the emotion of a protein robot. The only time I witnessed a disturbance of her perfectly glazed persona was when, after she described a functioning Orthodox cathedral, I asked if there were also synagogues in Kyiv and she flushed a deep red and retorted angrily, "Of course, there are synagogues here! There are many!" I've long considered myself to be an atheist, but the thought of my grandparents escaping the pogroms urged me to make this query.

Antanas informed us that we had places reserved for lunch that afternoon at the hotel restaurant. Arriving at the scheduled time, we stood at the dining room entrance while negotiations proceeded: Antanas displaying the paper with our prepaid reservations and the tuxedoed maître d' firmly stating over and over, "Nicht platz!" with his arms crossed. After enduring this impasse for a few long minutes, Antanas reached into his pocket for some hard currency, and the ambience changed drastically. The door swung open, and the smiling overlord of dining gestured expansively to welcome us, after which another tuxedoed gentleman brought us to our table in the huge and completely empty dining room. More tourism followed during the afternoon, with a high point being a funicular ride to the historic Upper Town where we enjoyed a dramatic view of the Dnieper River. That evening, there was a "special dinner" being held in our honor by a local restaurant, where we would be served the city's signature dish, Chicken Kyiv. The modern hall was illuminated by black light and highlighted by colored neon. Cheesy electronic disco in a minor key at high volume filled the air, drowning out all possibility of conversation and lending an uncertain festivity to the occasion.

We had been given a driver for our two days in Kyiv. He had a huge grin seemingly permanently plastered to his face. In fact, "plastered" might have been an apt description for his general state of being, as he exhibited a grand aura of alcohol consumption. Driving to the theater for soundcheck on the day of our concert, we were treated to a cassette playing amateurish old-time swing, "Mack the Knife," "Autumn Leaves," and other chestnuts. The music featured trombone, and he kept turning around to inform us proudly that it was him playing. He would also "swing" the steering wheel in time to the music, sending the car careening somewhat rhythmically from left to right in the dense traffic. Between the trombone solos, he would tell us over and over, again turning around to face the rear as the car lurched forward, "I love jazz, please invite me to America, I love jazz." We were quite relieved to reach the hall intact.

The concert hall was huge and ornate in a futuristic way, with seats for perhaps two thousand people. On the stage were doppelgangers for the Tesla amps that, once again, we thought we'd left behind only as a bad memory. Such a majestic stage demanded proper equipment, but it was not to be. Troupers all, we carried on, and as the concert proceeded, we could somewhat forget about the physical sound onstage and let the music take us. We had the next day free for walking around the city, prompting Peter Hollinger's expression of disgust: "You Americans with your showers and your tourism." Peter, a fantastic musician with a sardonic cast, was interested in neither. After dinner, we were driven to the train station and trundled on to the Express, a twelve-hour ride bringing us to Moscow, our handlers grinning and bidding us adieu. Though the train looked quite worn and battered from the outside, the compartments were elegant and comfortable with cushioned wooden furniture and gilt and brass fixtures. A speaker mounted in the ceiling of the compartment offered multiple channels of non-stop political commentary in Russian but also one channel of cheesy electronic disco. It took some time to figure out how, but, to our great relief, we were able to turn it completely off. At one end of the train car sat a huge samovar attended by a hefty babushka in a smock. Biscuits and tea were available at any time of day or night. As we approached Moscow the next morning, the towers of the legendary Hotel Ukraina were the first things visible. We would be taken there for their breakfast buffet to feast on buckwheat blini.

After breakfast we were driven to the outskirts of town and to our Moscow lodgings, another private stay. We passed the Bolshoi Ballet and the Opera, as well as a few movie theaters all playing the cautionary tale *Hard Currency Prostitute*. Arriving at a shabby white high-rise apartment complex, we noticed that the walls were covered with graffiti and many doors and windows were cracked or completely missing. Our hosts were extremely gracious and welcoming and had a number of flats at their disposal, where we were comfortably accommodated. That evening we were treated to a variety of canned fishes and caviar with hot red pepper vodka, followed by entertainment: a bootleg copy of Ridley Scott's *Alien* with Russian narration overriding the original sound. More tourism the next morning (with Peter opting out). The Moscow subway system was an attraction in itself: beautifully engineered with each station having its own decorative theme—some cultural, some historic, some propagandistic. After a walk in Red Square, we visited the nearby and famous GUM department store, where I was able to find some albums of Azerbaijani folk and classical music.

On concert day it was planned that we would depart for the venue just after noon, as traffic would be slow. This was indeed the case, and it took nearly three hours of crawling before we reached a university hall where, we were told, Boris Yeltsin had spoken the week before. Once again, a beautifully appointed modern concert hall with completely dysfunctional sound equipment on stage. Entering the university complex, we spotted a trailer truck with a large Melodiya logo, the symbol of the state record company. Antanas informed us of their interest in recording the concert and releasing an LP of it. The deal being offered was classic: no money for recording and no royalties. Still, Ned and I both thought it would be a thrill to have a Russian vinyl release—but the others were opposed and vetoed it. One of the Melodiya engineers invited me in to see their mobile studio, and I was astounded to find that it was packed with top Western gear, including a Neve console from Britain, plus American Pultec equalizers and API compressors.

The concert was typical for our Soviet tour, with us attempting to make the most of a terribly unbalanced stage sound and unresponsive amplifiers. I might have been pleasantly surprised by recordings, but none were made. Perhaps the music did come together. We certainly felt that it achieved something approaching transcendence at passing moments, though we never experienced the sustained transit through the void that is a sign of successful improvised music. After the concert, our backstage room was crowded with well-wishers and autograph seekers. One young man was very insistent that I trade him my "New York punk boots" (ironic in that they were actually Romanian Army surplus though, yes, purchased from a little shop on Orchard Street in the Lower East Side), but I had to tell him over and over that they were the only shoes I had with me and I would not part with them. He finally offered to trade me a Russian army shirt for a set of my guitar strings, to which I agreed.

Back at the apartments we enjoyed a post-concert feast lubricated by plenty of that red pepper vodka, then a few hours' sleep before being carted back to the airport. Check-in and security were quick and uneventful, and soon enough we followed a recommendation from one of our hosts and installed ourselves at the stylish chrome-and-charcoal bar on the top floor of Departures. There, we could join the suits and pilots in breakfast libations of vodka, accompanied by toasts dotted with caviar and eggs for $0.02 per portion, cheesy minor-key electronic disco providing the perfect ambience. Well-fortified, we boarded the IL86 and clanked and rattled back to Berlin.

My next encounter with "Soviet jazz" took place at New York's Knitting Factory. Besides Boris Grebeshnikov, leader of the band Aquarium from Leningrad (now returned to the name St. Petersburg), one of the key figures in the Russian underground was pianist and composer Sergey Kuryokhin. In addition to his role as keyboardist for Aquarium, Kuryokhin led a more freeform band called Popular Mechanics. He visited New York in December 1990, and we performed together at the Knitting Factory in a quartet with Ned Rothenberg and drummer Bobby Previte. I'm not sure what his source of information was, but Sergey seemed confused by the direction of our improvised set, which was dark, loud, jagged, and rocking. After, he said to me, "I was expecting New York kitsch, and this was not it," to which I had to agree.

In 2007, pianist Anthony Coleman and I were invited by vocalist NetLenka to join her group Ethnica for concerts in St. Petersburg and Moscow. The plan was to present two concerts of improvised combinations of the players with an overriding esthetic of "world music meets free improvisation." I was suspicious of the approach, but the recordings of the group revealed a high level of musicianship. That, combined with good terms for our appearance, sealed the deal. Anthony was already in Europe with a different project and went to St. Petersburg a day in advance. My flight out of JFK was delayed due to bad weather and I missed my connection in Munich, resulting in eight hours of suspended animation. Though I had sent texts and emails to Anthony and NetLenka, I received no response, so that when I finally arrived in St. Petersburg at 2 a.m., I had no idea if anyone would be at the airport to meet me. There wasn't, so I took a taxi to the hotel, where there was a message waiting for me announcing that we would all meet at lunch the next day at a nearby restaurant. At lunch, introductions were made and a loose plan for our first concert was devised, which included a day of rehearsals in the theater before the day of the concert. Traffic in St. Petersburg was phenomenally slow and thus, a good portion of our time was spent sitting in cars. The hall was a pleasant surprise, with good acoustics and stage equipment. I'm philosophically opposed to rehearsing improvisation but was willing to go along with the prevailing stream of thought. The "ethnic" aspect of the ensemble translated to music that somehow teetered between the folkloric and kitsch. This is not to say that the players were bad. They were all extremely proficient, and it was clear that NetLenka was the star of the show for good reason, with her powerful voice and willingness to take stylistic excursions. Anthony and I agreed that we were the odd ingredient in this borscht, the wild-card spice. So be it.

The day of the concert, Anthony and I headed out to explore the downtown. There were some enticing little restaurants, including fast-food blini and kebab joints. We stepped into a department store, always a good way to take in local culture. Indeed, not far from the entrance was an area displaying a huge wall of stylish and disposable handguns, some with silencers—the perfect accessory for the cosmopolitan hitman. After, we found a Dagestani restaurant. Dagestan is home to a number of languages and nationalities and, thus, a meeting place for many cuisines. We enjoyed a *plov* and other delights before heading back to the hotel to meet the gang for the trek to the theater, again with hours spent in cars in standstill traffic. The concert was okay, though not memorable. All played well and there were elevated moments, but never the feeling of a unified sound.

We flew the next morning to Moscow, not on the state airline Aeroflot, but thankfully on a private carrier whose fleet used modern Airbuses and Boeings. The hotel was situated in one of the largest gambling casinos in Moscow. It was clean and modern, albeit a touch bizarre. The casino operated 24/7, and there were always limousines and showy automobiles ranging from Alfa-Romeos to tricked-out Hummers parked in front.

Our venue in Moscow was the auditorium of the Central House of Artist, a four-story gallery and exhibition space built in 1979.

Next door to the House of Artist was the Muzeon Art Park, with an enormous collection of objects across history and culture and many large pieces of Soviet-era statuary. Given the way Soviet iconography appeared in the Western press throughout the Communist era, the displays in this park appeared as pure kitsch, but of the most enjoyable variety.

Setup was quick, though even after fine tuning the sound remained strangely separated and with little juiciness, a quality that allows the music to feel more unified. It wasn't a question of reverberation—sometimes a useful tool in blending the sound—but one of the unusual acoustics of the room. It wasn't dry, just not acoustically resonant, probably a good room for lectures. Our concert reflected the sense of distance, with individual playing of a high order but very little group communication or melding of sound.

After soundcheck, a few visitors came to say hello, musicians that I had met in Moscow in 1990, including the enthusiastic trader desirous of my punk boots. Conversations turned to the state of things both in the US and in Russia. I was admonished (as a representative of the USA!) that Americans loved Putin too much and that he was extremely dangerous and should be watched. I was also told about how many Russians are now nostalgic for the days of Communism, when food, medicine, and education were not dangled out of reach of the general population at the whim of the marketplace.

My call to return to the Sheremetyevo airport was at 3 a.m. for flights to Frankfurt and NYC. I offered my prepaid voucher to the driver and received a torrent of shouting in Russian. I assumed that there was a problem with the voucher or that a cash surcharge was being demanded. After a number of attempts, I was able to reach the manager of NetLenka, who spoke to the driver who, in his particular manner, was only asking if I needed a receipt.

32

China Times

In November 2005, I received an email out of the blue from guitarist John Myers, who was visiting Beijing, telling me how exciting things were there. He suggested that I get in touch with our old friend Michael Pettis if I had an interest in performing there. Michael ran a short-lived but high-impact little club in the East Village in 1983 called S.I.N. Club, where I had performed solo and with Carbon and which also saw performances of John's band Rat At Rat R, Sonic Youth, Swans, and many others. While some perceived the meaning of S.I.N. as decadent debauchery, in reality it stood for "Safety In Numbers," as Avenue C and 3rd Street at that time was a drug-sodden wasteland of burned-out buildings and even-more-burned-out junkies and dealers. S.I.N. was "membership-only," thereby working around licensing laws for the public sale of alcoholic beverages. The club operated only on Friday and Saturday evenings and attracted a loyal coterie of music fans for every show.

Michael now lived in Beijing, where he taught economics at Beijing University, and he had taken an interest in the underground punk and noise scene there. He was hoping to bring in New York musicians to work with the locals. We ironed out details and so it was planned that I would come in February 2006 with a concert at the Yugong Yishan club, two unannounced shows at smaller venues, and a talk at the Computer Music department of Beijing Music Conservatory. At the last minute, a show was added in Shanghai as well.

After seventeen hours of travel, we make our final approach with some wild lurching maneuvers over the craggy mountain peaks then down to the desert plain where Beijing sits. The air gets progressively browner and thicker as we finally land in the dense smog. I'm met at the airport by drummer/synthesist Shenjin (Shenggy) from Hang on the Box and guitarist Shou Wang (JeffRay) of Car Sick Cars, both leading bands of the burgeoning Beijing rock scene. Their duo is called White and they will open for me and we will also play improvised music together.

I'm brought to the hotel, which is in the north center near the Bell and Drum Towers, an older area above the Forbidden City and still filled with *hutongs*, narrow alleys of tiny shops and houses. Both Towers are imposing edifices built in the thirteenth century and originally used for musical purposes, later for telling the time. On my first morning there, I go for a walk in the Dongcheng area where the hotel is situated, just north of the Drum Tower and Bell Tower. One of the first things I discover is that Beijing drivers give little quarter to pedestrians, and a green "walk" signal just makes you an easier target. I am surprised to see huge SUVs whose operation seems to have the same effect on their drivers that these vehicles have in the USA, reducing intelligence, judgment, and empathy to a tiny smear. To cross the street, one must be fast and lucky. Close to the hotel are busy shopping streets with blasting hip-hop and young men in front of the shops with microphones trying to lure in customers, not so far off from the vibe in Times Square or 14th Street. I head down to the area of the lakes and wander around the *hutongs*. Later in the afternoon, Shenggy and Jeff come to the hotel to take me on a thirty-minute taxi ride over wide highways packed with careening cars and oblivious drivers to the Chingua district. As we drive, I'm struck by the vastness and grimness of the city, with row upon row of huge gray high-rise residences covering its expanse like a Philip K. Dick hallucination. Our rehearsal takes place in their practice room in a dingy rock club that felt quite like CBGB. Once we're set up, we have a brief discussion of what we're going to be playing. I suggest we improvise the entire set, and both are game. They're excellent musicians and have a wide knowledge of contemporary alt-rock styles, as well as a fondness for Krautrock, Velvet Underground, and other drony psychedelia, though they're less familiar with more extreme jazz vocabulary and extended techniques for guitar. We quickly find a common ground and dig in. By the end of the session we're confident that we'll be able to present a coherent groove-oriented set. It's dark as we head back to the area of the *hutongs*, and I notice that there is little neon to give even a false impression of festivity, except in a few places on the lake. The overall feeling is of a city desolate, or at least dormant. No doubt, this will all change in the coming years. The seat of government is in the old city, populated only by low buildings. I've been told that this is because of the paranoia of the government, which forbids the construction of edifices high enough to allow anyone to peer into the centers of operation.

Taking place on this second night is our first unadvertised show and the venue is the ?What Bar, literally a hole-in-the-wall just north of the Forbidden City. There's not much of a barrier between the inside and outside, and consequently it shares the frigid temperature of Beijing in February. It's a tiny place reminiscent of a Japanese "live house" or some low-level US punk bars and is the ancient home to the Beijing underground rock scene. The house drum kit is pretty tired, though a pair of Laney solid-state amps work surprisingly well. I've brought the solid-body eight-string, soprano sax, and my laptop, and while I prefer to have both bass and guitar amps, the twelve-inch Laney is more than adequate in the cramped confines of the ?What. The house is smoky and totally packed with thirty or forty people, a mix of local musicians, journalists, and foreigners, as well as a few soldiers in uniform. I inquire if they're there to monitor the proceedings for the government, but no, they're mostly there to buy, sell, and consume drugs. In fact, I'm surprised to see quite a bit of open exchange and consumption of various substances that might land someone in deep hot water, given the strict regulations. The evening begins with White and their set comprising analog synth drones, noise loops, and minimalist beats that expand into huge crescendi. The space is not conducive to using the computer, so for my solo it's the eight-string with my slides, spring bows, and a few pedals, including a looper. We finish with an improvised trio of jagged crashes, noisy loops, and freeform grooving to great response. This gig, like all that follow, is notable for the sea of red LEDs of recording: audio, video, still photos.

Daytime on February 24 is filled with a long walk guided by Shenggy through the Forbidden City, a theme park of artifacts from the bygone imperial eras, impressive in its size and magisterial sculpture. Later, we meet JeffRay and head off to the Dos Kolegas club for soundcheck. This venue is currently the unofficial home of Beijing's underground community of artists, musicians, and writers and is located in a somewhat remote area with a drive-in movie theater and bowling alley, a small lake, and a tiny strip of bars. Heat is also in short supply, but the equipment is quite a bit better. I also set up the computer for a solo Tectonics set. Soundcheck is efficient and satisfying, so we retire to the nearby bowling alley to dine in its surprisingly good restaurant then return to a packed house, over one hundred people jammed in, adding both heat and psychoacoustic resonance. Our set together is white hot, with the only problem being the difficulty in getting the sound engineer to turn down the monitor mix—it's BLASTING and gets louder as the set proceeds, with just touching a string threatening to unleash a wall of the unwelcome kind of feedback. At Dos Kolegas I meet Yan Jun, the one-man epicenter of the Beijing scene who, besides performing electronic music and DJing, operates a few small labels.

The final Beijing concert is on February 25 at Yugong Yishan, a well-equipped modern dance club with a capacity of a few hundred. In another surprise, there are a few African men in front of the parking lot hawking illicit consumables. The audience includes a large expat contingent of media types, fashionistas, and press crowding the bar who are there more to make the scene than to listen. Still, the area in front of the stage is packed with a crush of people who are focused on the music and wildly enthusiastic. Doro and Lu, the owners of the club, show us great hospitality and have a video crew shooting the show and doing a live mix—we can see it projected on a side wall.

This is a late, late night, and I return to the hotel in time to get just two hours of sleep before heading to the airport for our flight to Shanghai. At the airport, JeffRay and Shenggy skillfully steer us past the numerous "helpers"—private citizens who try to grab your baggage and aid you with check-in and then demand tips. They're completely unnecessary and a nuisance, but apparently a fixture at all of the nation's airports. Weather is bad over the mountains on our route, and the flight is two solid hours of bumping and shaking, rendering rest impossible. Our landing approach takes us over the harbor and city with spectacular views of a skyline packed with high-rise towers, each topped with an ornate phallic crown, a sure sign of success in business.

The streets in the area around our hotel are teeming with pedestrians packed into narrow channels by the carts of street sellers displaying their wares. One can find anything and everything: hardware, fruit, electronic components, magazines, clothing. They present a high contrast to the modern buildings just behind them and surrounding us. After lunch, we head to the Zhu Qizhan Museum for soundcheck. It's a recent building, tastefully slick, with an active program in contemporary art. Unfortunately, the backline has not arrived, rendering soundcheck impossible, so while the elements are rounded up, I run back to the hotel for a mini-nap and return in time for a quick setup and line check. The audience enters just as Jeff and Shenggy are finishing their check, and we break while a pot of excellent and much-needed coffee is cooked up by the director. There's a full house and the audience is young, the buzz tangible. They surround and spill over onto the stage, phones held aloft to grab pics of the music and each other. White's set is glowing radioactivity, and my solo set follows suit, charged up by the audience. We dig in for the trio, and the crowd demands more—we happily comply. We enjoyed the Beijing shows, but Shanghai feels different, looser, more psychic resonance. When the dust finally settles, we do a quick pack and bring the equipment to the hotel, then we're taken first to the Bund to view the waterfront skyline, a mix of modern architecture and European colonial antique illuminated with a kid's Crayola box of fluorescent-colored lights, and then to a late-night restaurant for yet another incredible meal. Too short a time at the hotel, then back to the airport, before another two hours of bouncing and lurching back to Beijing.

On return, there's just enough time for a quick shower and coffee at the hotel, then I trundle off to the Computer Music Center of Beijing Conservatory for my final event. Directed by Ken Fields, a former East Village neighbor, the CEMC has strong programs in sound art, electroacoustic music, composition, and conceptual approaches. I was invited to give a lecture-demonstration on various aspects of my work. After class, we head to a Xinjiang restaurant for a final meal in Beijing before my departure early the next morning. Xinjiang is a western province of China, and its population, the Uighur people, are Muslim. Writing in 2024, we have been witness to a nefarious process at work, with government suppression of the culture and language of the Uighur and the use of concentration camps for "re-education." We can't foresee this at the time, and so we enjoy the delicious Uighur cuisine, which shares many elements with that of Uzbekistan and Turkey. Post-dinner, we're off to a gritty studio in the outskirts where I am interviewed on-camera for a documentary film being made of this trip. In conversation, I express surprise that given China's censorious control of the internet, everyone I met seems to be quite up on the latest culture and world politics. I'm told that the censorship is "just for the peasants" and that the well-connected offspring of government officials, business people, and educators have fairly open access to web information.

I'm happy to return to Beijing again in April of 2007 for a residency at the D22 club, recently opened by Michael Pettis. A huge nor'easter has paralyzed travel on Sunday but by the time of my early Monday-morning departure via Chicago, the skies are flowing, if not completely smoothly.

The first concert is a collaboration with the Beijing New Music Ensemble, an open-minded contemporary music group founded by Eli Marshall, an American composer, pianist, and expat. He's assembled a talented and diverse group of players to perform the algorithmic score *SyndaKit*, including *gu-zheng* virtuoso Wu Fei, flutist Bruce Gremo (whom I know from NYC but have never played with), pianist Michelle Yip, tubist Mickey Wrobleski, saxophonist Nathaneal Gao, bassist Da Hwe, and percussionist Justin Padro. We rehearse at D22 from late afternoon into the early evening. D22 feels very welcoming with that 1980s East Village mix of coziness and alienated cool. The lighting is subdued, and the walls are reddish and black. There's a long bar and an upstairs balcony overlooking the stage. The sound system even looks 1980s: two giant speaker boxes with fifteen-inch woofers plus horns: powerful, loud, and clean. The stage sound is likewise well suited for making music. After we rehearse *SyndaKit* until it feels fluid, we break for a fiery Hunan meal then return to perform two versions of the piece in each set. Even though the musicians have only been briefly working with this composition and its approaches, they play it with fervor and excellent global listening.

The second evening at D22 begins with a solo Tectonics set in which a number of new drum grooves that I've been working on are introduced. Lots of saturated textures from the eight-string, and the new beats sound monstrous over the house sound system. After a short break, Bruce and Mickey join me for a quieter trio of microsounds and microrhythms. Mickey derives an extraordinary range of sounds from his tuba, and Bruce, in addition to his virtuosic *shakuhachi* and ceramic ocarinas, has brought his Cilia, an invented "virtual *shakuhachi*" controller that interfaces with the Max/MSP patches he's created on his laptop. Next up is a power trio with JeffRay and Justin—heavy beats and lots of ringing and droning overtone guitars, feedback, and non-pitched noise. We finish the evening with Bruce and Mickey joining for a more restrained, but no less intense, quintet. There is a brief rainstorm during the final set, and the combination of water and a strong wind has made the air clean and sweet (but not for long).

The next morning, Shenggy and JeffRay take me to the secondhand market in a poor northern part of the city—the towers look even more bleak, and there's no street life outside of the open-air kiosks. The market is mostly filled with vendors all selling the same fake "antiquities" cranked out in some factory in the hinterlands—it's hard to imagine that any of them are making money from this, judging by the vast supply of goods displayed and the dearth of purchasers. There's a man with an extensive collection of gongs and cymbals that look and sound fantastic. Another instrument shop has used *gu-jins*, *shengs*, and violins. I'd like to purchase a *sheng*, but none of them are in working condition. Tucked away in a corner is a one-man espresso bar built into a tiny cart. He makes a surprisingly good *ristretto*! I'm told that the Tibetans are the most impoverished population in Beijing and that many of the sellers in this market are from Tibet, including one offering hand-painted images of gods and demons on linen.

The Tectonics program begins the evening again, but on this day the set is shorter and denser. The material is being refined onstage as I play it—a trial by fire. As always, the presence of an audience changes the perception of duration and intensity—actually everything about how the music sounds, but more importantly, how it feels. After Tectonics, *gu-zheng* dynamo Wu Fei joins me for an improvised duo. In her hands, this ancient zither is capable of a huge range of sounds—delicate arpeggios, jagged glisses and scrapes, dense clouds, knocks and booms—and we dance around various strategies, always in sync. The Korean *samul-nori* (percussion group) Olssu Beida is up next with a short piece of their own—exciting and grooving—after which I join them. It takes us a few minutes to find the pocket as my feel of 12/8 is quite different from theirs, but we finally lock in to a straight-eighth pattern that launches us into a rocking fifteen minutes with a number of textural and rhythmic shifts. JeffRay and I then perform duo—our first time in this format and it works very well with the saturated sounds looping and blending with mutual provocation. For the finale, Yan Jun joins us on electronics, along with Mickey on tuba and Eli Marshall on an old pump-harmonium residing in the club. The resultant piece is cloudy, bittersweet, and atmospheric, sometimes reminiscent of Japanese *gagaku* or a psychedelic Morton Feldman, a fine way to end the series. There's a late hang at the club, two hours of sleep, then off to the airport for my flights to San Francisco and on to NYC.

In 2009 I experience a quick return to China for a performance of Christian Marclay's *Screenplay* at the eMedia Festival in Xuhui Park, Shanghai on October 22. *Screenplay* is both a score for the musicians and a work of video art which I've enjoyed playing on a number of occasions in the past, either solo or with shifting musical partners. I've just returned from London and have had barely fifteen hours at home including a quick run to my studio for some admin work and fresh guitar strings. It's not nearly enough time at home, but a gig is a gig. At 6 a.m. I'm off to LaGuardia for my flights to Chicago and from there to Shanghai. Happily, I sleep a good portion of the sixteen-hour flight, travel fatigue having taken its toll. There's a long immigration line and wait for the baggage, but I'm out after a little over one hour and the driver is waiting to bring me directly to soundcheck. Shanghai is humid and thick, the air smoggy and odorous, but the tropical warmth feels good after all that flight time. Greetings with Christian, Lydia Yee, Wu Na, Yan Jun, Bruce Gremo, and organizer Defne Ayas and I'm off to set up my equipment and check the sound for our trio. Wu Na with her *gu-qin* and Peking Opera percussionist Wang Li Chuan are already on stage, and it takes just a few moments to build up my compact equipment: eight-string, soprano sax, laptop, and a few pedals. Because of the logistics of the day, it's decided that I'll forego the use of guitar amplifiers and go direct into the PA. Getting power to the stage is problematic, but it's finally up; we check the sound and video monitors quickly and all seems to be fine. I run to the hotel for a quick shower and a big cup of Medaglia d'Oro instant espresso and back to the hit. The concert is free to the public, so the large crowd is quite diverse, with most enjoying the comic circus of the opening band. The first version of *Screenplay* is performed by Bruce Gremo on the Cilia, Ben Hauge on laptop, and Yan Jun narrating and using a small mixing board for non-instrument synthesis. We begin our set smoothly, but as the set develops the computer suddenly sounds wrong—I gesture to the sound engineer for more level, but he makes it quieter. Onstage the sound is too diffuse from the monitors for my guitar, but I can hear Wu Na acoustically, and of course, the percussion cuts across everything. The set feels good, though it's sonically frustrating for me. One learns that it's better to just go with the flow in such situations and not worry about one's own sound. We finish to a great response. As I'm packing my gear, I discover that one channel of my computer had been unplugged from the DI boxes somewhere in the confusion between groups, hence the bad sound—my electronic tracks for *Screenplay* rely heavily on stereo separation. This seems to have been unnoticed by all but me—so it goes.

There's only enough time for a few hours' sleep at the hotel before rising to catch the van that is taking us all to the airport for our flight to Beijing.

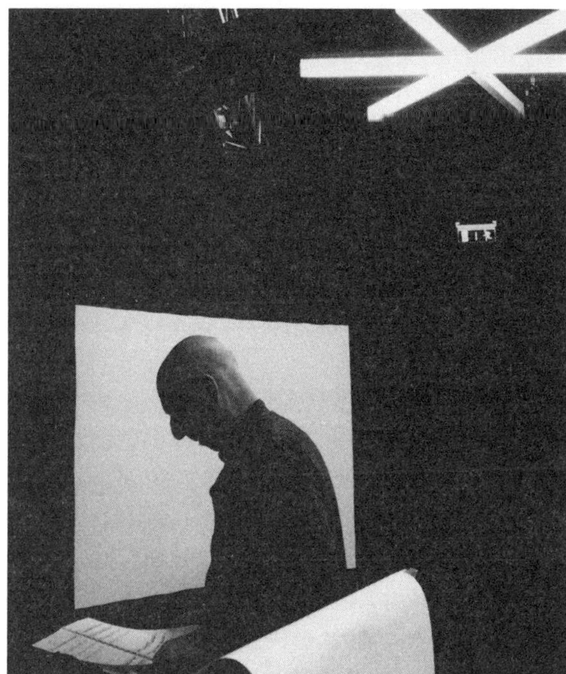

Figure 18
E♯, Kosice, Slovakia (2018). Photo by Lukas Kuzma.

Back on the ground and in a van, heavy traffic slows us down on the way to the hotel, but we have an hour there to chill and drink coffee before heading to D22 for the soundcheck.

There will be two groups performing *Screenplay* this evening: Bruce Gremo with guitarist JeffRay and saxophonist Li Tie Qiao, and my trio with Wu Na and Wang Li Chuan. We split the small stage so that we can all remain set up simultaneously. Christian deals with the less-than-powerful projector—scrubbing the lens with Windex to free it from the accumulated cigarette smoke helps enormously—and pretty soon we're ready to go, with both groups benefiting from the punchy stage sound. After a short break, JeffRay, Bruce, Li, and John Myers join me onstage for a long, dense, drone-filled improv. I'm happy to leave the smoke-filled club and return to the hotel at 0130, then sleep until well into the next afternoon—a rare treat. The final night is filled with a number of bands and combinations of players for a festive end to the trip.

Back in NYC, I have thirty hours to spend at home and at the studio before heading back to the airport for a flight to Germany for a festival in Mannheim, where I'm the featured soloist with the Barry Guy Orchestra. It's a great gig, but the trip is a blur: flight, nap, concert, nap, back on a plane, then home. The next day, I'm at work in the studio when gravity beckons me to the couch. It's late afternoon and getting dusky. At a certain uncertain point, I emerge into a murky half-sleep in the fully darkened room, a loud rumbling sound filling the air, the couch vibrating. As I slowly regain consciousness, a mild panic sets in. I have no memory of getting on another plane: where am I going? What am I doing? As clarity returned, I had to laugh at the realization that I was actually in NYC on my couch in my studio, the rumbling caused by a truck idling outside. Happy to have two weeks without travel!

♯

It's another five years before I return to China, this time to the Tomorrow Festival in Shenzhen, May 17, 2014. I must ask, is the weather getting worse in general thanks to climate change, or is it just my luck to mostly have flights on stormy days? Rain and fog in NYC as we take off from LGA with a bumpy ascent, but fairly calm all the way to rainy Chicago. Landing is something else though, riding the roller coaster for a few white-knuckled moments. Couple of hours to kill in the lounge then heading off to Shanghai in a 747. Four hours are spent hanging out in PVG, and I am more than ready to move on to Shenzhen. As departure time approaches, there is no call for boarding until the last moment, when it is announced that the flight will be delayed due to very strong thunderstorms in Shenzhen. There's a mad rush to the podium by the assembled passengers: free food is being given out because of the delay. Total chaos with people pushing in and elbowing the competition to get at that grub. We finally get the call for the flight, almost three hours later. The seat-belt signs are never turned off during the two-hour fifteen-minute duration, and it is moderately turbulent throughout, but nothing too drastic. However, as we lurch down to Shenzhen we pass through an area of storms, and the cabin is intermittently lit by strong lightning flashes about ten kilometers to our east. We weave around cumulonimbus towers, illuminated by lightning and the light of the nearly full moon visible through gaps in the clouds. It is all quite a dramatic and thrilling ride, but I am happy to finally land, some twenty-eight hours after taking off from NYC.

Thirty years before, Shenzhen was a quiet fishing village, now in 2014 a sprawling city of twenty million with booming industries including the notorious Foxconn complex. We drive to the OCT-Loft district, a "culture-area," lush with vegetation including mango, lychee, and mangosteen trees, where I am taken to meet Fei, the garrulous and welcoming director of the festival and proprietor of Old Heaven, a fantastic bookstore masquerading as a record store and functioning as a cafe. I ask Fei about the popular perception of Shenzhen, versus what I see as a quiet green college town. He smiles and gestures, "Everything is over that hill on the other side, that's hell on earth!"

Post-breakfast, I meet with translator Shang-Shang, with whom I go over the outline for my lecture and discuss the basic elements of my talk. The topic is "Current Strategies for Composition and Performance," a catch-all to explain my work of the moment. I would begin describing the solo format and its manifestation of a mix of composition and improvisation—a direct link from Inner Ear to sound. Next would come improvisation in duo or groups and the notion of duet as conversation expanding to the complication of large-ensemble improvisation, where the interactions are defined by socioacoustics, whether tangible or not. From structured improv I would segue to algorithmic composition and self-organizing systems, including discussion of the importance of interactive feedback in *SyndaKit*, and then to graphic notation with display and discussion of the recent graphic scores-as-movies *Foliage* and *Sylva Sylvarum*.

During the talk, there is some heated commentary by one audience member who just doesn't get how graphic notation could be valid and how isn't it just a pretty picture and how *Foliage* is just a product of technology. I try to explain and clarify these issues by pointing out that anything in the signal chain between eye and ear will have an effect on one's creative process, and yes, at its worst, a graphic score might just be a pretty picture, but at its best it could be a powerful way of communicating abstractions from composer to the performer. I also explain that music and technology have always been inextricably linked, from the first simple percussion instruments to the piano, the instruments of the modern orchestra, and finally to synthesizers and computers. Despite this, he remains quite argumentative and resistant, so, with time limited, I move us on to the final section, a presentation of through-composed works for string quartet, orchestra, and opera, and discussion of my approaches to these media. I pepper the lecture with slides of some fully notated scores and examples of music played back from my laptop, including *SyndaKit*, the latest string quartet *Tranzience*, and the orchestral *Calling*. This seems to quiet my skeptical critic. There are more questions

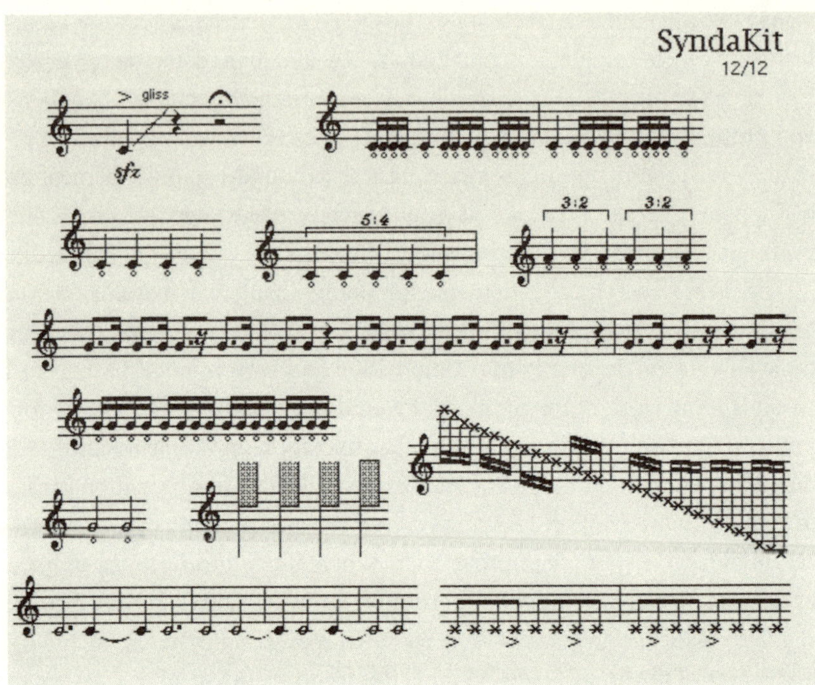

Figure 19 Score, *SyndaKit*, "Page 12" (1998).

from others and talk and then I move to the nearby B10 club for soundcheck for the evening concert.

Opening the evening is Xiao He's solo set. Xiao plays the *ruan*, a four-string fretted lute with steel strings. His *ruan* has been retrofitted with a Shadow midi-pickup and controller unit plus a microphone. He runs everything through various pedals, a Roland Loop-Station, and a laptop running Logic MainStage. He's able to layer and loop sounds from his instrument and voice, as well as samples and synth-sounds. Xiao is a dynamic presence on stage, and his music ranges from delicate to bombastic, mystical to comedic. We have been asked if we would consider a spontaneous duo, and so the staging is such that we are both able to remain fully set-up. I perform a sixty-minute set that mixes elements from both *Momentum Anomaly* and the *Haptikon* compositions. The audience attention and response are extremely gratifying, and when I finish, Xiao He joins me onstage. Pretty quickly, we are into a deep conversation in sound, lasting about thirty minutes.

We convene the next morning (not too early) at the bookstore for coffee, then Fei drives us downtown to one of the ancient villages that now comprise Shenzhen for a delicious dim sum breakfast, after which we go to visit a tea master at her *cháguǎn*, or teahouse. She's a big supporter of the festival and of contemporary culture in Shenzhen and a gracious host. We are treated to the proper preparation of five courses of hand-picked and dried teas, ranging from green tips at the beginning through aged white tea leaves, yellow, red, and then finishing with oolong. Her serenity and concentration make for a beautiful atmosphere, and the cumulative effect of the various teas causes an elevated state. As we depart the tea house, Xiao He proclaims, "We're drunk on tea!" We then return to B10 where I do an extensive interview in front of an audience. The festival's activity for that evening is a screening at the bookstore of *Amin*, a densely packed and moving documentary by Iranian director Shahin Parhami about the activities of Amin Aghaie, a Qasqari musician and ethnomusicologist whose life's work is to preserve the Qasqari musical traditions, though faced with many negative pressures. It's a riveting and powerful film, well worth seeking out.

33

Vong Co

Music of Longing

Apocalypse Now! For many Americans, the Kubrick film is the definitive version of that chunk of history defined as the Vietnam War (or as it's known in Ho Chi Minh City and environ, the American War). Its rock soundtrack forged an indelible connection between the daily travails of the American occupying soldiers and their sonic soul food. 1965 was the year that the presence of American "advisers" in Vietnam and the definition of their role there was beginning to make front-page news in the US, mostly as a propaganda effort to convince the home front that the boys were over there to stop the inevitable march of Communism from Southeast Asia, through the Philippines, and into everyone's suburban backyard. In other words, the long-discredited Domino Theory.

I was fourteen in 1965 and in our social studies classes, we absorbed the prevailing doctrine and were expected to regurgitate it correctly in order to get As. In private, we knew it was a load of horseshit. Our deprogramming was music: we were listening to Dylan, The Yardbirds, The Stones, The Beatles ("I Feel Fine"!), The Who, and, when we could sneak the records past parental censors, Frank Zappa's Mothers of Invention and The Fugs, an uncompromising and frequently obscene group of peace-creep poetic outcast hippie-punks led by Ed Sanders and Tuli Kupferberg. 1965 also saw the release of the Smithsonian Folkways recording *Music of Vietnam*, a collection of folk and traditional musics from various regions of the country. It found its way into our local library, and to my unlearned ears, it was thrilling in its lo-fi exoticism and panoramic sweep, ranging from tribal sounds played on xylophones and zithers to sophisticated songs colored by dramatic glisses and bends woven into delicate webs of interplay.

Cut to 1988 and a cassette appeared in the mail from Ohio-based musicologist Terry Miller, who had recorded a variety of selections performed by Vietnamese exiles living in his area. He was wondering if I might release it on my zOaR label. It was a compelling compilation overall, but what really hit my ears were a couple of tracks that included guitars played in a way that I'd never heard before. Clean-toned and displaying a variety of vibratos and bending techniques, it was difficult to ascertain whether they were acoustic or electric. I was astounded at how reminiscent the guitars were of the *dan tranh*, a Vietnamese plucked zither closely related to the Chinese *gu-qin* or Korean *kayagum*. In later research I found that guitars began to be adapted for use in Vietnam in the 1930s, with the wood of the fingerboard heavily scalloped leaving high frets very much like those of a sitar. These adapted guitars are known as *ghita phím lõm*. At that time I had been in discussion with SST Records about zOaR operating under their umbrella, and this collection would be one of the first releases. However, with great turmoil overwhelming the relations between SST and its artists and dooming our co-op venture, *Eternal Voices: Traditional Vietnamese Music in The United States* was not released until 1993, and then by New Alliance.

I was often on tour in Europe during the '90s, and a day off in Paris would give me the opportunity to play *flâneur*. The thirteenth and eighteenth arrondissements were favorite places to wander, and I would haunt the Vietnamese and Arab shops in search of cassettes, whether folk, pop, or Algerian *rai*. Most of the Vietnamese music I found was sentimental ballads with traditional accompaniment. I was told that these ballads were *vong co*, translating to "nostalgia for the past" or "longing for the old traditions." There were often electric guitars or lap steels bathed in reverb blending in with *dan bao*, the iconic Vietnamese monochord with a sound like a theremin; *dan tranh*; the lute *dan kim*; and a bright and staccato wooden block, the *song loan*, used to count cadences and denote phrases. The bent strings and glissandi gave the music an intensely emotional cast, deep beauty and sadness. The songs featured introductions and breaks rich with melodic improvisation, often quite virtuosic. In her exhaustive study of *vong co*, *The Syncretic Art and History of Vietnamese Vọng Cổ Music*, Clair Hoang Khuong Nguyen speaks of the importance of the title of the piece in setting the mood and emotional ambience, a trait inherited from Confucian and traditional music from China. This overriding "sentiment" shapes the improvisational choices of the musicians as they perform introductions as well as interludes between verses, all designed to enhance the feeling of the piece. More than just the sequences of notes, the listeners to this music prize the emotional underpinnings as manifested in the improvisations. The music usually begins with a simple folk melody composed of a limited set of pitches, yet soon they are greatly expanded by the way notes are approached, bent, vibrated, slid, and attacked for an emotional range seemingly without limit. A close cousin could be heard in the extended improvisations of free jazz and psychedelic rock.

During certain periods of my life, insomnia has been my friend, with the hours between three and four in the morning especially ripe for discovery and revelation. Whether it be seeds of compositional strategies or approaching the completion of a project long in the works, that period before dawn is often where the action is. Sometime in 2011 during an insomniac couch session, I began finding YouTube videos of solo performances of *vong co* played on electric *ghita phím lõm*, reminiscent of Delta blues but also revealing DNA strands of Indian and Chinese music and psychedelic guitar—evidence of past foreign incursions. (Other evidence of this process may be found in the presence in almost every Vietnamese town of a bakery turning out perfect baguettes in the French style.) The improvisations were based on the traditional melodies, but creative extrapolation was to be expected in the manifestation. The basic songs might be heavily ornamented with myriad ways of attacking a note, and the improvisations may use pentatonic scales and diatonic modes, but never in predictable patterns and ornamented with bends and vibrato. The electric guitars were sometimes clear-toned but often distorted and appeared to be the mutated offspring of a Fender Stratocaster or Teisco Spectrum. My theory is that during the war years, the widespread presence of American military personnel listening to rock on the radio and even playing guitars themselves was the catalyst for this opening up of orchestration to electricity in the traditional music. The electronic processing of the guitars is not a gimmick, but operates in the service of the vocality of the lines, a textural and nearly vocal counterpoint. I was so taken with *vong co* guitar that I began looking to acquire a *ghita phím lõm*. Another late session online led me to one such instrument, and after its arrival in a few days, I was plugging it in at Studio zOaR. This particular Strat derivative had "Adam" written on the headstock, and with built-in fuzz and a harsh and choppy envelope filter, it could produce a wide range of unusual sounds. To know the notes and their position on the fingerboard is one thing, but to be able to truly play *vong co* guitar with all of its expressive bends, turns, slides, and ornaments is another.

Of the many *vong co* guitarists heard and seen on YouTube, my favorite is the prolific Hoàng Phúc, a master of traditional and modern Vietnamese music. Considered a leading pedagogue, he is also an effortless virtuoso who peels off astounding runs of fractal complexity and deeply affective power, all the while keeping his extreme cool. His readings of the original songs have a burning intensity or a sweet lilt, feelings sustained in his improvisations. Solos that would cause most Western guitarists to display terminal "guitar face" are played with a completely stoic demeanor, though with a piercing glare that lets you know how serious this music is. The guitars in his collection all display high "fetish" quality, including a wicked-looking double-neck. It's my dream to visit Vietnam and take some lessons with him in *vong co*!

34

Non-asymptotic

This is the conclusion of *Feedback*, that point in this process of writing and reading that I can assert with full confidence is non-asymptotic. No matter how many infinite points there are between the first and last words in this chapter or between the final word and the punctuation that follows it, the words themselves will come to a complete stop. The words have reached completion, but on another level the stories will progress in their own asymptotic way, maintaining their own trajectories, as do the stories of music, sound, art, and artists and the worlds that they inhabit.

So many of my friends and colleagues act from a singular and admirable point of determination, the determination that we all do what we do because we have no choice as we have found deep resonance with our path. Inevitability. It may meander and diverge, even contradict itself and go in reverse at times, but ultimately it is the only byway on which we journey.

There are those who feel an artistic approach is trivial and selfish in the face of the crises of our modern world. People live under constant threat of annihilation or experience it in its most horrible fullness thanks to the machinations of politicians and corporate entities. There is vast wealth being accumulated by very few, more than enough to ensure that no person on this planet need go hungry, without housing or medical care, or without education. We are inundated daily with disinformation and the crassest of marketing strategies, even to the point of having our entire existence scanned and eavesdropped to further the gains of unholy commerce.

I'm certainly not a Luddite, but I fear that the avalanche of breathtaking milestones in AI seems as ominous as it is brilliant and portends a deeply negative transformation of human life, rendering humanity's goals irrelevant to the larger agenda of corporate control and profit. Writing this in the days after the US presidential election of 2024, it is easy to feel overwhelmed by a tsunami of lies, ignorance, and amoral manipulation resulting in the crowning of an incompetent and felonious liar, grifter, and adjudicated sex-

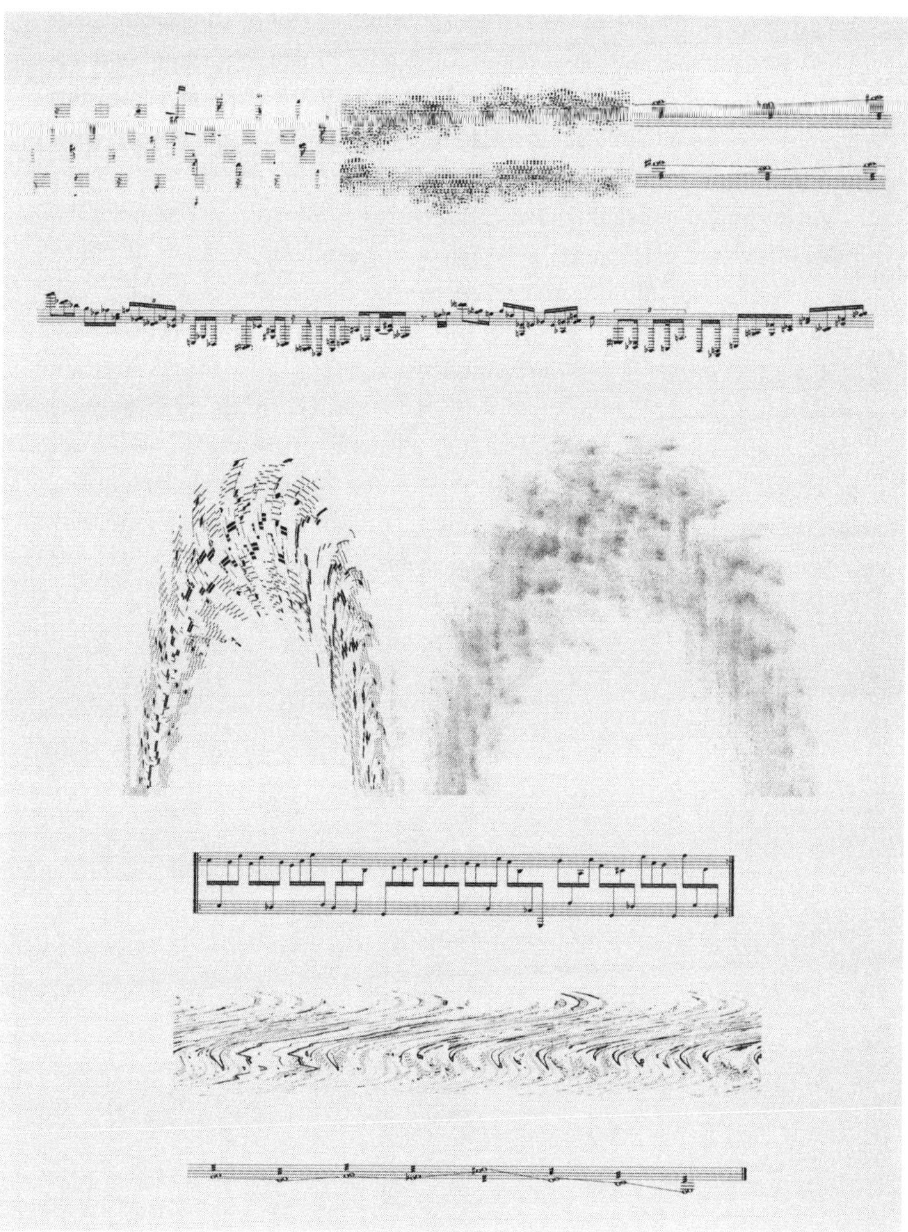

Figure 20 Score excerpt, *Correlation Engine* (2017).

ual offender as "leader of the free world" with a cabal of equally vile technocrats, oligarchs, and "servants of the people" operating behind and underneath the scenes for their own ends. But are there additional strategies besides despair and solipsistic isolation on the one hand and overt protest and screed on the other? Can the opposition take other forms?

Artists function as antennae, commentators, investigators, generators, processors, and instigators, even when not explicitly focused on political concerns. Sound initiates psychoacoustic chemical change. Our work in music and sound can be a great positive force in all of our ecosystems, whether it is disseminated in the high-speed arcs and instant gratification of popular culture or inside the slower arcs of other channels, perhaps more obscure or esoteric. Sonic strategies will always be of great value, even if not perceived immediately or on the surface. Music and sound can be utopian, inspirational, strengthening, energizing, and can catalyze transformation in consciousness in any part of the spectrum.

To be continued . . .

SELECTED DISCOGRAPHY

Solo and Leader

Aggregat, Dialectrical (Clean Feed, 2016)
Momentum Anomaly (New Atlantis, 2013)
Octal, Books I–III (Clean Feed, 2007–2012)
Sharp? Monk? Sharp! Monk! (Clean Feed, 2005)
Quadrature (zOaR, 2004)
The Yahoos Trilogy (zOaR, 1985–2004)
The Velocity of Hue (zOaR, 2003)
Tectonics, Errata (Neos, 1998)
Tectonics, Field and Stream (zOaR, 1996)
Cryptid Fragments (zOaR, 1992)
Ganging the Wave (zOaR, 2022)
Steppe (zOaR, 2023)
Mandocello (zOaR, 2024)
Mandorle (zOaR, 2024)
Hudson River Compositions: 1973–74 (zOaR, 2025)
Crowds and Power: Live at The Kitchen, NYC 1982 (zOaR, 2025)

Orchestra Carbon and Carbon

Transmigration at the Solar Max (Intakt, 2018)
The Age of Carbon (Intakt, 2012)
Void Coordinates (Intakt, 2009)
Radiolaria (zOaR, 1999)
SyndaKit (Neos, 1998)
Rheo~Umbra (Neos, 1996)
The Age of Carbon (Intakt, 1984–1996)
Interference (Atavistic, 1995)
Amusia (Atavistic, 1994)
Serrate (zOaR, 1992)
Larynx (Neos, 1988)

Orchestral and Chamber Music

Oceanus Procellarum (Cavity Search, 2017)
Tranzience (New World, 2016)
The Boreal (Starkland, 2015)
Oneirika (Zeitkratzer, 2014)
"Storm of the Eye," on *In 27 Pieces*, with Hilary Hahn (Deutsche Grammophon, 2013)
String Quartets, Vol. 2 (Tzadik, 2002–2008)
Racing Hearts / Tessalation Row / Calling (HR Media, 2003)
String Quartets, Vol. 1 (Tzadik, 1986–1996)
Occam's Machete (zOaR, 2023)
Plastovy Hrad (Infrequent Seams, 2019)

Opera

Port Bou (Infrequent Seams, 2016)
Binibon (Henceforth, 2011)
Em/Pyre (Opus 10, 2008)
A Modicum of Passion (Abaton, 2004)
Innosense (zOaR, 1982)
Filiseti Mekidesi (Infrequent Seams, 2020)
Die Grösste Fuge (Infrequent Seams, 2022)

Soundtracks

Calling All Earthlings (Cavity Search, 2023)
Incident (zOaR, 2016)
Q-Mix (zOaR, 2016)
Spectropia Suite (Neos, 2010)
Commune (zOaR, 2005)
Yellowman (zOaR, 2002)
Suspension of Disbelief (Tzadik, 2001)
Figure Ground (Tzadik, 1997)

Terraplane

Century (zOaR, 2021)
4am Always (Yellowbird, 2014)
Sky Road Songs (Yellowbird, 2012)
Forgery (Intuition, 2008)
Secret Life (Intuition, 2006)
Do the Don't (zOaR, 2003)

Blues for Next (zOaR, 2000)
Terraplane (zOaR, 1994)

Collaborations

Tectonics: Songs from A Rogue State, with Eric Mingus (zOaR 2023)
Chansons du Crepuscule, with Hélène Breschand (Public Eyesore, 2017)
Rub Out the Word, with Steve Buscemi (Infrequent Seams, 2016)
Tectonics: Fourth Blood Moon, with Eric Mingus (Yellowbird, 2016)
Crossing the Waters, with Melvin Gibbs and Luca Niggli (Intakt, 2013)
Let Her In, with Nels Cline (Public Eyesore, 2013)
Electric Willie, with Henry Kaiser, Glenn Philips, Eric Mingus, Melvin Gibbs (Yellowbird, 2010)
The Prisoner's Dilemma, with Bobby Previte (Grob, 2002)
Anostalgia, with Reinhold Friedl (Grob, 2002)
High Noon, with Christian Marclay (Intakt, 2000)
GTR OBLQ, with Vernon Reid and David Torn (Knitmedia, 1998)
Blackburst, with Zeena Parkins (Victo, 1996)
Jajouka New York, with Bachir Attar (zOaR, 1990)
Bone of Contention, with Semantics (SST, 1987)
Hara, with David Fulton (zOaR, 1978)

Compilation Producer

I Never Metaguitar, Vol. I–IV (Clean Feed, 2010–2015)
Secular Steel (Gaff Music, 2004)
State of the Union 2.001 (zOaR, EMF) 2001
Volume, Bed of Sound (PS1, 2001)
State of the Union III (Atavistic, 1999)
State of the Union II (MuWorks, 1992)
Real Estate (Ear-Rational, 1990)
Island of Sanity (No Man's Land, 1986)
State of the Union I (zOaR, 1982)
Peripheral Vision (zOaR, 1981)

ACKNOWLEDGMENTS

A few sections of this book first appeared in abbreviated form as articles in other media.

With the permission of the now-archived online journal *Please Kill Me*:
"Peter K. Siegel—Quietly Changing American Music"
"Hubert Sumlin: Howlin' Wolf's Secret Weapon"
"Skull Forming: Tim Wright after Pere Ubu"
"Vong Co: Guitar Sounds from Vietnam to the U.S."

A version of "A Gig's a Gig" appeared as part of the article "What If Touring Ended" in the online journal *Perfect Sound Forever*.

An excerpt of "A Conversation with John Fahey" was originally published in the *Knitting Factory Knotes*, January 2001.

Much thanks to the Wesleyan crew: Suzanna Tamminen, Ally Findley, Hannah Krasikov, Ron Kuivila, Rebecca Maher, Paula Matthusen, and Stephanie Elliott Prieto.

My gratitude to these dear friends and esteemed colleagues who over the years have offered their enthusiasm, support, and suggestions across many realms: American Academy in Berlin, Werner Aldinger, Laura Andel, Sergio Armaroli and Francesca Gemmo, Jonathan Berman, Pavel Borodin and Anna Cherednichenko/In Situ Art Society, Glenn Branca, Helene Breschand, Karl and Isabella Bruckmaier, Marco Cappelli, Stefanie Carp, Peter Cherches, Anthony Coleman, Pedro Costa, Gareth Davis, Angelika Donhärl and Gottfried Düren/arToxin Gallery, Toni Dove, Luke DuBois, Julius Eastman, Joel Eckhaus, Evan Eisenberg, Morton Feldman, Scott Fields, Suzanne Fiol, Paul Fox, Foundation for Contemporary Arts, Reinhold Friedl, David Fulton, Bruce Gallanter/Downtown Music Gallery, Richard Gehr, Melvin Gibbs, Michael Goldman, Manuel Göttsching/Ilona Ziok, David Grubbs, the Guggenheim Foundation, Ken Heer, Alanna Heiss and Fred Sherman, Doug Henderson, Lejaren Hiller, Roald Hoffman, Dave Hofstra and Lynne Tillman, Masa Hosojima and Donna Rataczak, James Ilgenfritz and Infrequent

Seams, Judith Insell, Nicholas Isherwood, ISSUE Project Room, Christopher Johnson, Al Kaatz, Wolf Kampmann, Charles Keil, Ed Keller and Carla Leitao, Rainer Kern, Jin Hi Kim, Saul Koll, Harry Lachner, Ron Lawrence, Yoon-Ji Lee, Jonathan Lethem, Bernd Leukert and Clair Lüdenbach, Mary Ann Livchak, Alberto LoFoco/AKAMU Agency, Christian Marclay and Lydia Yee, Joe Mardin, Hope Martin, Gillian McCain and Alan Bisbort /*Please Kill Me*, Don McKenzie, Ed McKeon, Eric Mingus, Tracie Morris, Clair Hoang Khuong Nguyen, Charles K. Noyes and Kalina Ivanov, Keisuke Oki, Massimo Ongaro, Felipe Orrego, Matthias Osterwold, Wendy Oxenhorn/Jazz Foundation of America, John Palmer, Zeena Parkins, Carol Parkinson/Harvestworks, Michael Pettis, Steve Piccolo, Bobby Previte, Jenn Reeves and Bill Wu, Retrofret Guitars, Marc Ribot, Veniero Rizzardi, David Rothenberg, Roswell Rudd, Jim Staley/Matt Mehlan and Roulette Intermedium, Jen Sacks, Andreas Scherrer/Company of Heaven, Bert Shapiro and Charlotte Freeman, Howard Sharp, Kassie Sharp, Sonny Sharrock, Adam Shatz, Chandra Shukla, Peter K. Siegel, Ola Strandberg, Mort Subotnick and Joan LaBarbara, Dave Sulzer, Edwin Torres, Rick Turner, Yasuhiro Usui, Chris Vine, David Weinstein, Sean Wilentz, Amy Williams, Kenneth Wissoker, Jack Womack, Tim Wright, Michiyo Yagi and Mark Rappaport, and Kate Yourke.

Special thanks to our twins Lila and Kai for keeping me sharp; my mother, Eugenie Sharp; and my father, the late Bernard Sharp.

And above all, to Janene Higgins, who, throughout our deep entanglement, has been muse, collaborator, advisor, and my great joy and love.

Feedback is dedicated to my sister, Denise Gail Sharp (1952–2022).

INDEX

Page numbers in *italics* refer to illustrations.

ABOUT THE AUTHOR

ELLIOTT SHARP is an American composer, multi-instrumentalist, producer, and performer. A central figure in the avant-garde and experimental music scene in New York City for over forty years, Sharp has released over one hundred and sixty recordings, ranging from orchestral music to blues, jazz, noise, no wave rock, and techno music.

Sharp leads SysOrk, Orchestra Carbon, Terraplane, and Tectonics and has pioneered the use of fractal geometry, chaos theory, and genetics in musical composition and interaction. Sharp was awarded the Berlin Prize for Music Composition for 2015 and a Guggenheim Fellowship in 2014. His composition *Storm of the Eye* appears on violinist Hilary Hahn's Grammy-winning album *In 27 Pieces*. Sharp has been featured on National Public Radio and at such festivals as the Venice Biennale, New Music Stockholm, Donaueschingen, and Au Printemps–Paris. He is the subject of the documentary film *Doing the Don't*. His first book was *IrRational Music* (Terra Nova Books/MIT Press, 2019).